Supernatural Out of the Box

ALSO OF INTEREST AND FROM MCFARLAND

*A Supernatural Politics: Essays on Social Engagement,
Fandom and the Series* (edited by
Lisa Macklem and Dominick Grace, 2020)

Approaching Twin Peaks: *Critical Essays on the Original Series*
(edited by Eric Hoffman and Dominik Grace, 2017)

The Science Fiction of Phyllis Gotlieb: A Critical Reading
(Dominick Grace, 2015)

Supernatural Out of the Box

Essays on the Metatextuality of the Series

Edited by LISA MACKLEM *and* DOMINICK GRACE

McFarland & Company, Inc., Publishers
Jefferson, North Carolina

This book has undergone peer review

LIBRARY OF CONGRESS CATALOGUING-IN-PUBLICATION DATA

Title: Supernatural out of the box : essays on the metatextuality
   of the series / edited by Lisa Macklem and Dominick Grace.
Description: Jefferson, North Carolina : McFarland & Company, Inc.,
   Publishers, 2020. | Includes bibliographical references and index.
Identifiers: LCCN 2020023869 | ISBN 9781476673424 (paperback : acid free paper ∞)
   ISBN 9781476639734 (ebook)
Subjects: LCSH: Supernatural (Television program : 2005–)
Classification: LCC PN1992.77.S84 S877 2020 | DDC 791.45/72—dc23
LC record available at https://lccn.loc.gov/2020023869

BRITISH LIBRARY CATALOGUING DATA ARE AVAILABLE

ISBN (print) 978-1-4766-7342-4
ISBN (ebook) 978-1-4766-3973-4

© 2020 Lisa Macklem and Dominick Grace. All rights reserved

*No part of this book may be reproduced or transmitted in any form
or by any means, electronic or mechanical, including photocopying
or recording, or by any information storage and retrieval system,
without permission in writing from the publisher.*

Front cover image © 2020 Shutterstock

Printed in the United States of America

*McFarland & Company, Inc., Publishers
   Box 611, Jefferson, North Carolina 28640
      www.mcfarlandpub.com*

Table of Contents

Introduction—Unpacking Supernatural: *What's in the Box?*
LISA MACKLEM *and* DOMINICK GRACE   1

Part One: "As meta as meta gets"

The Reality of Text Is Manifold: Performances of Writerliness in *Supernatural*'s "The Real Ghostbusters"
STELLA CASTELLI   15

"I so miss being an atheist": God, the Darkness and the Show That Wouldn't Die
ERIN M. GIANNINI   28

"There is no singing in 'Supernatural'!" The Meta as Narrative Device
STEPHANIE A. GRAVES   42

Part Two: "A cruel, cruel, capricious god"

God Is Dead and the Death of the Author: Theorizing Divine Absence in *Supernatural* Season Five
KWASU DAVID TEMBO   57

The Author, the Audience and the Almighty: *Supernatural*'s Chuck Shurley as Metatextual Mirror
EDEN LEE LACKNER   75

"You don't have to be a monster. You have a choice": *Supernatural*, Free Will and the Deterministic Concept of Monstrosity
ANNIKA GONNERMANN   90

vi   Table of Contents

Part Three: "Our lives are not for public consumption"

"Where's the pie?" Nostalgic and Apocalyptic Foodways in *Supernatural*
  KELLI WILHELM — 107

A Cicatricial Romance: Metanarrative, the Textual Wound and a Grotesque View in *Supernatural*
  LINDA HOWELL — 120

"I have my version and you have yours": Folklore, Narrative and the (Re)Telling of *Supernatural*
  KARI SAWDEN — 135

Part Four: Breaking Out of the Box

"Why are you the boy who hates Christmas?" "A Very Supernatural Christmas" as Nostalgic Holiday Special
  KEVIN J. WETMORE, JR. — 151

Strap In for the Scariest Hour in the History of Television: "Ghostfacers" as Parody of Paranormal Investigative Show
  KEVIN J. WETMORE, JR. — 162

Not All Monsters Are Universal: Gothic Parody in "Monster Movie"
  KHARA LUKANCIC — 178

Pamela Barnes as Pastiche: *Supernatural*'s Rock Muse and Blind Seer
  KATHLEEN POTTS — 193

Appendix One: Episodes Cited — 209
Appendix Two: Main and Major Characters — 217
About the Contributors — 223
Index — 227

Introduction

Unpacking Supernatural:
What's in the Box?

LISA MACKLEM *and* DOMINICK GRACE

In the era of Peak TV, how does a television show manage to stay on the air for fifteen seasons? This might be particularly unlikely for a genre, horror show, and yet *Supernatural* is in the top 50 of all-time longest-running United States first-run syndicated drama television series. The only two scripted series above it on this list are the westerns *Death Valley Days* and *Gunsmoke*, and there is something of the western in the story of two all–American boys driving around the country "saving people, hunting things, the family business," even if they do drive a 1967 Impala instead of ride horses. It's no coincidence, perhaps, that two episodes of *Supernatural* are actually "western" episodes or that Dean Winchester is thrilled to be sent back to the Old West and gets to pretend to be a real cowboy—like Clint Eastwood. Even though Bon Jovi doesn't truly classify as the classic rock that Dean is fond of, the brothers still sing Bon Jovi's "Wanted Dead or Alive" in the season three finale episode, harmonizing with Bon Jovi as he sings of a cowboy riding a steel horse.[1] The reference to "the family business" invokes the American Dream of heading west and upholding the American ideals of opportunity through hard work and sacrifice. The Winchesters work hard and sacrifice, but they do it without accruing fame or fortune. These are just some of the metatextual elements that have gone into keeping this series appealing and relevant for so many seasons. The essays in this volume seek to examine the multiple layers of textuality to be found in *Supernatural*.

According to the *Oxford English Dictionary*, metafiction is "Fiction in which the author self-consciously alludes to the artificiality or literariness of a work by parodying or departing from novelistic conventions […] and narrative techniques." Gérard Genette includes metatextuality with paratextuality under the more general heading of transtextuality. According to Genette, metatextuality involves one text commenting on another whereas paratext refers to anything that accompanies the core text, "such as an author's name, a title, a preface" (1). While Genette is concerned with written texts, these terms apply very well to visual media, and they are especially evident in *Supernatural*. Rather than incorporating a generic title sequence, *Supernatural* uses a title card that changes with each season, a reflection of the major story arc for that season. However, specific episodes also feature special title cards, such as the burning map for "Frontierland" (6.18) that mimics the opening of the television western series *Bonanza* or the opening card to "Clap Your Hands If You Believe" (6.09) that mimics the opening sequence of *The X-Files*. Opening credits themselves are parodied for "Changing Channels" (5.08). Viewers have also come to expect a season recap before the final episode of each season that is set to the unofficial theme song of *Supernatural*: "Carry On Wayward Son" by Kansas. Even the choice of song and band are meta, as the Winchesters are from Lawrence, Kansas, carrying on their father's legacy as monster hunters. The band even played the song at the *Supernatural* San Diego Comic-Con panel in 2017. Incorporating the actual story of *Supernatural* within the text of the show itself in the form of the novels about Dean and Sam Winchester is truly a hybrid of meta and paratextual referents or more properly, an example of the show's bold use of intertextuality. It's also difficult to tease out whether incorporating the production of itself within an episode in "The French Mistake" (6.15) is meta or paratextual, and again, this likely falls more clearly into the category of intertextuality. Intertextual elements are perhaps easier to discern, as when the writers comment on other genres and texts outside of *Supernatural* itself.

The terms surrounding textuality are somewhat fluid. Jonathan Gray, for instance, includes a great deal of material that occurs outside of any single media product as part of its paratext. His definition includes elements such as "posters, videogames, podcasts, reviews, or merchandise" and even genre (6). Taking such a broad view of the term may reduce the ability to examine the more nuanced ways in which *Supernatural* plays with textuality. Strictly speaking the "Supernatural" novels should be paratext, yet, in the context of the show it is fruitful to think of them as metatextual as well, when considering Genette's definition of metatextuality as a "transtextual relationship" in which a commentary is linked to the text it comments upon (Macksey quoted in Genette xix). Furthermore, it is especially relevant to tease out those instances of hypertextuality that include "all forms of imitation, pastiche, and parody" (xix), according to Genette. It is important to also recognize Genette's definition of intertextuality that considers the co-presence of two or more texts and Genette's use of architextuality which links the texts to the "various kinds of discourse to which it is a representative" (xix). While each of these terms may not be teased out from the more broad uses of paratext and metatext within this volume, it is useful to understand the nuances that underly references that occur within the show (paratext generally) and those that come from without (metatext in the general sense). This richness of textuality is only one of the elements that has contributed to *Supernatural*'s long run.

Some of *Supernatural*'s success has to be attributed to being in the right place at the right time. Had *Supernatural* been on any of the other major networks in 2005, it's very likely it would not have survived its first season. Even so, it was primarily fan campaigns that saved the show from cancellation for at least its first three seasons, as the show attracted a small but dedicated fanbase from the first season. Beginning on the now-defunct WB network in 2005, *Supernatural* likely benefited from the network shake-up that saw the WB transformed into a limited liability joint venture between CBS and Warner Brothers Entertainment in 2006. The new network would not have wanted to produce an entirely new slate of untried programs. The CW was one of the first networks to truly embrace the new, more reciprocal relationship between industry and viewers: a small but loyal audience that was invested in the show. The audience of *Supernatural* was interested in reaching out to writers and producers of the show in addition to supporting it through campaigns to keep the show on the air. In turn, the writers and producers reached out to fans through social media and direct contact at conventions and other events: a dialogue that eventually led to fans being included within the show itself. This relationship and on-going dialogue was not without its own misunderstandings, however.

The way viewers interact with television has changed remarkably in the last 15 years. Julie D'Acci points to "the impact of new technologies, especially the Internet" on television and posits the need to incorporate new ways of thinking about television that are "dedicated to analyzing the interworkings of industry, programming, and everyday life" (421). In particular, she advocates "a revised circuit model as a matrix for defining the field's object of inquiry and a guide for methodological study" (424). The emergent model for television now is one in which the hegemonic control of material by networks is being challenged. D'Acci defines hegemony as "the process by which various discourses in a social formation come to achieve positions of relative power in negotiations and struggles with other discourses" (434). Specifically, D'Acci's model focuses on the relationship between cultural artifact, production, reception, and socio-historical context. Traditionally, production is perceived as controlling all the power over a television series, but with the advent of the Internet, greater than ever fan engagement has increased the power that fans can exert upon the cultural artifact.

Supernatural has a unique ability to engage its audience in a dialogue, participating in Henry Jenkins's concept of convergence culture. Jenkins states that "convergence represents a paradigm shift—a move from medium-specific content toward content that flows across multiple media channels, toward the increased independence of communications systems, toward multiple ways of accessing media content, and toward ever more complex relations between top-down corporate media and bottom-up participatory culture" (243). This last component is especially relevant here, as *Supernatural* relies on its fans to understand what is at play between the show and its viewers. Breaking the fourth wall allows both the show and the fans to continue to negotiate the unique space that has been created between them.

Several essays in this volume explore some of the aspects of this fan-producer negotiation. It's also never been easier to research an obscure reference to understand the multi-layers of the metatext, given the number of websites devoted to exhaustively detailing all aspects of the shows on which they focus. Some shows, and *Supernatural* is exceptional in this regard, have answered such fan interest with acknowledgments of fandom within the shows themselves—breaking the fourth wall between artifact and audience. Breaking the fourth wall is a way for production to speak to fans about their shared relationship and reward fans for paying attention and is also an acknowledgment by production of the expertise fans have about the show and its production. The initial breaking of the fourth wall led to some disgruntled fans seeing their portrayal as a rebuke directed against some of their engagement with more controversial fan practices. Other fans saw this portrayal as part of a normal learning curve as producers and writers learned more about fans and their engagement with media.

Something had to attract the interest of the viewers to inspire such dedication. When asked what makes a successful television show or movie, industry professionals almost always shrug and declare that there is no way to predict what will be the next breakout success story. In fact, the entire process of bringing a show to air makes something new and innovative almost impossible. When *Supernatural* first aired, it seemed like a typical horror anthology with a monster of the week format—a woman in white, a wendigo, ghosts, and a handful of urban legends. However, underlying all this was a story about the Winchester family and the brothers' search for their missing father—a better hook than "Hook Man" (1.07). When asked what makes a successful TV show, Jeff Bezos said, "remarkable storytelling will always find an audience."[2] One thing that has remained constant with *Supernatural* through five showrunners is a consistently talented writers' room that is willing to think outside the box to keep the show fresh over its long run, and an audience that is more than willing to jump out of that box with them.

Dean Winchester asks, "What's in the box?" in "The Magnificent Seven" (3.01), to the befuddlement of his brother Sam and their surrogate father and mentor Bobby Singer, but to the delight of fans who revel in the show's wry meta elements. Sam and Bobby don't get the reference, but fanboy Dean and the audience do. Dean is, of course, quoting Detective Mills, Brad Pitt's character in the thriller *Se7en* (1995), directed by David Fincher. There's even an obvious link between the two titles. In addition, it seems likely that Sheriff Jody Mills, whose family also dies horrifically like Mills's wife in the movie, may also take her name from the film. Throughout its fifteen seasons, *Supernatural* has reveled in breaking out of the limitations usually implied by a television show, especially a genre show, breaking out of its own textuality in numerous ways and on numerous levels. Casual viewers will likely understand Dean's reference, which he accompanies with an impersonation of Pitt, but likely only more dedicated fans will pick up on the more subtle meta-elements. However, the extra elements are more of a reward for those dedicated fans rather than a barrier to the uninitiated viewer. Pop culture references abound, but there are also numerous storylines that weave in writing, television production, and fandom, as well as genre bending from horror into the western, as already mentioned, as well as comedy and even cartoons. Fans of all kinds are welcome here.

The genre-bending began early with season one's "Hell House" (1.17), which played the horror for laughs with the introduction of inept ghost hunters Ed Zeddmore and Harry Spengler. Their names are also an homage to characters in *Ghostbusters* (1984). The episode features a prank war between the two brothers, which mirrored the onset pranking between actors Jensen Ackles and Jared Padalecki. Ed and Harry also work on an even more metatextual level as they are trying to secure a reality television deal for themselves, and the storyline is referencing the entertainment business itself and reality television which script writers eschew. In season three's "Ghostfacers" (3.13), Ed and Harry actually shoot their reality TV show, complete with handheld, shaky cameras. This episode was the first to air after a lengthy writers' strike and was the writers' way of commenting on the trend of reality shows, by the airing of which studios avoid having to pay writers. It also lampoons the myriad of ghost-hunting shows on air. (See the second essay by Kevin Wetmore in this volume for an analysis of that episode.) This episode really rises to what Genette refers to as architextuality. Reality stars even make an appearance in later episodes, with Paris Hilton guest starring in "Fallen Idols" (5.05)—also played for laughs—and Snooki guest-starring as a crossroads demon in "Blade Runners" (9.16).

Other episodes that are largely comedic include "Bad Day at Black Rock" (3.03), "Wishful Thinking" (4.08), "Hunteri Heroici" (8.08), and "Scoobynatural" (13.16), the latter two of which are especially significant examples of *Supernatural*'s meta propensities. These last two episodes not only involve explicit meta elements but also rely on cartoons. "Hunteri Heroici" relies on

Warner Brothers cartoon tropes, like anvils falling on people, disappearing holes, and guns that furl out a BANG sign rather than shooting actual bullets. The episode features a character named Fred Jones—after one of the lead characters in *Scooby-Doo*. *Supernatural* goes full-cartoon in "Scoobynatural" when the brothers actually find themselves inside a *Scooby-Doo* episode, and the bulk of the episode is a cartoon rather than live action. Naturally, Dean is a huge fan of the cartoon and remembers the episode they find themselves in, which helps to solve the mystery. They also rely on their experiences in a previous episode—"Changing Channels"—to help them solve the case.

The ability to recreate itself is one of the reasons the show remains fresh for both the writers and the audience. The writers turn frequently to the subjects of writing and television production, drawing often on their own experiences with *Supernatural* itself. "Hollywood Babylon" (2.18) sees the brothers investigating a ghost on the set of a horror movie. The episode features many references to the difficulties writers and producers had experienced in the course of producing *Supernatural*, such as notes from executives wanting the show to be "brighter" and failing to understand the artistic and thematic necessities of the horror genre. In "Changing Channels," Sam and Dean find themselves moving through a series of different television shows as the Archangel Gabriel attempts to convince them to "play the roles they were born for." The episode moves seamlessly from references to a thinly veiled *Grey's Anatomy*, to *CSI Miami* (and an hilarious send up of David Caruso), to *Three's Company*, to *Knight Rider*, and even a Japanese game show and a commercial for a genital herpes medication. The writers don't reserve their send ups for other shows, however, and are prepared to laugh at themselves. Ben Edlund, executive producer and writer of "The French Mistake," calls the episode "as meta as meta gets."[3] In the episode, Sam and Dean are transported to an alternate universe where they are Jared Padalecki and Jensen Ackles, playing Sam and Dean on the television show *Supernatural*. The scene in which Sam and Dean find themselves trying to act is being directed by Robert Singer, the showrunner is Sera Gamble, and creator Eric Kripke is called in to come to Vancouver to rein in Padalecki and Ackles, who seem to have lost their minds. In the episode, due to SAG-ACTRA requirements, only Ackles, Padalecki and Misha Collins appear as analogues of themselves. Collins insisted that the Misha Collins portrayed in the episode be as "douche-y" as possible. While Singer, Gamble, and Kripke are portrayed by actors, Kripke was eager to be killed off and insisted that his "character" wear his signature running shoes. On the commentary track for the episode, Gamble explains how they are able to get so far out of the box:

> We often, throughout the episode, say, well, we're on season six, whatever, moving on, but when you are on a show on season six, you have a fanbase that is loyal, and you're glad that they're loyal and you're thankful that they're loyal and the least that

we can do is do an episode that acknowledges that they know more than the average viewer about the show so we were able to do this because they know what we're talking about and that's a cool thing.

It's perhaps not surprising that a show in which the writers reflect upon the production process also encourages the writers to muse about writing itself and the sometimes contentious relationship that the writers have with the audience.

In "The Monster at the End of This Book" (4.18), Dean and Sam discover a series of books about their lives written by Carver Edlund—an amalgamation of writers Jeremy Carver (who would eventually go on to become the showrunner for seasons eight to eleven) and Ben Edlund. The brothers soon learn that this is the pseudonym of Chuck Shurley—who turns out to be God, making one of his rare mainstream television appearances. Chuck is also the stand-in for Kripke—the creator of the show—and in "Swan Song" (5.22), Chuck tells the viewers in a rare voice over that "[e]ndings are hard" before disappearing at the end of the episode as Kripke also bows out as showrunner. Seasons eight and nine feature as main villain the appropriately named Metatron, the scribe of God trying to write himself into the position of God—in effect plotting in both senses of the word. Season ten's 200th episode is yet another recursive metanarrative, featuring a high school student trying to mount a musical adaptation of the Carver Edlund novels. Only half of the musical is really based on the novels, however, with the director relying primarily on fan fiction for the second half, and fan fiction as writing appears right alongside the novels in "The Monster at the End of This Book."

Fans actually show up in season one, and play an important role in "Hell House," because it's the fans of Ed and Harry's website that bring the Tulpa to life—much as the fans of *Supernatural* were able to breathe life into their favorite show. The depiction of fans and fandom has not always met with approval by the actual fans of the show. Dean, however, is depicted as a fanboy early on. He is star-struck by Tara in "Hollywood Babylon" and Dr. Sexy in "Changing Channels." There are layers of reference sprinkled throughout "Hollywood Babylon," such as when Dean gushes to Tara that he loved her in *Boogeyman* (2005). Her response is "What a terrible script, but thank you!" Tara's acceptance of fan–Dean is a reflection of the producers' acceptance of their own fans. The joke in Tara's comment is that *Boogeyman* is a real movie and was written by Eric Kripke. (However, Elizabeth Whitmere, who plays Tara, did not in fact appear in *Boogeyman*.) Dean is also a fan of Elliot Ness in "Time After Time" (7.12) and the old west in "Frontierland." Dean is disappointed when both of these time travelling episodes reveal that the object of his fannish passions doesn't live up to his expectations. Dean discovers that he quite enjoys the fan practice of LARPing (Live Action Role-Playing) in "LARP and the Real Girl" (8.11), and Dean and Sam are mistaken for LARPers, recursively playing themselves, in "The Monster at the End of This Book." Dean and Sam first encounter fans of Chuck's novels online. However, fan fiction–writing superfan Becky is called on by Chuck to deliver a message to Dean and Sam in "Sympathy for the Devil" (5.01). She later lures them to a fan convention in "The Real Ghostbusters" (5.09) that mimics real-world fan conventions for the show. Fans have not always been happy with the portrayal of fans onscreen and particularly criticized the portrayal of Becky in her first and last appearances as of this writing. In "Season Seven, Time for a Wedding!" (7.08), she drugs Sam and places a spell on him before declaring herself a loser and exiting the show. It's clear that the writers have not always understood the fans even while appreciating their passion. Fan portrayal in the show is complex and multi-layered, much as real fans are in real life.

In "Mint Condition" (14.04), Dean is trying to deal with the after-effects of having allowed the Archangel Michael to possess him, and is holed up in his room eating junk food and binging on horror movies; both are his comfort food. Sam uses a case to help him get over it, and the case itself focuses on the healing aspects of fandom. Sam can't understand Dean's fascination over horror movies—they live them every day! The case itself turns out to be a comic book store owner's ghost possessing various objects from the store, including the life-size replica of the Hatchet Man, a fictional horror movie villain that Dean just happens to be a fan of. The episode is typically meta with character Samantha paralleling Sam and character Dirk paralleling Dean. Dean confides in Dirk that he had a difficult time growing up and that sometimes it was nice to just check out and watch horror movies, knowing that the bad guys were going to lose. Many fans have expressed similar feelings about watching *Supernatural*.

In short, despite its horror trappings, *Supernatural* has been decidedly postmodern in its liberal use of pastiche, meta, intertextuality, and generic slippage. This collection is interested in exploring the ways *Supernatural* breaks boundaries and utilizes the full range of textual possibilities. While this book is divided into sections with essays grouped by thematic categories, the essays also speak to each other across these arbitrarily imposed parameters.

Supernatural's invocation of metafictive conceits has become a mainstay of the show and marks the most obvious way in which the show breaks out of the box of television conventions. Therefore, essays in Part One, "'As meta as meta gets,'" delve into the show's meta elements. Stella Castelli's "The Reality of Text Is Manifold: Performances of Writerliness in 'The Real Ghostbusters'" focuses on one episode, "The Real Ghostbusters," treating it as paradigmatic of how *Supernatural* uses metafictive devices to break out of the box. Castelli reads the episode in Barthesian terms as writerly—as not merely open to but demanding active engagement—in its blending of levels of diegesis. The episode challenges assumptions about narrative authority by including embedded narrative but more importantly by bringing Chuck Shurley (as noted above, the author of the series of books that document the lives of Sam and Dean—and, it is ultimately revealed, God in human form) to a fan convention, populated by enthusiasts who engage with "Supernatural" (Chuck's series of books) in their own terms, just as fans of *Supernatural* do, together with Sam and Dean, the "real" characters stuck between these conflicting models of authority over their lives. Erin M. Giannini, in "'I so miss being an atheist': God, the Darkness and the Show That Wouldn't Die," focuses on the fan side of the equation, though also invoking the show's use of God, by casting the conflict between God and Amara (God's sister and the major antagonist of season eleven), as reflective of the tension between creators of the show and fans of the show over control of the narrative. Stephanie A. Graves narrows the focus in her essay, "There is no singing in 'Supernatural!' The Meta as Narrative Device," exploring in depth the meta elements of *Supernatural*'s 200th episode, "Fan Fiction" (10.05), one of the most overtly and self-consciously meta episodes of the show to date.

In Part Two, "'A cruel, cruel, capricious god,'" Kwasu David Tembo and Eden Lee Lackner delve more deeply into how specifically the show's invocation of God is relevant to its metatextual concerns. In "God Is Dead and the Death of the Author: Theorizing Divine Absence in *Supernatural* Season Five," Tembo examines in detail the show's exploration of the relationship between narrative, destiny, and free will. In "The Author, the Audience and the Almighty: *Supernatural*'s Chuck Shurley as Metatextual Mirror," Lackner also digs into the narrative layers of the show, explicitly tackling the equation between Chuck Shurley as God within the diegetic world of *Supernatural* and of Erik Kripke, as creator of the show, as its extradiegetic God. Annika Gonnermann's "'You don't have to be a monster. You have a choice': *Supernatural*, Free Will and the Deterministic Concept of Monstrosity" ties together several of these ideas by delving into the show's Gothic roots to explore its complex conceptualization of monstrosity: is it inherent, imposed, and/or culturally determined? *Supernatural*, she argues, ultimately reflects a deterministic vision, a surprising position for a show produced in the United States of America, which prides itself on belief in freedom.

The essays in Part Three, "'Our lives are not for public consumption,'" deal with how the show engages with larger cultural questions, notably in how it negotiates its relationship with fandom. In "'Where's the pie?' Nostalgic and Apocalyptic Foodways in *Supernatural*," Kelli Wilhelm picks up on a fan-favorite aspect of the show (Dean Winchester's obsession with pie) to read the show in light of the cultural power of food both to encourage community and to enforce hegemonic and oppressive structures—especially germane in season seven, in which food is used as a weapon by the season's antagonists, the Leviathans. Linda Howell reads the show through the lens of trauma theory in "A Cicatricial Romance: Metanarrative, the Textual Wound and a Grotesque View in *Supernatural*," arguing that the show's meta elements, specifically in its insertion of an author/god into the show, can be understood as a metaphorical wound that represents the complex and sometimes combative relationship between show and audience. This question of authority over the narrative is picked up by Kari Sawden in "'I have my version and you have yours': Folklore, Narrative and the (Re)Telling of *Supernatural*." This essay explores how the show challenges hegemonic narrative by arguing that its folkloric and scriptural elements make explicit the show's repeated invocation of narrative control as a major motif; the notion of a master narrative is undercut when narrators are multiplied.

Part Four, "Breaking Out of the Box," analyzes how *Supernatural* explores what Genette refers to as hypertextuality through the use of parody, pastiche, and satire, especially of the tropes of television. In "'Why are you the boy who hates Christmas?' 'A Very Supernatural Christmas' as Nostalgic Holiday Special," Kevin J. Wetmore, Jr., reads the *Supernatural* episode "A Very Supernatural Christmas" (3.08) as a meta-episode specifically in relation to the ubiquitous Christmas specials that crop up on television during the holiday season; from its opening shot, borrowing the CBS "Special Presentation" logo, through to its conclusion, this episode functions as a knowing commentary on and subversion of the genre of the Christmas special. Wetmore's second contribution, "Strap in for the Scariest Hour in the History of Television: 'Ghostfacers' as Parody of Paranormal Investigative Show" similarly investigates *Supernatural*'s deconstruction of so-called reality ghost-hunting shows in "Ghostfacers." Wetmore demonstrates how the episode depends on the tropes of such shows by building the episode as a frame narrative around the Ghostfacers' attempt to make a pilot episode of their own ghost-hunting show, thereby interrogating *Supernatural*'s own exploitation of horror tropes. In their essays, Khara Lukancic and Kathleen Potts broaden the consideration, dealing with how *Supernatural* plays on the tropes of film and even of Aristotelean narrative. In "Not All Monsters Are Universal: Gothic Parody in 'Monster Movie,'" Lukancic explores the "Monster Movie" episode (4.05), even the title of which addresses its meta elements, by considering it in terms of Gothic parody, specifically of the Universal monster movies that inform the actions of the episode's antagonist. The effect of this episode, Lukancic argues, is to signal the more significant breaking of conventional horror boundaries that were to follow later in the season and subsequently in the show. Potts, by contrast, focuses on the character of Pamela Barnes, in her essay, "Pamela Barnes as Pastiche: *Supernatural*'s Rock Muse and Blind Seer," seeing Barnes as a postmodern pastiche figure invoking everything from rock groupie to Aristotelean protagonist and thereby ending up, paradoxically, as a new myth of rock 'n' roll chick as reluctant hero.

Within the context of this book, *Supernatural* required us to think somewhat outside the box when considering the component parts within the box. Consequently, references to the show *Supernatural* are rendered in italics while references to the book series "Supernatural" written by Carver Edlund appear within quotation marks. Each essay ends with a Works Cited list, but publication information on each of the episodes is contained within an appendix at the end of this volume. Likewise, a second appendix lists the major characters and who played them. Within the essays, episodes are referenced by season and episode number. For instance, episode one of season one appears as (1.01).

Notes

1. Complete song lyrics can be found in multiple places online.
2. Quoted in Lauren Moraski, "What It Takes to Make a Hit TV Show," CBS News (23 November 2015), online: https://www.cbsnews.com/news/what-it-takes-to-make-a-hit-tv-show-today/.
3. Ben Edlund. "Commentary for 'The French Mistake.'" *Supernatural: The Complete Sixth Season*. Warner Brothers, 2011. Blu-Ray.

Works Cited

D'Acci, Julie. "Cultural Studies, Television Studies, and the Crisis in the Humanities." *Television After TV: Essays on a Medium in Transition*, edited by Lynn Spigel and Jan Olsson, Duke UP, 2004, pp. 418–445.
Edlund, Ben. "Commentary for 'The French Mistake.'" *Supernatural: The Complete Sixth Season*. Warner Brothers, 2011. Blu-Ray.
Gamble, Sera. "Commentary for 'The French Mistake.'" *Supernatural: The Complete Sixth Season*. Warner Brothers, 2011. Blu-Ray.
Genette, Gérard. *Paratexts: Thresholds of Interpretation*. Translated by Jane E. Lewin, Cambridge UP, 1987.
Jenkins, Henry. *Convergence Culture: Where Old and New Media Collide*. NYU Press, 2008.
Moraski, Lauren. "What It Takes to Make a Hit TV Show." CBS News, 23 November 2015, https://www.cbsnews.com/news/what-it-takes-to-make-a-hit-tv-show-today/.

PART ONE

"As meta as meta gets"

The Reality of Text Is Manifold
Performances of Writerliness in Supernatural's *"The Real Ghostbusters"*

Stella Castelli

> If theatre and life are inseparable, our behavior is a series of roles. And if we are merely playing roles there is no "original" to the mimesis; we are caught in an inescapable condition of imitating a false idea [...]
> —Davis and Postlewait, *Theatricality*, 10–11

> Hotel Manager: "You guys are really into this."
> Sam Winchester: "You have no idea."
> —*Supernatural*, "The Real Ghostbusters" (5.09)

The CW's *Supernatural* has broken out of the box many times over the course of its run. Episode nine of season five, "The Real Ghostbusters," may be read as a synecdoche of the show's repeated performance of heightened self-referentiality as well as self-reflexivity. *Supernatural* has stepped beyond its frame on so many occasions, one may consider the show's willingness to break with its own narratology an inherent part of its appeal. We may recall "The French Mistake" (6.15), in which protagonists Sam and Dean Winchester find themselves astonished on the set of the television show of their "real lives," or "Changing Channels" (5.08), in which the protagonists jump between parodies of television shows. Bridging different notions of the metatext we also find episodes such as "Mystery Spot" (3.11), which draws on the popular 1993 film *Groundhog Day*, having Sam relive the same day over and over again, inscribing intertextuality into its materiality. Over its run, *Supernatural* has developed a long tradition of breaking the narratological norm. This heightened awareness of a metatextuality which is inherent in the show has allowed for the television format to become an extensively open, *writerly* text. A movement into the meta generates narrative space, which is to say, it produces a canvas onto which further text can be written, expanding the narrative. Metatextuality broadens the narrative space not just in its vertical, linear expansion but also in its horizontal, exponential expansion, above and beyond the previously established diegesis. The essence of *Supernatural*, then, is its self-referential quality which in a sense turns the show into a potential *perpetuum mobile*, a self-sufficient text that, rather than remaining *readerly*, becomes *writerly* in its metatextuality. By means of exploring the meta of the text in all its forms, the show not only draws attention to itself by means of the *mise-en-abyme*. In overtly being metatextual, the show employs its own materiality in order to further its narrative, continuously drawing on what (initially) lies outside its scope. A particularly telling example of this dynamic is offered in the aforementioned episode "The Real Ghostbusters," in which said textual extension beyond its diegetic boundaries is executed by means of a narratological expansion over different layers of diegesis. Contrary to the hierarchical structure narratology demands, these diegetic layers do not remain stable within a parallel configuration and therefore allow for the text to expand in manifold directions and in doing so, do not merely draw attention to the text itself but offer fruitful ground for the text to multiply itself.

Inherent in the title "The Real Ghostbusters" is the possibility of a number of diegetic levels—pointing to the fact that there will be real as well as non-real ghostbusters, which sets up the dually structured narration already in its title. The same dichotomy between real and non-real ghostbusters—or as it will turn out, diegetic and hypodiegetic levels respectively—holds true for the ghosts themselves as well as the case of the episode, structuring the plot along a doubled narration. The episode opens with Dean and Sam, the proverbial "real" ghostbusters, frantically pulling up at the Pineview Hotel. Upon their arrival, a somewhat puzzled Dean spots a row of cars, exact replicas of his beloved Chevrolet Impala. This marks only the first instance in which *Supernatural*'s "The Real Ghostbusters" is mirroring itself by means of evoking the double in various forms. As the protagonists enter the Pineview Hotel they find themselves confronted with a multiplicity of artificial renditions of themselves and other characters based on their actual lives. The protagonists become attendees of a "Supernatural" convention based on the diegetic "Supernatural" books which are being written by prophet Chuck Shurley, employing the pseudonym Carver Edlund. These books are based on their lives. The convention is designed for fans of the books and features the live action role-playing game "The Big Hunt" in which participants are meant to enact the roles of the many different characters found in the "Supernatural" books and solve an artificial, supernatural case. From a narratological perspective, we find a diegetic layer added to the tale with said hypo-fictional case "The Big Hunt." Within Sam and Dean's diegesis, the show *Supernatural* which features the two brothers Sam and Dean Winchester tackling dark supernatural forces all around the U.S., we then find the incorporation of a hypodiegesis of the enactment of the "Supernatural" books. As these two diegetic levels converge, the actual, diegetic Sam and Dean meet their hypodiegetically cosplaying counterparts, who stage their actual lives in artifice. The "Supernatural" books generate a heterotopic space which allows for the enactment of the "Supernatural" fantasy within the diegetic realm of the television show *Supernatural*. Within this framework, Dean and Sam's "real" is questioned as they observe their reality being performed as a fiction.

In his seminal text, *S/Z*, literary theorist Roland Barthes draws a distinction between *readerly* and *writerly* texts—the latter offering a plurality of possible interpretations for the reader, wherefore the reader does not remain passive but rather begins to perform the text, to write him/herself:

> The writerly text is a perpetual present, upon which no consequent language [...] be superimposed; the writerly text is *ourselves writing*, before the infinite play of the world [...] is traversed, intersected, stopped, plasticized by some singular system [...] which reduces the plurality of entrances, the opening of networks, the infinity of language [5].

Writerliness then refers to the way in which the reader assumes agency; by interpreting a text the reader begins to inscribe a plurality within said text. Within the *writerly*, then, Barthes elaborates on a certain plurality of connotation inscribed in a given text, turning the reader into a laborer and the text into a canvas:

> [M]y task is to move, to shift systems whose perspective ends neither at the text nor at the "I": in operational terms, the meanings I find are established not by "me" or by others, but by their systematic mark: there is no other proof of a reading than the quality and endurance of its systematics; in other words: than its functioning. To read, in fact, is a labor of language [10–11].

Supernatural's "The Real Ghostbusters" may be read as a physical performance of Barthes's notion of writerliness, reflecting not only on its own genre as a television series, but opening it up to further genres and further diegeses. In the episode, we find the readers of the "Supernatural" books who explicitly turn the text into their own *writerly* performance. The episode layers the diegesis of *Supernatural* with a hypodiegesis of "Supernatural." These doubly layered diegeses or dichotomous fictional "realities," then, rather than remaining static, eventually begin to interact with each other while their boundaries begin to blur—offering plural expansion of the text rather than a singular linearity. While mixing different diegeses by means of turning them into a performed *writerly*, the text interlaces multiple "Supernatural"/*Supernatural* realities and thus moves into a form of metatextuality, commenting on itself, its genre and its continual constructive reproduction.

This notion of writerliness is also inherent in the serial form of the television show itself. Based on its structure, which draws on the pleasures of repetition, the television series is a writerly text par excellence, potentially repeating itself endlessly. In *Populare Serialität—Narration—Evolution—Distinktion*, Frank Kelleter elaborates on the expansive nature of serial narration, making the claim that the repetitive aspect of the serial is subject not only to a vertical but also horizontal expansion. In the sense of the *writerly* as outlined by Barthes, Kelleter elaborates on how the serial generates text almost exponentially—in its own textuality but also within its broader realm of fan fiction, merchandise and respective spin-offs throughout various genres and therefore assumes a pluralistic hybridity (20–25). Considering that "The Real Ghostbusters" makes use of said horizontal expansion of the serial as a form of *mise-en-abyme*—internalizing the external, its own "what comes after" and incorporating said external within an intrinsic hypodiegetic level—renders its potential for the *writerly* particularly poignant.

Before closely examining the way in which *Supernatural* not only employs but mixes narrative levels we must define said multiple diegeses. In *Narrative Fiction*, Shlomith Rimmon-Kenan distinguishes between narrative levels in narrative fiction, making the claim that within a story (diegesis) another story (hypodiegesis) can be told. Within this narratological structure there remains, according to Rimmon-Kenan, a hierarchy amongst these various diegeses: "Such narratives within narratives create a stratification of levels whereby each inner narrative is subordinate to the narrative within which it is embedded" (92). Rimmon-Kenan elaborates on this hierarchical dynamic, claiming that the narrator resides within a higher level of the story that is told: "Narration is always at a higher narrative level than the story it narrates. Thus, the diegetic level is narrated by an extradiegetic narrator, the hypodiegetic by a diegetoic (intradiegetic) one" (93). In cinematographic narratives, the camera assumes the position of the extradiegetic narrator. It is the camera that tells the audience of the diegesis. Within "The Real Ghostbusters," we are then faced with an additional layer of narration, a *mise-en-abyme*, triggered by the "Supernatural" convention itself, which tells the Sam and Dean story within the Sam and Dean diegesis in the form of a hypodiegesis. "The Big Hunt" becomes the story within the story, albeit both stories are told by the same narrator, the camera.

Medially tied to a single narrator, we nonetheless have a narration along two diegetic levels. If we define the narrative of Sam and Dean as the diegesis, the narrative of their manifold replicas and staged antagonists live action role-playing "The Big Hunt" become the hypodiegesis, the narration within the narration, its *mise-en-abyme*. The proverbial real ghostbusters, Sam and Dean, operate within the diegesis of the television show *Supernatural*. The contrasting fake ghostbusters, the attendees of the "Supernatural" convention who merely perform Sam and Dean within the diegesis, operate within the hypodiegesis of "The Big Hunt," which is simultaneously generated by the television show *Supernatural*. The camera as narratological entity is split along the diegetic levels, telling two tales. While we perceive all story lines through the lens of the same camera, Chuck, as the prophet, assumes the role of the extradiegetic narrator of Sam and Dean's story (while becoming the intradiegetic narrator of the hypodiegesis when posing as Carver Edlund, author of the "Supernatural" books), opening the Sam and Dean story up to the heterotopic space of "The Big Hunt." While Dean accepts Chuck's role as prophet, he does question his role as author who produces the hypodiegesis, selling their story for economic gain: "Who gave you the rights to our life story?" To which Chuck answers: "An archangel and I didn't want it." While the legitimacy of Chuck's exploitation of the "Supernatural" story may be questionable, its metatextual incorporation in the television show allows for an increased production of textuality. It is not merely the establishment of two diegetic layers but the interference with the diegetic hierarchy which, in a *writerly* fashion, generates more narrative. These intersecting diegeses break with the parallelism of the narratological structure and are therefore able to assume agency, adding more narrative.

In his 1936 essay "The Work of Art in the Age of Its Technological Reproducibility" Walter Benjamin elaborates on the loss of what he terms the "aura" of a work of art once it becomes technologically reproducible. What is at stake in a technological reproduction, according to Benjamin, is the authenticity of the original which is no longer present in its imitation, as he states: "In even the most perfect reproduction, one thing is lacking: the here and now of the work of art—its unique existence in a particular place. It is this unique existence—and nothing else—that bears the mark of the history to which the work has been subject" (103). While the attendees of the "Supernatural" convention are not technological, identical reproductions of Sam and Dean, they do, in a similar manner as outlined with regard to the technologically reproduced work of art, lack the history which marks the actual Sam and Dean Winchester. The consequential question is that of authenticity of an original which is rendered fraudulent by a reproduction thereof. In the case of "The Real Ghostbusters" this notion begins to threaten not only the protagonists who are being reproduced but even more so the diegesis which is being reproduced by the hypodiegesis. While the text opens itself up and becomes more *writerly*, it simultaneously threatens its own aura as an authentic, original work of art, which is inscribed within the doubly mirrored narrative in the episode.

As the protagonists face themselves being performed, it is Dean who increasingly questions not only the performability of their lives but also the appeal of their existence when he states: "In fact I think that the Dean and Sam story sucks. It is not fun, it's not entertaining, it is a river of crap that would send most people howling to the nuthouse. So, you listen to me, their pain is not for your amusement." Benjamin elaborates on the notion of proximity as a form of meeting a desire of engulfing an aura, an object's uniqueness: "The desire of the present-day masses to 'get closer' to things, and their equally passionate concern for overcoming each thing's uniqueness by assimilating it as a reproduction" (105). *Supernatural* shows awareness of this aspect, while simultaneously dismissing its gravitas by means of pointing towards its own fictionality with one of the role-players, Demian, stating, "I don't think they care because they're fictional characters." This statement also attempts to break the fourth wall—as the audience of *Supernatural*, the viewer also takes pleasure in the pain of Sam and Dean in a cathartic sense. While for an instant *Supernatural*'s fictionality is heightened, it is brought back to the diegesis with Dean stating, "Oh they care, believe me, they care a lot," to which Sam responds, "He takes the story very seriously." In this reflection of their authenticity, which is made possible only by means of crisscrossing diegetic levels, the authentic Sam and Dean and the unauthentic, "auraless" Sam and Dean begin to affect each other. As Benjamin states, the reproducibility of an object (or subject in this case) not only renders the replicas auraless but further jeopardizes the original, resulting in a devaluation of the original work of art: "And what is really jeopardized when the historical testimony is affected is the authority of the object, the weight it derives from tradition" (103). *Supernatural*, then, skillfully turns this potential devaluation into comic relief, illustrating self-awareness and therefore reinstating its authority as text. Having had their authenticity and originality established over the course of five previous seasons, Sam and Dean remain unharmed albeit temporarily threatened by the replicas they are faced with while their artificial reality remains authentic throughout in the sense outlined by Benjamin:

> In the film studio the apparatus has penetrated so deeply into reality that a pure view of that reality, free of the foreign body of equipment, is the result of a special procedure—namely, the shooting by the specially adjusted photographic device and the assembly of that shot with others of the same kind. The equipment-free aspect of reality has here become the height of artifice [...] [105].

Benjamin further emphasizes the significance of representation as a tool of penetration:

> Hence, the presentation of reality in film is incomparably more significant for people of today, since it provides the equipment-free aspect of reality they are entitled to

demand from a work of art, and does so precisely on the basis of the most intensive interpenetration of reality with equipment [116].

It is not the technical which penetrates the narrative in this case, but the additional layer of narrative—a copy not only of the protagonists but of the narrative itself—which puts its authority into question only to reinstate itself and within this act, further its own narrative.

Within these diegetic layers penetrating each other, abandoning the hierarchical parallelism outlined by Rimmon-Kenan, the narrative finds its nurturing ground in the *writerly* sense while simultaneously reestablishing a potential loss of authenticity by means of contrast of the authentic and the unauthentic. While the protagonists are forced to observe a performance of their actual lives, they themselves also step inside the hypodiegesis—which along the lines of Benjamin's elaborations on the truthfulness of the aura within a copy, also brings the question of theatricality into play. Sam and Dean, then, are not merely mirrored in a surplus of counterparts but in the sense of Kelleter's horizontal expansion of the text. This notion becomes particularly apparent in the scene in which Sam and Dean contemplate the destruction of the bones of the real ghosts when they overhear a fake Sam and Dean discussing the fake case. The real ghostbusters notice the realness of the map that their fake counterparts obtained. As they approach their counterparts, Sam states that "it's real," meaning the map. As Sam reassures the audience of the authenticity of the map, it is the dramatic irony which renders this scene particularly writerly—as the show adds the comedic counterparts uttering "we get to be Sam and Dean" in "The Big Hunt" while the real Sam and Dean merely get to enact the supporting characters of Rufus Turner and Bobby Singer. The narrative and resolution of the case is furthered by their counterparts, feeding into Barthes's elaboration on the *writerly* text. It is Sam who then makes a claim for Dean taking the story of the "Supernatural" books very seriously while trying to maintain the illusion which is enacted in the hypodiegesis as a means to assure the safety of Demian and Barnes. In fact, it is Dean who is most concerned with the factuality of their lives, unwilling to play along in the hypodiegesis, continually questioning the (un)reality of the hypodiegesis with utterances such as "Real enough for you?" or "This isn't make-believe." "[I am] Dean. The real Dean." Notably, it is then also Dean who eventually instrumentalizes the hypodiegesis in order to vanquish the ghosts and bridges the two diegetic levels which then are no longer merely parallel but interactive, feeding each other's narration. While Dean proves most reluctant with regard to performing the artifice of "Supernatural," he seems most aware of the diegetic levels at play and never slips into performing the hypodiegesis. Remaining at the superior level of diegesis throughout also allows him to come up with a plan that instrumentalizes the hypodiegesis in order to contain the diegetic, "real" situation, and, on a narratological level, to advance their narrative by means of letting the text expand horizontally.

Crafting an episode which centers on live action role-playing has the question of authenticity inscribed in itself by definition. The hotel manager himself states, "Guess you convention folks wanted authenticity" as he informs the protagonists that "The Big Hunt" is rooted in a diegetic actuality of a real ghost. Inscribing an inherently theatrical text such as a television program with further theatricality heightens the complexity of imitation as outlined by Benjamin. In *Theatricality*, Tracy C. Davis and Thomas Postlewait make a similar observation with regard to a lack of authenticity in the theatrical rendition, stating that "[t]he theatre may imitate life (or some ideal), but like a metaphor the representation is always removed from its model, falling short of it" (5). The problematic aspect with regard to the diegetic levels in this particular episode lies with the recipient's awareness of that which is performed and that which is not (within its respective layer). In their elaborations on the theatrical, Davis and Postlewait claim that

> [w]hen the spectator's role is not to recognize reality but to create an alternative through complicity in the "heightening" of the breakthrough into performance, then both performer and spectator are complicit in the mimesis. [...] It means that mimesis may not mislead, because when caught up by it the actors and spectators agree to forgo truth. This "mimetic conundrum" implies that performers and spectators are still true to themselves, though, paradoxically the representation may lack truth [6].

This agreement is shattered in "The Real Ghostbusters" by means of its interwoven structures. While the actors and spectators of both the diegesis and the hypodiegesis are in agreement to forgo the truth, the authenticity, which is implied throughout the episode by their manifold references to *Supernatural*'s fictionality (on both levels) it is the representation which tampers with its own authenticity in crossing its diegetic levels. In a number of instances, the audience is temporarily left alone in judging whether evidence is real or false. The question which is at stake is not only that of authenticity but also that of reliability. As Rimmon-Kenan states, "A reliable narrator is one whose rendering of the story and commentary on it the reader is supposed to take as an authoritative account of the fictional truth" (101). Sam and Dean become the only reliable authority of authenticity on all diegetic levels based on their—in terms of Benjamin—imprinted history. In turn, Sam and Dean themselves are considered reliable because of their authenticity. By means of contrasting the hypodiegetic fake with the diegetic real in instances such as Demian who is performing Dean not expecting authenticity: "That's not a plastic skeleton, that's a skeleton skeleton" and Barnes, his fake Sam counterpart, who remarks, "You just dug up a real grave," Sam and Dean's authenticity is not only reaffirmed but continuously restored. As the episode progresses, hypodiegetic fake Sam and Dean find themselves under attack by the diegetic real ghost, which is to say that the hypodiegetic characters become part of the diegesis. This continual doubling of characters, plot and diegetic levels then begins to obtain a haunting quality which is reminiscent of Sigmund Freud's "The Uncanny."

Freud makes the argument that something is rendered uncannily frightening when it harbors qualities of both the strange as well as the familiar: "the uncanny is that class of the frightening which leads back to what is known of old and long familiar" (220). He further elaborates on this quality outlining a form of tampered familiarity which produces the uncanny:

> In order to grasp the concept of the uncanny, the German expression "unheimlich" is best to describe it: The German word "unheimlich" is obviously the opposite of "heimlich" ["homely"], "heimisch" ["native"]—the opposite of what is familiar; and we are tempted to conclude that what is "uncanny" is frightening precisely because it is not known and familiar. Naturally not everything that is new and unfamiliar is frightening [...] something has to be added to what is novel and unfamiliar to make it uncanny [220–221].

We have a number of instances within "The Real Ghostbusters" which evoke the uncanniness, for example, inherent in the ghosts: "Many people experience the feeling [the uncanny] in the highest degree in relation to death and dead bodies, to the return of the dead, and to spirits and ghosts" (Freud 241). However, while there are two layers of dieses which both feature ghosts, uncanniness becomes particularly apparent in the fact that we have a doubled layering of the same and in that sense also find inscribed into the episode the figure of the double—the doppelgänger which incorporates said strange familiarity. Read in connection to Benjamin, Freud's uncanny doppelgänger poses a threat to a subject's authenticity by means of shattering a perceived individuality: "Or it is marked by the fact that the subject identifies himself with someone else, that he is in doubt as to which his self is, or substitutes the extraneous self for his own. In other words, there is a doubling, dividing and interchanging of the self" (234). This notion which is played with throughout the episode is picked up in a scene right at the beginning. Live action role-player Demian approaches the real Dean saying, "Hey Dean, looking good," to which Dean replies, "Who the hell are you?" which is met with "I'm Dean too, duh." As diegetic levels begin to overlap, the replicas of Sam and Dean become more and more uncanny, which eventually results in reinstating the authenticity of the real Sam and Dean Winchester as hierarchically superior to their replicas. Within the diegesis—the fictitious reality of *Supernatural*—the doubles revert back to their actual selves, exposing the hypodiegesis as mere play and reestablishing the authority of the real ghostbusters. It is not only the ghosts—real and fake—which obtain an uncanny quality, but the interlayering of diegetic levels themselves, which come to haunt each other. In consequence, as diegetic levels are no longer set up in a parallel structure, this notion of interlayering diegetic levels also allows for the production of more text, rendering the horizontal nature of the serial even more *writerly*.

The overt writerliness within "The Real Ghostbusters," which produces more narrative by means of incorporating a hypodiegesis that seeps into the diegesis and assumes authorial agency, eventually also furthers the overarching narrative of the show. As the episode comes to an end, Becky Rosen shares information which she derived from the "Supernatural" books as to the location of the Colt—the quest for which is an overarching theme of the season—thereby offering an additional piece of the puzzle. As Becky is saying goodbye to Sam, she references the "Supernatural" books and states, "In chapter thirty-three of 'Supernatural,' *Time Is on My Side*, there was this girl Bela [...]. She stole the Colt from you and then said she gave it to Lilith, remember?" The "Supernatural" books, however, reveal to the diegetic reader that Bela never gave the Colt to Lilith but, as Becky further reports, "she never really gave it to Lilith. There was this one scene where Bela gives the Colt to a demon named Crowley [...]." Within the overarching narrative of the fifth season of *Supernatural*, Becky reveals a crucial piece of information to Sam which aids in their stagnated quest for the Colt. By embedding this hypodiegetic piece of information within the diegesis of the "The Real Ghostbusters," a statement which advances their diegetic plot, *Supernatural* repeats the intersecting of diegetic layers in order to generate narrative on a larger scale. This renders *Supernatural*'s tendency to step outside the box both narratologically productive as well as self-reflexive of its genre.

Supernatural as a television series, then, becomes a repetition of patterns. Ralph Waldo Emerson's 1841 essay "Circles" is centered on the idea that in nature—and by extension culture—everything is built upon a circular, cyclical dynamic. Emerson states that "[t]he eye is the first circle; the horizon which it forms is the second; and throughout nature this primary figure is repeated without end" (225). Starting with the pupil of the eye, Emerson elaborates on the fact that nature is built upon circles around which new circles are drawn: "Our life is an apprenticeship to the truth that around every circle another can be drawn; that there is no end in nature, but every end is a beginning; that there is always another dawn risen on midnoon, and under every deep a lower deep opens" (225). It appears that the serial depiction offers this dynamic of writerliness to its reader as long as its repetition remains performative and constructive rather than static. The system of the serial narrative is inherently pluralistic in its linearity which positions the serial in the realm of the *writerly*—or rather, within serial depiction, we find a notion of writerliness inscribed which both aids and presupposes its performative repetitiveness. Drawing on Emerson's elaborations said writerly dynamic becomes an intrinsic aspect of the television series, which continually draws a new circle around itself:

> The man finishes his story,—how good! how final! how it puts a new face on all things! He fills the sky. Lo! On the other side rises also a man and draws a circle around the circle we had just pronounced the outline of the sphere. Then already is our first speaker not a man, but only a first speaker [227].

Tying this circular dynamic, which first and foremost produces by means of drawing outside its scope to the repetitive aspect of serial narration, it becomes evident that it is *Supernatural*'s heightened metatextual nature which renders its narration productive beyond its previously established boundaries. The incorporation of a "Supernatural" convention within *Supernatural*, along with the reduplication of manifold fake Sams and Deans, can be read as a form of performative repetition which constructively produces rather than merely imitates text. The LARPers do not remain a mere repetition of the protagonists but become a repetition with a twist, which in its imitation repeats something that was formerly not there and therefore renders itself productive. If we connect this notion to Barthes's elaborations on writerliness, we can see that the factual, "real" ghostbusters, as well as the doubled diegeses in which they reside, have become a *writerly* text themselves, a canvas for the expansion of their tale.

On a purely formal level, the *mise-en-abyme* within the text performs this accumulative circularity in its structure. The artificial, fictional "Supernatural" within the television series *Supernatural* can partially be read as somewhat of a glue amongst the different diegetic levels and partially also as a tool of self-reflexivity. This form of self-reflexivity, a form of meta-serial reflection reverting back to its own seriality, confirms the series' performative circularity. This notion of overstatement points to the aesthetic of the serial narration as a whole, which we find described in Stanley Cavell's "The Fact of Television":

> To say that the primary object of aesthetic interest in television is not the individual piece, but the format, is to say that the format is its primary individual of aesthetic interest. This ontological recharacterization is meant to bring out that the relation between format and instance should be of essential aesthetic concern [79].

This concept of essential aesthetic concern for the relation between format and instance which we find in *Supernatural* further highlights the writerliness of the text—it appears that within *Supernatural* we find a successful entanglement of both the format as well as the individual piece, which feeds into the serial progression of the show. In *Supernatural*, form and content perform simultaneously, each aspect feeding into the other, eventually stepping beyond a previously established circle into a new one, turning metanarrative into diegetic narrative. By means of inverting a hypodiegesis, letting it seep into the diegesis and instrumentalizing the evoked metatextuality as a means of furthering the overarching plot, "The Real Ghostbusters," in Emersonian terms, also draws a new circle around a previous diegesis and offers a canvas for the creation of a broader narrative. As we read in Emerson, "[e]very ultimate fact is only the first of a new series" (227). Embedded in the serial format of the *Supernatural* narrative, we find its heightened metatextuality a further authorial voice which continually establishes new narratological strands—or, in the sense of Emerson, narratological circles, which—once in position—will only come to be overwritten by another next, a new circle.

In conclusion, it can be stated that the doubled layering of diegetic levels in "The Real Ghostbusters" as well as their eventual interaction with each other heightens the writerliness of the text. By means of stepping outside the box on numerous occasions, *Supernatural* not only becomes self-reflexive but is further able to produce more text and advance its narrative—in Kelleter's sense horizontally so. Said pluralistic hybridity of the text is particularly present in those episodes of *Supernatural* which move beyond their diegetic level, outside their body. As the show moves into its meta level it repeatedly uses the resulting temporary diegetic instability in order to generate narrative while eventually reinstating its authenticity and diegesis. It is within this structurality that the genre of the serial in general and *Supernatural* in particular is at its most *writerly*. "The Real Ghostbusters" becomes an ideal synecdoche of this notion as it employs the writerliness in a horizontal manner, internally expanding itself and, by means of this internal expansion, generating more canvas for an external expansion of *Supernatural*. In "The Real Ghostbusters" this becomes evident in the additional piece of the puzzle that is revealed within the hypodiegesis of the "Supernatural" books and furthers the overarching diegetic narrative. By drawing on this pluralistic hybridity, the episode manages to circumvent the threat of becoming unauthentic in its reproduction. The performance of the hypodiegesis, then, not only displays awareness of itself as double but also becomes uncanny, simultaneously strange and familiar. It is the strange quality that harbors the unauthentic, which is not only highlighted but instrumentalized as a means to reaffirm the authority of the diegesis. In employing the hypodiegesis in order to reaffirm and advance the diegesis, the text manages to step outside its initial scope and broaden its own circularity. Drawing on the aesthetics of its own genre as a television show, *Supernatural*, in being metatextual, actively performs its own writerliness.

Works Cited

Barthes, Roland. *S/Z*. Translated by Richard Miller, Hill and Wang, 1974.
Benjamin, Walter. "The Work of Art in the Age of Its Technological Reproducibility." *Walter Benjamin: Selected Writings, Volume 3, 1935–1938*, edited by Howard Eiland and Michael W. Jennings, Harvard UP, 2002, pp. 101–133.

Cavell, Stanley. "The Fact of Television." *Daedalus*, vol. 111, no. 4, 1982, pp. 75–96.
Davis, Tracy C., and Thomas Postlewait. *Theatricality.* Cambridge UP, 2004.
Emerson, Ralph Waldo. "Circles." *Nature and Selected Essays*, Penguin Books, 1982, pp. 225–238.
Freud, Sigmund. "The Uncanny." *The Standard Edition of the Complete Psychological Works of Sigmund Freud.* Translated by James Stratchey, The Hogarth Press, 1955, pp. 219–252.
Kelleter, Frank. *Populäre Serialität: Narration—Evolution—Distinktion. Zum Seriellen Erzählen Seit Dem 19. Jahrhundert.* Transcript, 2012.
Rimmon-Kenan, Shlomith. *Narrative Fiction.* 2nd Edition. Routledge, 2002.

"I so miss being an atheist"

God, the Darkness and the Show That Wouldn't Die

Erin M. Giannini

Supernatural season ten's musical episode "Fan Fiction" (10.05) marks the first appearance of the "Supernatural" book series author/prophet and God Chuck Shurley since he disappeared in a burst of light at the end of season five's "Swan Song" (5.22). "Fan Fiction" features a high school musical version of the first five seasons, written, directed by, and starring Marie, based on the "Supernatural" book series. While much of the narrative remains the same as depicted in the show's canon, Marie's version does touch on the subtextual romantic elements in the relationship between Dean Winchester and the angel Castiel, and adds a second act—in the absence of a readily available continuation of the book series—that takes place in outer space.[1] At the end of the episode, Chuck appears, having claimed the ticket Marie left for him, and tells Marie that her version is "not bad."

This tacit endorsement of "transformative works" or "fan fiction" is something of a shift within the series; the Kripke era offers numerous examples of the series' problematic relationship with fans, from the shapeshifter in "Monster Movie" (4.05), who uses his love of classic horror to stalk a local woman, the convention featured in "The Real Ghostbusters" (5.09) filled with complaining fans, to the increasingly problematic representation of Becky Rosen, "Supernatural" fan fiction author (which stretches beyond Kripke's tenure as showrunner). Between season five, when Becky is introduced as an author Chuck contacts to convey a message to Sam and Dean ("Sympathy for the Devil," 5.01), and her final appearance in the post–Kripke seventh season ("Season Seven, Time for a Wedding!" 7.08), her characterization becomes increasingly predatory, including magically drugging and marrying Sam.[2] As

Cait Coker and Candace Benefiel argue, "one may reasonably assert that portraying Becky as a misguided loser who is unable to relate to the world except through her obsession with Sam, is a slap on the wrist from the series producers, telling all the Beckys out in the audience to sit back and let the big boys run the show" (109). Coker and Benefiel argue that male fans, such as Demian and Barnes[3] in "The Real Ghostbusters" are portrayed as both harmless—they role-play to escape their boring lives—and helpful (they help Sam and Dean defeat the ghosts haunting the convention), underscoring the gendered nature of this portrayal (Coker and Benefiel 108). That does not, however, take into account that Becky does provide vital information—gleaned from her fan activities—within the same episode, tempering the episode's implicit critique of Becky in a way that season seven's portrayal of Becky as stalker and near-rapist does not.

In that respect, the ways in which fandom is portrayed within the series—disgruntled, naive, or having a tenuous grip on reality—can be attributed to the Kripke era of the series: "The Monster at the End of This Book" (4.18) not only introduces the concept of Wincest (fan fiction positing the brothers as lovers), but also, as Coker and Benefiel contend, positions fans as potentially predatory (97–110)—i.e., Chuck asks of Sam and Dean, "Is this a *Misery* thing?" when they appear at his house. "Sympathy for the Devil" and "The Real Ghostbusters" portray fans as deluded or silly. Yet the more toxic portrayals—Becky's kidnapping and near-rape of Sam in "Season Seven, Time for a Wedding!" or vampires targeting *Twilight* fans to either feed on or turn ("Live Free or Twihard," 6.05)—actually aired during Sera Gamble's tenure as showrunner, one that was characterized by negative fan reaction to narrative and character choices. For example, the website "Supernatural Snark" offered recaps and reviews of season seven under the subtitle "Sera Gamble is a moron"; however, this was not changed to "Jeremy Carver is a moron" for the reviews of seasons eight through ten ("Can We All Stop Pretending…," 2012). The negativity inherent in the gullible teens of "Live Free or Twihard" in season six and Becky's predatory behavior in season seven could arguably be the writers' and showrunner's response to this type of feedback, and the personal nature of the attacks on Gamble.

This may be the reason why the series does not acknowledge the fans again in depth until the aforementioned musical episode of season ten; the intervening four seasons may have mellowed both the writers and the characters' response to fandom. Even Dean, who was freaked out by the concept of fan fiction in season four, offers the cast of the musical a rousing pep talk before they go on stage in "Fan Fiction": "This is Marie's 'Supernatural.' So, I want you to get out there, and I want you to stand as close as she wants you to, and I want you to put as much sub and add text, as you possibly can."

It is the following season, however, in which the initial shift in showrunners and the idea of who "owns" *Supernatural*'s text is addressed in depth. The rise of the Darkness, who sucks the souls from her victims and seems unnaturally focused on one brother over another, as well as her challenge to and near destruction of Chuck (now revealed as God), both echoes and subverts the criticisms of Gamble versus Kripke, as well as the unforeseen length of the series itself. By having the Darkness embody the worst fan criticisms of Gamble's narrative choices (soulless, prurient, destructive), and the eventual God/Darkness detente that closes out the season, season eleven stands as a low-key metanarrative examination of creation, destruction, and ownership of the series itself, and how it may contribute to the series' longevity.

"All your favorites, all your chosen. They are suffering": Passing the Producer Baton

In 2001, Joss Whedon handed the reins of his series *Buffy the Vampire Slayer* to Marti Noxon, who had been with the series for three years and had written some of its best-regarded episodes.[4] Whedon had another series in production, *Buffy* spin-off *Angel*, and was working with Tim Minear to create *Firefly* for 20th Century–Fox. It made sense to delegate, and Noxon had a good understanding of the series. At the end of Whedon's last season as showrunner (season five), the eponymous heroine had sacrificed herself to save the world ("The Gift," 5.22). Season six, therefore, deals with Buffy's well-meaning but ill-fated resurrection by her friends, who convinced themselves they were pulling her out of Hell ("Bargaining, Part 1," 6.01) but in fact ripped her out of a heavenly dimension ("After Life," 6.03). Buffy's resulting trauma and sense she "came back wrong" ("Smashed," 6.09, and "Dead Things," 6.13) is expressed in depression and using sex with her enemy, Spike, as a palliative. The fact that the season's villains are entitled male nerds who escalate from robbery ("Flooded," 6.04) to attempted rape and murder ("Dead Things," 6.13), means that season six is one of the darker seasons of a series that always walked a tightrope between humor and horror. Season seven deals particularly with the Slayer mythology, introducing the "Potentials" (i.e., young women who could become the next Slayer when the current one dies) and the "First Evil," bent on destroying the Slayer line and the world.

Fan criticism of these storylines was often brutal and personal. An analytical piece in the *New York Times*, focused on viewer/fan interactions with content, quoted a fan who posted:

> "I think Marti Noxon should be on BtVS. And I think Drusilla and Spike should tie her up and torture her, then kill her in the most painful way possible. Then hacking

her body beyond recognition so there could be no possible way to make her rise from the grave. Then they should STAMP on the bits" [qtd. in Sella 2002].

While Noxon now jokes about her status as "show killer"—her Twitter bio reads: "I ruined Buffy and I will RUIN YOU TOO" (Anders 2014)—she does admit it was painful to read such comments at the time (Sella 2002).

On both a narrative and production level, *Supernatural*'s sixth and seventh seasons mirror *Buffy*'s. In the final moments of "Swan Song," Sam Winchester, serving as Lucifer's vessel and engaged in an apocalyptic battle with the Archangel Michael, takes control of his body and throws himself into Hell (taking Michael with him) in order to save the world. Like Buffy, Sam returns from his afterlife markedly different: cold, distant, and violent. It is eventually revealed that only Sam's body returned from Hell; his soul is still there ("Family Matters," 6.07). He is incapable of feeling anything, and he requires neither sleep nor food. This soullessness is expressed in various ways, including being a ruthless "hunter" (e.g., having no qualms about using humans as bait), including his own brother ("Live Free or Twihard"); an inability to make a connection with anyone ("Unforgiven," 6.13); and no feelings of remorse, even when attempting to kill those close to him ("Appointment in Samarra," 6.11). Like Buffy, Sam is aware he came back "wrong" ("You Can't Handle the Truth," 6.06), but he does not know how to fix it. When his soul is returned, it is with a caveat; a "wall" has been built in his mind to block his memories of Hell. If that wall fails, the torture and torment he suffered in Hell will return and, at best, render him non-functional, and at worst, kill him ("Appointment in Samarra"). Unlike the angel and demon storyline that dominated the final two seasons of Kripke's era, season six focuses on life after the apocalypse: Dean (temporarily) settles down in suburbia ("Exile on Main Street," 6.01), and Sam deals with the aftereffects of his sacrifice. In many respects, this allowed the series to take a more personal approach; the first half of the season is devoted to the changed dynamic between the brothers, with few opportunities for more light-hearted narratives.

As with Noxon (Mathis 2013), Gamble's episode work was known for its ability to tease out the emotional resonance and pain inherent in the lives of the characters and their interactions with one another. In an interview, Padalecki joked that when he gets a Gamble script, "It usually means I'm getting naked, crying, or getting naked AND crying" ("Jared and Jensen Attend..." 2008). Season six's dark, noir feel is in line with many of the episodes Gamble wrote during the first five seasons, including Dean's confrontation with his future in Hell and his inability to have a normal life ("Dream a Little Dream of Me," 3.10); an episode in which a seeming victory over the season's antagonist, Lilith, ends with a wholesale slaughter ("Jus in

Bello," 3.12); and Sam having to kill a woman he loves after she is infected by a werewolf ("Heart," 2.17).

Like Noxon, Gamble's second and final season as showrunner also expanded both the series' mythology and the stakes; Purgatory was added to the pantheon of afterlives within *Supernatural*, as were the Leviathans: vicious monsters bent on devouring everything. While season seven's antagonists do target the brothers, their goal is global: to turn the planet into an abattoir. That this plan is enacted through the Leviathans staging a corporate takeover and implementing their plans using fast food additives (such as high-fructose corn syrup) underscores Gamble's contention that "corporations are scarier than the government" ("Survival of the Fittest," 7.23, commentary). Indeed, the effect of the Leviathans' corporate power on Sam and Dean is, for this series, fairly quotidian, but resonant with real-world analogues (see Giannini 83–96). By posing as the brothers and committing violent crimes ("Slash Fiction," 7.06), the Leviathans manage to strip them of their identities, their extralegal sources of income (credit card fraud, pool hustling), their beloved Impala, and finally, their mentor/father figure Bobby Singer ("How to Win Friends and Influence Monsters," 7.09).

The challenge of taking over a series in which the protagonist had sacrificed him-/herself to avert an apocalypse is something that both Noxon and Gamble had to deal with; that is, resurrecting a series whose narrative had reached an, if not the, endpoint. Resurrecting Sam (and Buffy), and the difficulties both have in adjusting to post-death life, serves as a metonym for the narrative difficulties both Noxon and Gamble faced with their respective series. *Supernatural* (and *Buffy*) had been building to their fifth seasons' arcs since the third season. Dean goes to Hell in "No Rest for the Wicked" (3.16), kicking off the apocalypse storyline that would dominate seasons four and five; Buffy has a prophetic dream in "Graduation Day, Part 2" (3.22) that makes reference to her impending death in "The Gift" (5.22). Perhaps owing to the impossibility of following this up, Gamble's era was characterized by narrative arcs that only lasted a single season, using a structure for season six that later series *Agents of S.H.I.E.L.D.* would adopt: three or more short-term, but related, narrative trajectories that would feed into a larger arc: Sam's soullessness and the collection of souls; the introduction of the Campbell family and the collecting of alpha demons; and the emergence of the "mother of all" demons, the search for Purgatory, and the war in heaven.

Using this structure to follow up a fairly tight three-season arc, however, gave season six the impression of being disjointed, and Gamble abandoned it for season seven, focusing primarily on the Leviathan storyline. Given her reputation for "bringing the pain" it is perhaps not surprising that her final season as showrunner was characterized by the aforementioned losses and ended with Dean and Castiel trapped in Purgatory and Sam alone. The viewer response to Gamble's character and narrative choices, however, often verged on the insulting. The announcement that she was stepping down was greeted with "Bye Bitch" (user "Chiknttrazinni") and accusations that she "drove the show headfirst into the ground" (user "abbiemills") ("Is the real life…" 2012). Others were even more brutal, accusing Gamble of pruriently favoring Padalecki/Sam over Ackles/Dean:

> You don't agree that Sera Gamble actively took every possible chance to humiliate Dean in Season 7 to make Sam come off more heroic? Two words: BALLET SLIPPERS. Sera's a self-confessed Sam Girl and HOLY SHIT did she ever make it obvious ["Video: Top 10…"].

In essence, the commentator is accusing Gamble of both objectifying Sam and feminizing Dean. Michael Fuchs suggests, regarding not only the introduction of female characters—and possible love interests—within the series, but also Gamble's tenure as showrunner, that female fans (who comprise the majority of the series' fandom) may feel "an anxiety of being dispossessed of these characters, onto whom fans have projected all sorts of fantasies and whom fans have employed as vehicles for subversive practices" (Fuchs para. 23). This anxiety, Fuchs argues, extends to the reaction to Gamble's tenure. That is, while Kripke explicitly positioned himself as a "fanboy" of various media properties, including the classic rock he insisted, over network objections, be included within the series ("Paley Festival Panel Discussion" 2006), Gamble's similar status as "fangirl" was not given the same "reification" as "one of us" that Kripke was allowed (Wexelblat 225). Indeed, despite revealing that she wrote *Twin Peaks* fan fiction and considered herself a Trekkie (Larsen and Zubernis 214), she was accused of letting her fannish-ness, with regard to Sam, drive her narrative decisions (as suggested in the comment above, among others). As Cory Barker points out, an *Entertainment Weekly* story announcing Gamble's new role had nearly 300 comments, a majority of which, in Barker's words, "questioned Gamble's ability to write and run the series" and "pushed for the promotion of supposedly 'non-biased' writers like Ben Edlund" (Barker, par. 10).

While this reaction could be, Fuchs suggests, the result of patriarchal "cultural indoctrination" (i.e., the assumption of male mastery over a text), he is "not convinced." Rather, he suggests that Gamble as a "fangirl" as opposed to a "fanboy" auteur does not allow the female fanbase to "subvert" the text (through fan practices such as fan fiction featuring the brothers as lovers) because it is already subverted through having a female fan as showrunner. That is, it is inherently feminized, through the supposed reification of "SamGirls" over "DeanGirls" by Gamble, and therefore does not offer the same opportunity for female fan creators to subvert its masculine qualities (Fuchs para 30–31), a reading that is somewhat suggested by the aforementioned comment regarding the episode "Out with the Old" (7.16) in which Dean is drawn to a cursed pair of ballet slippers because of a secret desire to dance, which he defensively attributes to the "hot tutu-on-tutu action" of Darren Aronofsky's *Black Swan* (2010).

Rhonda Nicol offers a somewhat different take, however, analyzing how the series engages with issues of masculinity as performance and the concept of feminism within a predominantly male series, and suggesting that the vehemence displayed by some fans may have been responding to seeing their own (potential) objectification of the male leads reflected in Gamble's narrative and visual choices. As Nicol argues about the episode "Live Free or Twihard," Dean, who is frequently the repository of masculine gate-keeping, is violently objectified and assaulted by a vampire, which allows the series to "tak[e] Dean on a journey that moves him from an unproblematized masculine authority to a vulnerable feminized position of abjection and back again" (Nicol 165). While Gamble may have been accused of focusing on Sam at the expense of Dean during her seasons, moments such as this represent vital character shifts for Dean, particularly in terms of showing the "cracks" in his hypermasculine attitudes.[5] Not only does Dean serve as both father and mother to Sam, but he has sacrificed himself for those he loved ("All Hell Breaks Loose, Part 2," 2.22) and wishes for a normal life of nurturing and family ("What Is and What Should Never Be," 2.20; "Dark Side of the Moon," 5.16). In the post–Kripke era, Dean's masculine performance has been undermined not only by the aforementioned turn in "Live Free or Twihard," but by his increased comfort in displaying a softer side: his claim that he is "nesting" as he prepares a meal for Sam after they move into their first permanent accommodations ("Trial and Error," 8.14) since their mother's death 30 years earlier ("Pilot," 1.01); his comfort in displaying himself in short-shorts as he washes his car ("Baby," 11.04); or even his ability to care for infants ("Two and a Half Men," 6.02; "Form and Void," 11.02). This "softening" perhaps may be why his toxic and rage-filled behavior as a demon at the start of the tenth season ("Black," 10.01; "Reichenbach," 10.02) was more shocking than it would have been earlier in the series' run; that this led directly to the release of the Darkness offers a particular narrative response.

Thus, in keeping with the series' long-standing responsiveness and metanarrative practices with regard to its fans, season eleven addresses the shift in characterization and the Gamble era in particular through the introduction of the ultimate DeanGirl: Amara.

"We're bound, Dean": Chuck vs. Amara for the Soul of the Series

At the end of the ninth season of the series, Dean is killed by rogue angel/false deity Metatron. That Dean had agreed to take on the Mark of

Cain in order to kill season nine's primary antagonists ("First Born," 9.11) means that this death is not permanent; Dean is resurrected as a demon in the final moment of the season finale ("Do You Believe in Miracles?" 9.23). Even cured of his demon-ness ("Soul Survivor," 10.03), however, the Mark continues to influence his behavior, making him increasingly violent and unable to be killed without becoming a demon again. He appears to make a deal with Death to remove him from Earth to prevent him harming others, while Sam makes a deal with King of Hell Crowley, and his mother, the witch Rowena, to remove the Mark. It is Sam's plan that goes forward, removing the Mark and releasing an entity known as the Darkness ("Brother's Keeper," 10.23).

Representing the biggest shift to the series' mythology since the introduction of the angel Castiel in season four ("Lazarus Rising," 4.01), the Darkness/Amara is revealed to be God's sister, locked away at the dawn of time so God could create everything ("Our Little World," 11.06). The Mark Dean bore was the lock, and removing it set her free to exact revenge upon her brother; it also meant that Dean was connected with and unable to destroy her. Throughout the season, Amara grows more powerful, ingesting human souls to feed herself, and formulates a plan to destroy God's creations to make him reveal himself.

While season five's "Swan Song" suggested that the prophet/author of the "Supernatural" book series Chuck Shurley was God, "Don't Call Me Shurley" (11.20) confirms this when he reveals himself to a now-human Metatron and asks him to help edit his autobiography, having no interest in stopping his sister. When he eventually changes his mind, Amara nearly kills him before the two reach a detente and disappear to work out their differences, leaving the earth to its own fate again ("Alpha and Omega," 11.23).

There are several elements at work that lend themselves to an interpretation of the season-long arc as a meditation on who authors the series itself, as well as the more personal shift between Kripke and Gamble as showrunners. Both season six and season eleven address this, with season six's "The French Mistake" (6.15) being the more direct example. In that episode, the brothers are thrust by the angel Balthazar into an alternate reality in which they are merely actors—Jensen Ackles and Jared Padalecki—in a series entitled "Supernatural," set in a world with no demons, angels, or gods. What follows is metatextual madness: Sam and Dean unsuccessfully attempting to act, director "Bob Singer" shaking his head and mumbling "Season 6," and Padalecki's real-life wife, Genevieve Cortese, appearing as his wife. "You married fake Ruby?" is Dean's shocked question when they arrive at the Padalecki estate, referencing Cortese's role as a demon during *Supernatural*'s fourth season.

"The French Mistake" not only references in-series narrative and production issues; as a "fiction about fictions" (Gass 11), it also touches on other media properties. The episode title is a likely reference to the fourth wall breaking finale of the film *Blazing Saddles*, in which cowboys and townspeople burst into a Busby Berkeley type musical number entitled "The French Mistake," and the episode's final showdown with the angel Virgil visually and narratively references some of the final scenes of *The Godfather*, explicitly mentioned by the angel Balthazar at the start of the episode.

There are two scenes in the episode that are particularly germane to this analysis. Following Sam and Dean's disastrous attempts at acting, Bob and the writing staff put in a call to showrunner Sera Gamble (voiced by Hilary Jardine):

> SERA: Okay. Uhh…. Maybe it'd help if I—I'll fly up and talk to them.
> JIM: You know, I'm not sure Jared and Jensen … know who she is, strictly speaking. She's, you know, new. No offense.
> SERA: Right.
> BOB: Yeah, I think what we might need at this stage is for Kripke to come up himself. He created the show. They'll listen to him.
> SERA: How's that make me look? I'm supposed to be running this thing. Besides, Eric is off in some cabin somewhere writing his next pilot ["The French Mistake"].

The eventual outcome of Kripke's set visit—he's gunned down along with most of the crew—essentially leaves Gamble in charge by default; the original author of the text is literally dead. Actualizing the death of the author within the episode is not only an element of the metafictional conceit of the episode, but also speaks to the series' continuing life after this "death." It could also be read as a message to the fans: Kripke may still be around (he wrote season six's finale episode), but *Supernatural*'s ownership and authoring can and will be transferred.

Season eleven is a more sustained meditation on this subject. By 2015, Jeremy Carver had been the showrunner for four seasons. Further, with the debut of the eleventh season, *Supernatural* had not only become the longest-running genre series in U.S. television history, but also had officially run longer without Kripke in charge than with him. In that respect, season eleven is easily viewed as a companion season to season six.[6] Amara, released from her prison, not only goes on a murderous rampage among the faithful to draw God's attention—killing parishioners in a Catholic church, raining blood and lightning on an end-times group ("Our Little World")—but is empowered by sucking the souls out of humans.

The choice of a supernatural creature powering itself through souls has its genesis, unsurprisingly, in season six. Numerous episodes within season six make reference to someone—revealed at the midpoint of the season to be Castiel—gathering souls from Heaven, Hell, and Purgatory, including preventing the *Titanic* from sinking in order to harvest the souls of its passengers and their descendants ("My Heart Will Go On," 6.17). The final episodes of the season reveal that Castiel, working with Crowley, has been doing this to gain enough power to defeat the Archangel Raphael, who wishes to restart the apocalypse that the brothers, Bobby, and Castiel prevented in the previous season. Castiel does defeat Raphael by ingesting all these souls, then declares himself God and demands humans bow down to him ("The Man Who Knew Too Much," 6.22).

While Castiel's temporary status as God allows the series to make some pointed statements—he visits a church in which the pastor is preaching against homosexuality and tells him, "I am utterly indifferent to sexual orientation. On the other hand, I cannot abide hypocrites like you, Reverend" ("Meet the New Boss," 7.01)—the power consumes him, and he is forced to give it up, unleashing a new threat (the Leviathans) before disappearing ("Hello, Cruel World," 7.02). More importantly, it underscores the importance of souls as power within the series narrative. Sam's soulless status throughout the first part of the sixth season is also germane to season eleven's plot; not only does it allow him to recognize the cause of several murders ("Thin Lizzie," 11.05), but it is also an opening salvo on the season-long meditation on creation and the nature of power.

This works on multiple levels throughout the season. It is revealed that God locked away his sister because he wished to create the world; while the discourse around Amara's behavior, as well as Amara's own contentions, suggests that she was only interested in destruction (as God's opposite), she eventually confesses she was hurt that she was not enough for him and admits the beauty of what he had created ("Alpha and Omega"). Amara is not a being who can create; she is shown destroying and reacting, but not necessarily offering an alternative creation to that her brother produced. That being said, her final act before disappearing is in itself an act of both creation and destruction: she brings Sam and Dean's mother, Mary (Samantha Smith) back from the dead, at the same age she was when she died, an age that her own sons are nearing (late '30s/early '40s). While this turn allows any number of narrative possibilities to play out in subsequent seasons, it also represents an act of destruction: Amara, in essence, "de-fridged" Mary Winchester, whose death as recounted in the pilot set the entire narrative of the series in motion.

It is in this respect that the series is making a direct reference to the initial shift in showrunners between seasons five and six. By casting a woman in the role of Chuck's sister/opposite in a series as male-oriented as *Supernatural*, the parallel to the Kripke/Gamble switch is an easy one to make, particularly given the aforementioned responses to Gamble's narrative and character choices. Given that Chuck is the author of the "Supernatural" series who literally disappears as he writes "The End" on the final book of the series,

"Swan Song," it is clear that he is a stand-in for Kripke, for whom the episode "Swan Song" was the final one of his era. This reference is less direct in season eleven than it was in "The French Mistake," in which Bob Singer tells Gamble that "the boys don't really know you," and yet throughout the season, Amara can only "react" to what Chuck has created; when she attempts to kill Chuck, she nearly destroys the world. As it was under Gamble's tenure that Sam was brought back from Hell without a soul, having Amara gain power through the removal of individual souls seems a narrative choice that is a direct line back to season six. Souls have always played a large role in the series' narrative, particularly as currency (e.g., the Crossroad Demons who make deals with humans to trade their souls in exchange for success, power, etc.); Castiel's season six quest to gather souls fits within that structure, particularly the constant references throughout the season as to the number and quality of souls he was procuring. As for Amara, she initially uses souls to grow from newborn to adult, then to increase her power, reducing them to a commodity in a similar way to both crossroad deals and Castiel's use of them to power himself.

Yet, given the meta nature of the series in general, and of season six's "The French Mistake" in particular, one can read the commodification of "souls" within the series as "viewers" for two related reasons: setting "The French Mistake" within the production and filming of the series, with constant references to its low viewership, and the actual drop in viewing numbers during the Gamble era. While this drop off could be attributed to the shift in tone through the shift in showrunners, seasons six and seven are the only seasons which aired on Fridays, a notoriously difficult time slot. Yet the idea of Amara "destroying" Chuck's world—including consuming his "chosen"—is in line with the aforementioned viewer response to parts of Gamble's era as showrunner, as well as Kripke's "abandonment" of the series following season five. That Chuck is meant to be an avatar of Kripke is made explicit during his conversation with Metatron in "Don't Call Me Shurley": "I started a new series of books.... *Revolution* ... but I don't think it's going anywhere." *Revolution* was a short-lived series co-created by Kripke and JJ Abrams; it ran for two seasons (2012–2014) on NBC before being cancelled. Chuck's answer to Metatron's impassioned plea as to why Chuck "abandoned us," however—"You disappointed me. You all disappointed me"—is not backed up by any public statements Kripke made regarding the series or its showrunners following his departure. That being said, it is arguable that had Kripke stayed on as showrunner, he may have taken the characters in different directions than subsequent showrunners did. As the "God" of *Supernatural*, however, Kripke created the show and then walked away, allowing the narrative and character to progress without his direct intervention.

Conclusion

When Sam and Dean discover their lives are on display for consumption through the "Supernatural" book series, they are determined to track down the author, despite the fact that he is reclusive, and hides behind a pen name (Carver Edlund, a combination of writers/producers Jeremy Carver and Ben Edlund). To find him, Sam and Dean must prove their fan credentials to the publisher, Sera Siege (Keegan Connor Tracy), including being quizzed on little known facts about themselves and displaying their anti-possession tattoos.

In essence, Sera Siege, both fan and producer (publisher) whose name, like Carver Edlund's, is a combination of writers Sera Gamble and Julie Siege, serves as a gatekeeper, limiting access to Chuck to only the most worthy. As discussed above, however, when Gamble herself was elevated to a level equal to that of Kripke, the discourse shifted in a negative direction, implying that she was a force of destruction, sucking the soul out of character and narrative, much as Amara feeds off of souls and nearly destroys the world Chuck created.

Yet the season ends not with a decisive victory for Chuck/God or Amara/the Darkness, but rather an acknowledgment that both light and dark are necessary to maintain existence, and both deities remove themselves from the equation. In that respect, the low-key metanarrative of season eleven seems to cement more firmly what the episode "Fan Fiction" implied: *Supernatural*'s story does not solely belong to its creators and writers; while Chuck might be "disappointed" with his creations, their fates are no longer solely in his hands. This ability to share authorship may be the key to its surprising longevity.

NOTES

1. While it is not entirely clear whether it is meant as an intentional call-back, at the end of season ten, Death offers to take Dean away from earth where he will be safe from harming himself or others due to the effects of the Mark of Cain curse ("Brother's Keeper," 10.23), lending an amusing weight to Marie's interpretation.
2. Becky's return in season fifteen postdates completion of this volume
3. The names "Demian" and "Barnes" are themselves a metatextual reference to the names of the recapper and the discussion board moderator, respectively, of the *Supernatural* section of the former website *Television Without Pity*, which at the time was well-known enough to merit references within more than one series, including *Veronica Mars*.
4. As Matthew Pateman points out, even in Noxon's first year as a writer on *Buffy* (season two), she not only wrote six of that season's twenty-two episodes, but Whedon tapped her to write "Surprise" (2.13), the first of a two-parter that essentially served as a "second pilot" for the series (Pateman 33).
5. See Coker and Benefiel's analysis of Dean as "good" fan—that is, one who "quotes and references, and even idolizes, but does not create" (para. 2), as opposed to the more immersive fan practices such as fan fiction (as Marie and Becky create). In particular, Coker and Benefiel examine the way such practices—creation vs. non-creation—are considered

particularly gendered within fandom and seemingly within the *Supernatural* writers' room (Coker and Benefiel 2019).

6. This "revisiting" of previous seasons could be read as a mark of and reason for the series' longevity. As is addressed in this essay, the end of season eleven reverses the inciting event of the series, with season twelve an extended examination of the result of that action. season thirteen revisits, through an alternate dimension, the apocalyptic storyline and battles of seasons four and five, with the final episode of the season reversing Dean's initial refusal to serve as vessel for the Archangel Michael in season five by having him give his consent eight seasons later ("Let the Good Times Roll," 13.23). Season fourteen examines the fallout from this decision.

WORKS CITED

"After Life." *Buffy the Vampire Slayer: The Complete Sixth Season,* written by Jane Espenson, directed by David Solomon, Twentieth Century Fox Home Video, 2004.

Anders, Charlie Jane. "Has a Producer Ruined Your Favorite TV Show? That's Nothing New." *i09*, 14 October 2014, https://io9.gizmodo.com/has-a-new-producer-ruined-your-favorite-tv-show-thats-1646275078. Accessed 2 February 2018.

"Bargaining, Part 1." *Buffy the Vampire Slayer: The Complete Sixth Season,* written by Marti Noxon, directed by David Grossman, Twentieth Century Fox Home Video, 2004.

Barker, Cory. "SamGirls and DeanGirls: Anti-fan Fans in Supernatural." Popular Culture Association/American Culture Association Annual Conference, 22 April 2011, San Antonio Marriott Rivercenter/Riverwalk Hotels, San Antonio, TX, https://corybarker.com/2011/04/26/pcaaca-2011-samgirls-and-deangirls-anti-fan-fans-in-supernatural/. Accessed 14 March 2018.

"Can We All Stop Pretending That Dick Roman Was/Is Awesome Now? Seriously, It's Getting Old Now. Just Stop. Stop." *Supernatural Snark*, 8 June 2012, https://supernaturalsnark.wordpress.com/tag/sera-gamble-is-a-moron/. Accessed 20 March 2018.

Coker, Cait, and Candace Benefiel. "The Hunter Hunted: The Portrayal of the Fan as Predator in *Supernatural.*" Supernatural, *Humanity, and the Soul: On the Highway to Hell and Back*, edited by Susan A. George and Regina Hansen, Palgrave MacMillan, 2014, pp. 97–110.

_____, and _____. "'It's a Guilty Pleasure': Gendering Cultural Consumption, Masculine Anxiety, and the Problem of Dean Winchester." *Metafiction, Intertextuality, and Authorship in* Supernatural, edited by Ana Klimchynskaya, McFarland, 2019, forthcoming.

"Dead Things." *Buffy the Vampire Slayer: The Complete Sixth Season,* written by Steven S. DeKnight, directed by James A. Contner, Twentieth Century Fox Home Video, 2004.

"Flooded." *Buffy the Vampire Slayer: The Complete Sixth Season,* written by Jane Espenson and Douglas Petrie, directed by Douglas Petrie, Twentieth Century Fox Home Video, 2004.

Fuchs, Michael. "*Supernatural*'s Showrunners, Creative Teams, and Fans: Television Authorship in the Age of Participatory Culture." *Auteur TV*, edited by Ralph Poole and Saskia Fürst, Winter Verlag, forthcoming, http://fuchsmichael.net/index.php/news/47-publication-news/116-supernatural-television-authorship. Accessed 14 March 2018.

Gass, William. "Philosophy and the Future of Fiction." *Syracuse Scholar*, vol. 1, no. 2, 1980, pp. 1–13.

Giannini, Erin. "'This Isn't Wall Street, This Is Hell!' Corporate America as the Biggest *Supernatural* Bad of All." Supernatural, *Humanity, and the Soul: On the Highway to Hell and Back*, edited by Susan A. George and Regina Hansen, Palgrave MacMillan, 2014, pp. 83–96.

"The Gift." *Buffy the Vampire Slayer: The Complete Fifth Season,* written by Joss Whedon, directed by Joss Whedon, Twentieth Century Fox Home Video, 2003.

"Graduation Day, Part 2." *Buffy the Vampire Slayer: The Complete Third Season,* written by Joss Whedon, directed by Joss Whedon, Twentieth Century Fox Home Video, 2003.

"Is the Real Life, or Is This Just Fantasy?" *Oh No They Didn't*, 4 April 2012, https://ohnotheydidnt.livejournal.com/67937747.html. Accessed 20 March 2018.

"Jared and Jensen Attend the Salute to 'Supernatural' Convention." *Buddy TV*, 18 November 2008, http://www.buddytv.com/articles/supernatural/jensen-and-jared-attend-the-sa-24609.aspx. Accessed 20 March 2018.

Larsen, Katherine, and Lynn Zubernis. *Fandom at the Crossroads: Celebration, Shame and Fan/Producer Relationships.* Cambridge Scholars, 2012.

Mathis, Cori. "Bringing the Pain: An Examination of Marti Noxon's Contributions to *Buffy the Vampire Slayer.*" *Joss in June: Selected Essays,* Special issue of *Slayage: The Journal of the Whedon Studies Association* vols. 11.2–12.1, no. 38–39, Summer 2014. http://www.whedonstudies.tv/uploads/2/6/2/8/26288593/mathis_slayage_11.2-12.1.pdf

Nicol, Rhonda. "'How Is That Not Rape-y?': Dean as Anti-Bella and Feminism Without Women in *Supernatural.*" Supernatural, *Humanity, and the Soul: On the Highway to Hell and Back,* edited by Susan A. George and Regina Hansen, Palgrave MacMillan, 2014, pp. 155–167.

"Paley Center Panel Discussion 2006" [Blu-Ray extra]. *Supernatural: The Complete First Season,* Warner Home Video, 2010.

Pateman, Matthew. *Joss Whedon.* Manchester UP, 2018

Sella, Marshall. "The Remote Controllers." *New York Times,* 20 October 2002, https://www.nytimes.com/2002/10/20/magazine/the-remote-controllers.html. Accessed 2 March 2018.

"Smashed." *Buffy the Vampire Slayer: The Complete Sixth Season,* written by Drew Z. Greenburg, directed by Turi Meyer, Twentieth Century Fox Home Video, 2004.

"Surprise." *Buffy the Vampire Slayer: The Complete Second Season,* written by Marti Noxon, directed by Michael Lange, Twentieth Century Fox Home Video, 2002.

"Survival of the Fittest" [commentary track]. *Supernatural: The Complete Seventh Season.* Warner Home Video, 2012.

"Video: Top 10 Supernatural Episodes." *The Agony Booth.* 7 March 2013, http://www.agonybooth.com/top-10-supernatural-episodes-cw-kripke-16729. Accessed 14 March 2018.

Wexelblat, Alan, "An Auteur in the Age of the Internet: JSM, *Babylon 5,* and the Net." *Hop on Pop: The Politics and Pleasures of Popular Culture,* edited by Henry Jenkins, Tara McPherson, and Jane Shattuc, Duke UP, 2002, pp. 209–225.

"There is no singing in *Supernatural*!"
The Meta as Narrative Device

Stephanie A. Graves

> "Look, Mr. Edlund. Yes, I'm a fan. But I really don't appreciate being mocked. I know that 'Supernatural's' just a book, okay. I know the difference between fantasy and reality."
> —Becky Rosen, "Sympathy for the Devil" (5.01)

Meta-, the Greek prefix meaning *after, beyond, adjacent,* and perhaps most tellingly, *self,* is part of the inescapable fabric of our postmodern world. Although metatextuality has become somewhat commonplace in this postmodern cultural landscape, there is arguably no show on television, past or present, that has both explored and delighted in the many incarnations of self-referentiality to the degree with which CW's *Supernatural* has. While self-reflexivity is a hallmark of *Supernatural*, throughout the run of the show, the creators have stepped outside of the realm of mere self-referentiality and explored the entire landscape of the meta: metafictionality, metatextuality, metareferentiality, and metafilmicality, or, a more appropriate portmanteau, metatelevisuality. However, these postmodern moments (some—including the writers—might say *indulgences*) are not a means of distancing the viewer; to the contrary, they are a clever and savvy way to expand the creative space the show occupies while rewarding the ardent fan base *and* parodying itself for its own metatelevisuality—that is, the show's awareness of and diegetic nods to television as an organizing concept and, especially, to its own construction as a TV show. *Supernatural* conforms to the storytelling model identified by Jason Mittell as the "complex narrative," which is marked by a turn from episodic structures to a blend of concomitant episodic and serial through-lines and often featuring a "heightened degree of self-consciousness in storytelling mechanics"; additionally, the show is well-known for the "narrative spectacle" Mittell describes as a "narrational bravado" that violates "the program's own storytelling conventions in a spectacular fashion" (53, 46). Through the various meta devices employed throughout *Supernatural,* the show consistently calls attention to its own constructedness, to the materiality of the medium of television fandom, and to the very nature of the phenomenology of narrative itself.

"Dude, you just got whaled on by Paris Hilton!"[1]

Supernatural is, in the most reductive sense, a television show about two brothers, Sam and Dean Winchester, who fight the many guises of evil in the world—"saving people, hunting things," as Dean succinctly puts it ("Wendigo," 1.02). They do so in a 1967 Chevy Impala, set to a classic rock soundtrack, with a large dose of attitude, an astonishing collection of fake IDs and other credentials, and an extensive collection of weapons. Although the show initially began as fairly conventional Monster of the Week (MOTW) fare, there is a larger overall story arc that instills the narrative complexity to which Mittell refers. Subsequent seasons generally follow this template, with assorted MOTW encounters tempered with overall season arc storylines, yet as the show has progressed, it has become increasingly interested in self-referentiality as a narrative device. As far as narrative, genre, and self-referential structure are concerned, *Supernatural* owes a large debt to Joss Whedon's *Buffy the Vampire Slayer* (WB/UPN, 1997–2003), which similarly organized larger narrative arcs across MOTW episodes. However, unlike *Buffy,* or shows such as *The X-Files* or *Fringe* that are very much rooted within the world (or worlds) of their own creation, *Supernatural* expands to occupy the "real" world—our world—as well, deploying mimesis as a creative tactic and admitting to both itself and its audience that while it crafts its own world(s), it exists within ours. The creative team behind the show continually pushes the envelope of self-reference, expands the boundaries of its own created universe, and explores the many guises of meta.

One fundamental way the show tears down the fourth wall of its existence is through an ongoing series of intertextual references—clever nods to the world outside the diegesis, which acknowledge to viewers that the writers are aware the show does not exist in a vacuum, and furthermore reward fans for their cultural literacy and comprehensive pop culture knowledge. Since intertextuality—that is, references to other texts through allusion or quotation—creates a matrix of signification, *Supernatural* is then able to wield its rich intertext as a narrative shorthand to establish generic and thematic connections. As early as the first season, writers were appealing to viewers' knowledge of urban legends and ghost stories, such as the episode "Bloody Mary" (1.05), which explores the traditional ghost story about chanting "Bloody Mary, Bloody Mary" into a mirror in order to summon a ghostly spirit. Similarly, in the episode "Hook Man" (1.07), a series of deaths replicate popular urban legends, including the titular tale of the man with a hook for a hand that terrorizes teenagers making out in parked cars, as well as the fabled, "Aren't you glad you didn't turn on the light?" message being scrawled in a roommate's blood. Season two's "Tall Tales" (2.15) taps not only urban legends but also tabloid headlines; on a college campus, Sam and Dean contend with a haunted classroom building, an "alien abduction," and a sewer alligator before Bobby Singer points out they are dealing with a Trickster figure (later revealed to be the angel Gabriel in disguise). Likewise, in season three's "Bedtime Stories" (3.05), fairy tales are used as the framing device for the plot, and the writers capitalize on cultural familiarity with tales such as "The Three Little Pigs" and "Hansel and Gretel." There is even—almost inevitably—a "slenderman" episode: "#thinman" (9.15) plays with the widely-known meme of Slenderman, a modern legend that got its genesis in a 2009 SomethingAwful.com forum (Dewey). The use of these speculative narrative devices foregrounds the importance of cultural funds of knowledge for both the show and the audience.

Further rooting the *Supernatural* diegesis within the extradiegetic, the characters continually make references to popular culture within the story, which grounds the show as a part of the culture upon which they comment, revealing the homologous structure that is such a strong governing force in the narrative. This tendency manifests as a kind of obsessive cataloguing in the diegesis of cultural shorthands, tropes, and references. The traditional elements of horror films are particular favorites, which makes sense given the show's generic positioning—classic horror creatures from Dracula to Godzilla to Bigfoot are mentioned fairly often—but Sam, Dean, and company are conversant with a wide range of pop culture knowledge, from Celine Dion to Bob Marley, *The Shining* (1980) to *Deliverance* (1972), *Buffy* to *Ally McBeal*, *Twilight* (2008) to the Incredible Hulk. A long-running joke in the show involves the Winchesters posing as assorted government officials in order to gain access to crime scenes; Dean often introduces himself and his brother with the aliases Agent X and Agent Z, in which X and Z are classic rock musicians.[2] The show even parodies itself for this tendency—in "Slash Fiction" (7.06), Frank Devereaux suggests that if the boys wish to keep a low profile they should ditch the rock star aliases and try "Tom and John Smith" from now on. The obsessive deployment of these references to everything from music to superheroes to movies reflects the mimetic grounding of the show within the real world—an appeal to verisimilitude. These created characters exist inside a universe that is fleshed out by the same trappings of culture as ours, blurring the boundary between this fictive world and ours.

Intertextual even in its paratextual aspects, the episode titles themselves—splashed on screen in a typewriter font at the beginning of each episode, as if placed there by the scriptwriter's device, and therefore textually evident within the episode—demand of the audience a certain fluency with popular culture in order to both recognize the reference and situate it within the narrative thrust of the episode. Season four's Halloween episode, "It's the Great Pumpkin, Sam Winchester" (4.07), references the classic Charlie Brown Halloween special, and "It's a Terrible Life" (4.17) features a plot inspired by the classic Jimmy Stewart film *It's a Wonderful Life* (1946). In season five, "The Curious Case of Dean Winchester" (5.07) references the F. Scott Fitzgerald short story (turned into a 2008 film starring Brad Pitt) in which a man ages backwards; the episode features a prematurely-aged Dean as the result of a run-in with a witch. "Two Minutes to Midnight" (5.21), in which Dean is on the verge of being dragged to Hell, is the title of a song by heavy metal band Iron Maiden, the lyrics of which refer to impending doom. Season five's "99 Problems" (5.17) is titled after a popular rap song by Jay Z, featuring a chorus in which the singer lists problems but asserts that a woman (though the term he uses is different) is not one of them. The lyrics of that song cleverly connect to the plot of the episode in which a woman posing as a Christian prophet is revealed to be the Biblical Whore of Babylon.

Likewise, "Sam, Interrupted" (5.11) directly references the film *Girl, Interrupted* (1999) (both are set in a mental institution), and "My Bloody Valentine" (5.14), set on Valentine's Day, features a series of gruesome and bloody deaths, but it is also an extratextual reference—that is, a reference to the world outside the *Supernatural* diegesis—to the 2009 film *My Bloody Valentine*, starring none other than Jensen Ackles. Season six includes "Mannequin 3: The Reckoning" (6.14), in which a mannequin factory is haunted by a vengeful ghost that causes the mannequins to come to life—a reference to the films *Mannequin* (1987) and its flop of a sequel, *Mannequin 2: On the Move* (1991), in which an enchanted mannequin comes to life to find true love. "My Heart Will Go On" (6.17) features the angel Balthazar altering history so the *Titanic* never sinks—merely because he cannot stand the Celine Dion theme song to the James Cameron film *Titanic* (1997). Season seven's "The Girl with the Dungeons and Dragons Tattoo" (7.20) introduces fan-favorite Charlie Bradbury, a savvy computer expert who helps Sam and Dean against the Leviathans; Charlie, named for classic science fiction author Ray Bradbury, is a particular site of polysemy; she is both a reference to hacker-savant Lisbeth Salander from Stieg Larsson's novel *The Girl with the Dragon Tattoo* (2005), as well as a self-proclaimed fangirl who has a tattoo of Princess Leia in a slave bikini astride a D20 gaming die—"I was drunk, it was Comic-Con,"

Charlie explains. That the *Supernatural* promotion machine itself is always a popular draw at Comic-Con makes this comment even more ironically amusing, as it bridges the distance between the show's diegesis and our reality.

This in particular is something the show does very well: it steps outside the world of its own creation and makes nods to a reality beyond its own narrative valance—special *wink-wink nudge-nudge* moments in which *Supernatural* acknowledges certain extradiegetic circumstances or occurrences and expects that viewers will contextualize these insertions. These inclusions act, as Richard-Laurent Barnett theorizes in his short essay "Metatextualities," as a "supra-strata" that participate in "the elaboration, construction, or, as some see it, the deconstruction of the work to which they are annexed or of which they are an unseverable component" (3). For example, at the end of season two's "The Usual Suspects" (2.07), Dean comments offhandedly, "I could really go for some pea soup," a remark that nods to the episode's guest star—Linda Blair of *The Exorcist* (1973) fame—and that film's notorious use of pea soup as vomit in her portrayal of a young girl possessed by the Devil. Similarly, in season five's "Fallen Idols" (5.05), Paris Hilton offers a very postmodern guest star turn as herself—or, rather, as the *form* of Paris Hilton taken on by the pagan god Leshii, who is driven by the need for people to idolize her. Written by Julie Siege, this episode not only employs the conceit of the monster assuming the form of Paris Hilton—an American heiress and reality TV star in the mid–2000s who styled herself to embody vacuous, frivolous femininity—it also takes pleasure in the visual spectacle of Paris Hilton beating the crap out of Dean. In this same episode, Dean references *House of Wax*, a 2005 horror film that starred both Paris Hilton and Jared Padalecki. When Dean tells Leshii/Paris, "I've never even seen *House of Wax*," the camera cuts away to Sam, who looks at Dean and slides his eyes to the side in a subtle acknowledgment of the metatextual reference to the constructed nature of *Supernatural* itself. This moment crystallizes the extratextual within the narrative, as well as points toward the phenomenon of "actor residue" and intertextual casting as theorized by John Fiske in *Television Culture* (7). A similar extradiegetic moment occurs at the beginning of "Hollywood Babylon" (2.18) when Sam and Dean are on a film and television studio tour; the tour guide drives the group past the set of *Gilmore Girls* (2000–2007)—a show that, like *Supernatural,* was a WB/CW network crossover—saying, "If we're lucky, we might even catch one of the show's stars!" At this, Sam cuts an uncomfortably guilty look toward Dean—a sly nod to viewers who recognize Padalecki as the actor who played Dean Forester on the first few seasons of *Gilmore Girls*. This moment conflates the extradiegetic with the metatextual—it both references the world outside the show while simultaneously referencing a constitutive element *of* the show that speaks from what Lauren Barnett calls an "outwardness from within" (3). The writers *expect* that viewers will catch the reference, and knowledgeable fans not only appreciate the appeal to their cultural literacy, but the inclusion of this extradiegetic concession also rewards viewers' pop culture fluency.

M. Night–Level Douchiness

Supernatural also brings self-referentiality to new heights. One of the most overt markers of this is Chuck Shurley's self assessment in "The Monster at the End of This Book" (4.18): "I mean, writing yourself into the story is one thing, but as a prophet? That's like M. Night–level douchiness!" The writers openly acknowledge the apparatus of the show itself through repeated references to the mechanics thereof. Oftentimes, these writerly nods serve to poke fun at the writers themselves. The previously mentioned "Hollywood Babylon," a metafilmic episode set on a sound stage where a horror movie is being filmed, features actual film director McG (real name: Joseph McGinty Nichol)—or, rather, the *character* of McG being portrayed by actor Regan Burns. The show returns to this conceit in season six's "The French Mistake" (6.15). In "Hollywood Babylon," McG is portrayed as a generic Hollywood hack director stereotype, and the other producers discuss his lack of talent and control on the set behind his back. The joke, of course, is that McG was in reality one of the executive producers of *Supernatural* up until 2013, yet the character of McG is presented farcically in the episode—a self-conscious, self-parodic move on the part of the writers. (Ironically, the actual McG briefly appears in the background while Sam and Dean speak to the "fake" McG.) Further, the episode also includes a reference to *Boogeyman*, a critically panned 2005 horror film for which Kripke wrote the screenplay; Dean tells actress Tara Benchley that he loved her in *Boogeyman*, to which she replies, "God, what a terrible script." Such self-referential inclusions metafilmically expose the mechanics of creating a horror vehicle and then mock the conventions thereof. Ben Edlund, who wrote "Hollywood Babylon" (and is responsible for many of what are termed the "meta episodes"), uses this framing technique to self-referentially poke fun at directors, producers, and yes, even writers. (After all, the villain in this particular episode turns out to be a disgruntled screenwriter.)

The season four episode "It's a Terrible Life"—written by season six and seven showrunner Sera Gamble—also mines *Supernatural*'s own artifice for source material and creates a hyperdiegetic parody of itself. In this episode, Sam and Dean are transported by the angel Zachariah into an alternate reality—one where they were never hunters or brothers, and do not know one another. However, they work for the same corporation: Sam a cubicle-dwelling peon and Dean a slick corporate executive in an expensive suit.

When a ghost begins punishing unproductive employees with violent deaths, Sam Wesson and Dean Smith (their alternate identities[3]) team up to fight it, and Sam's internet research on how to dispatch ghosts turns up the Ghostfacers website—run by ghost hunters Harry Spengler and Ed Zeddmore,[4] who Sam and Dean met in their own (primary) reality in season one's "Hell House" (1.17). Further blurring the lines between fantasy and reality, both www.ghostfacers.com and www.hellhoundslair.com (the website Harry and Ed curate in "Hell House") were active paratextual websites until 2013 (*Internet Archive*).

Supernatural is also rife with metatextual references to its cast and production team, and there is an obvious ironic glee behind these self-aggrandizing inclusions. Season four's "The Monster at the End of This Book" (4.18) introduces Sam and Dean to alcoholic, agoraphobic Chuck Shurley, who writes a series of books called "Supernatural" under the pen name Carver Edlund—an unabashed synthesis of the names of key staff writers Ben Edlund and Jeremy Carver. Similarly, the character of Bobby Singer mimetically evokes longtime series producer, director, and current series co-showrunner Robert Singer. Throughout the diegesis, banners and signs in the background set of the show often feature the names of set designers, graphics department members, costumers, and stunt coordinators. Lest viewers feel the creative team is too full of itself, the season six episode "The French Mistake," written by Edlund, places Sam and Dean into the "real world"—ostensibly *our* world—as actors Jared Padalecki and Jensen Ackles, who star in a television show titled *Supernatural*. In this reality, Dean/Jensen echoes what might be the reaction of the show's audience and asks producer Robert Singer (who is played by actor Brian Doyle Murray), "What kind of a douchebag names a character after himself?" Similarly metatextual, season twelve's "Somewhere Between Heaven and Hell" (12.15) acknowledges the appearance of actor Jeffrey Dean Morgan—who plays John Winchester—as the villain Negan on AMC's *The Walking Dead* (2010–present); Dean hefts a barbwire-wrapped baseball bat that deliberately references Negan's bat Lucille, declaring, "Man, Dad loved this thing!"

"That is some of the worst fan fiction I have ever heard!"[5]

Calling attention to the constructedness of fiction, metafictionality—fiction *about* fiction—is also a tactic *Supernatural* deploys with great success. In season six's "Live Free or TwiHard" (6.09), *Supernatural* satirizes the adolescent phenomenon of *Twilight*, featuring vampires who pose as sensitive victim figures (like author Stephenie Meyer's Edward Cullen) in order to capitalize on the popularity of the *Twilight* novels and movies—or, in this case, the surrogate titles *My Summer of Blood* and *Dream of the Vampires*—in order to lure in—and snack on—young girls obsessed with the series of books and films. The episode teaser is an amazing series of visual and dialogic references to the *Twilight* series: a young, pretty brunette girl in a plaid shirt—named Kristen, no less[6]—meets up with her "Edward," who gracefully catches her phone when she drops it and then broods appropriately. Later, she gets a paper cut and declares herself clumsy—a near perfect echo of the referent. The conceit, of course, is that she is only pretending, exploring a world of fantasy, whereas the man she is with is *actually* a vampire—one who uses online message boards to prey upon girls obsessed with the fictional world of vampires. Season nine's "Meta Fiction" (9.09)[7] makes this metafictional tendency explicit; the episode is narrated by the angel Metatron, who sits behind a typewriter, musing about how good stories are constructed. Metatron asks the audience, "What makes a story work? Is it the plot, the characters, the text? The subtext? And who gives a story meaning? Is it the writer? Or you? Tonight, I thought I would tell you a little story and let you decide." Metatron is explicitly referencing the constructed nature of the narrative—the fictional acknowledgment has literally *become* the narrative device.

Blending metafictional awareness with the metatelevisual, season five's "Changing Channels" (5.08), written by Jeremy Carver, again features the Trickster, who traps Sam and Dean inside a televisual simulacrum called "TV Land" where they have to participate in a soapy medical drama titled *Dr. Sexy, MD*,[8] a procedural cop show that deliberately evokes *CSI: Miami*'s embrace of terrible corpse-related puns and tendency to wear sunglasses at night, a kitschy 1970s-style sitcom à la *Three's Company* featuring a live studio audience, and an extreme Japanese game show involving a device called "The Nutcracker." One simulacrum features a *Knight Rider* parody that, rather than just featuring an upgraded Baby, instead turns *Sam* into the talking car. The line between what is part of the canonical world of *Supernatural* and what is the world of the viewer becomes even more ambiguous when an advertisement for a genital herpes treatment begins that appears to be part of our television conventions—the ad break—but is derailed by the appearance of Sam, who *very* begrudgingly announces, "I have genital herpes." In these ways, *Supernatural* both parodies and criticizes cultural convention through metatextual references to other TV genre tropes while simultaneously using metatelevisuality to craft a self-aware, complex "narrational bravado" that, even as it creates spectacle, necessarily contains a criticism of itself (Mittell 46).

This synthesis of metafictionality and metatelevisuality is evident in the Edlund-penned season four "Monster Movie" (4.05), in which classic horror tropes are explored, mocked, and mined for narrative value. In this episode—shot in black and white and featuring a classic monster movie-style score—

the brothers fight a shapeshifter who takes on the guise of those classic Hollywood movie monsters—Dracula, The Mummy, and the Wolf Man. The use of monochrome and the musical appeal to such classic source material illustrates the creative team's obvious verisimilitude with filmic historicity, but the inclusion of modern humor—such as a Dracula who orders pizza, but quizzes the delivery guy to make sure there is no garlic, and pays with a coupon—updates the material and grounds their appeal to classic horror conventions within their own created universe. *Supernatural* is consistently excellent at this acknowledgment of its generic heritage while it still pokes fun at these conventions—and its own complicit employment of them.

The show's tendency toward self-reflexive discourse as a narrational stratagem is foregrounded in episodes like the narrative duo of season four's "The Monster at the End of the Book" and season five's "The Real Ghostbusters" (5.09). "The Monster at the End of This Book"—wherein the Winchesters discover their lives have been published as a pulpy series of novels—forces the brothers to narratively engage with the cult fan practices that surround the diegetic book series, and simultaneously positions the apparatus of the show itself to acknowledge and critically respond to parallel extradiegetic fan practices. Thus, the episode narratively forces Sam and Dean to interact with a simulacrum of their own existence and to acknowledge an external communal interpretation of their lives, while also diegetically coercing them, as KT Torrey argues, "to embody some of that community's practices in order to gain access to critical information" (166). Building off this same metafictional thread, "The Real Ghostbusters," written by series creator Eric Kripke from a story by Nancy Weiner, features Sam and Dean being duped by Becky Rosen—a "superfan" of the diegetic "Supernatural" book series—into arriving at a "Supernatural" convention where Chuck is the keynote speaker. Extending beyond what would traditionally be considered metafictional, this episode instead incorporates so many narrative layers it might more aptly be termed *metasituational*. In "The Real Ghostbusters," Sam and Dean are dropped into a situation constructed entirely on the base *Supernatural* diegesis as told through the "Supernatural" books written by prophet Chuck. They are confronted with convention goers costumed not only as Sam and Dean, but also as their past adversaries—evil clowns, yellow-eyed demons, a hook man, etc. There is a live action role-playing game (LARP) where attendees hunt down a ghost, and much to Sam and Dean's consternation, among other convention activities, a panel on "The Homoerotic Subtext of 'Supernatural'" is scheduled.

Here Sam and Dean are presented with not only the diegetic trappings of their own narrative "lives," but also a metafictional mimesis of the show's actual fan practices, both of which are mocked heavily. When Fritz—a German convention goer costumed as the Hook Man—is confronted by a child's ghost (believing it to be part of the role-playing game), he says tiredly, "*Ja.* How original. 'Supernatural' bringing you more creepy children. Sigh." As evidenced by Fritz's deprecating reply, the writers use the episode as a means of acknowledging the show's occasionally repetitive use of tropes while also acknowledging that they are aware of the perception of these repetitions by their audience. Even the character of Becky—who herself writes Sam/Dean slash fan fiction based on the book series—is a diegetic acknowledgment of the extradiegetic fanbase who pores over minute details of the show, and each successive appearance of Becky is an acknowledgment of the fandom that exists outside—yet around—the show. While delivering a message from Chuck, she tells the Winchesters, "He's being watched. Angels. Nice change up to the mythology, by the way. The demon stuff was getting kind of old" ("Sympathy for the Devil"). It is clear that Becky serves as a synecdoche of the fans, and when she offers such gems as congratulating Sam and Dean on the addition of angels to the mythos or explaining where and when an item was last seen in the narrative, she represents the writers' acknowledgment of their collective awareness of the audience's viewing practices. In the later "Season Seven, Time for a Wedding!" (7.08), Becky's use of a demon's love potion to convince Sam to marry her makes a critical extratextual comment on the more fervently manic aspects of the fandom while also pointing toward a recursive, constitutive relationship between extratextual fan practices and fictional diegesis. Additionally, the episode—as evident from the title—pokes fun at serial narrative's formulaic tendency to include "stunt" episodes as a show ages in order to maintain viewer interest.

"*For whatever reason, our life is a TV show*"[9]

The use of these metafictional references lightens the gravitas of the show—after all, this is a television series that often deals in heavy subject matter, wrestling with notions of duty, loyalty, and free will—but it also acts as a way of acknowledging that in our postmodern world, simple narratives that inhabit only one plane are far less compelling than those that reach out into multivalent narratological spaces and reflect the interconnected nature of the contemporary world. By pushing the envelope of self-referentiality and the construction of what is "real" within the universe of the Winchesters, *Supernatural* expands the narrative space that a show can fill, creating an extensive hyperdiegesis that is explored through these metatelevisual devices. This is highly evident in season six's "The French Mistake," written by Edlund and directed by Charles Beeson. Named for the song in Mel Brooks's *Blazing Saddles* (1974) during which actors from the Western film crash through a movie studio wall into a dapper Hollywood musical featuring the song "The

French Mistake," the episode sends Sam and Dean crashing through a window and into a world in which they are actors named Jared Padalecki and Jensen Ackles who star on a TV show named *Supernatural*.

In this episode, "reality" takes on a peculiar and distorted guise; while Jensen and Jared play themselves, show producers Robert Singer and Eric Kripke are both portrayed by actors. Sam and Dean are both startled to find Jared is married to the actress who played the demon Ruby in season four—and in *our* actual reality, Jared Padalecki is in fact married to costar Genevieve Cortese Padalecki, who played the second incarnation of Ruby. So, while some constructs of the episode are based in our reality, others are simulacra, and these simulacra are most often used as opportunities to lampoon the cast, crew, and diegesis. Jensen's trailer sports an egregiously enormous fish tank, and Jared's house features a huge portrait over the fireplace of him in a cowboy hat riding a horse. Once again taking the opportunity to mock both themselves and the conventions of the show, the writers include the line, "We'd have to blow off the scene where they [Sam and Dean] sit on the Impala and talk about their feelings." Fictional Robert Singer scoffs, "Ha, right! You answer the hate mail!," driving home the writers' acknowledgment of the fandom's reaction to the narrative choices they make. This peculiar blend of constructed fiction and extradiegetic fact is rarely found on television, and it creates a strange facsimile of reality that bends around and bites its own tail like the mythical Ouroboros.

"Fan Fiction," the Robbie Thompson–penned 200th episode, takes a similar approach, although instead of a jump into the "real" world, the Winchesters find themselves involved in a hunt at an all-girls preparatory academy that turns out to be staging a theatrical adaptation of the book series, titled *Supernatural: The Musical*. The play's writer and director, Marie, is a fan of the Carver Edlund books, and she has developed a musical version of the Winchesters' lives—complete with the production values one would expect from a high school drama department. The show contains songs about the *Supernatural* storyline, including "The Road So Far" (a nod to the paratextual tag that accompanies recaps at the top of each episode) and "A Single Man Tear," which parodies the "feelings" scenes in the show that "The French Mistake" mocked seasons earlier. As in "The Monster at the End of This Book," Dean is dismayed to again be confronted by slash content in the (simulated) fan practices—when Dean asks Marie why the two actors playing "Sam" and "Dean" are standing so close together, she replies suggestively, "Reasons." He is later outraged to see the "actors" who play "Dean" and "Castiel" within the play intimately embracing. Marie explains that the second act explores the nature of "Destiel"—the extradiegetic portmanteau for the romantic relationship between Dean and Castiel that is championed by a vocal portion of the fandom—and she tells Dean, "You can't spell 'subtext' without S-E-X." At this,

Dean turns directly to the camera with an exasperated look on his face; this moment thus creates a recursive nexus of intertextuality, metatextuality, metafictionality, extradiegetic awareness, and a shattering of the fourth wall between the show's narrative, the play's reinscription of that narrative, and the viewer's consumption of these narrative layers. When Dean tells Marie what actually happens in the "narrative" after the Carver Edlund books ended, she laughs at him and tells him, "That is some of the *worst* fan fiction that I have ever heard!" As the entire cast assembles before the show, Sam asks, "Where's Chuck?," to which Marie replies, "Honestly, the author inserting themselves into the narrative thing, it's just not my favorite. I kind of hate the meta stories." Sam and Dean reply in unison: "Me too."

Once again, *Supernatural* exhibits what I would term a "mimetic bleed" that foregrounds both metatextuality and metafictionality as a narrative strategy while simultaneously gesturing toward the extradiegetic reception of the show itself, blurring the boundaries between the various levels of diegesis and leaving *Supernatural* to exist in a recursively constitutive limen.

"My head hurts"[10]

The many incarnations of meta-ness on *Supernatural* create a complex, varied, and often humorous landscape in which the show both explores and explodes the boundaries of the televisual narrative; as Dean laments in "The Monster at the End of This Book," "I'm sitting in a laundromat reading about myself sitting in a laundromat reading about myself. My head hurts!" In this way, *Supernatural* is an outlier in the dominant TV paradigm that tends to reward more predictable fare—like the romantic entanglements of medical staff or the pun-laden procedural police drama that *Supernatural* mocks in "Changing Channels." Is there any other show on TV that has created and sustained so many narrative valences? The world of Sam and Dean is encapsulated by the frame of the Winchester Gospels, by the world of TV parody courtesy of the Trickster, by fragmented and recursive timelines, by the jump into the "real" world of Jensen Ackles and Jared Padalecki, and by the *High School Musical* version of the *Supernatural* diegesis that is filtered through not only previous metafictional devices but also through the extratextual "reality" of fan practices. The word *supernatural*, at its core, means "above nature" or "existing outside of nature." How appropriate, then, that a TV show about things above and outside of nature explores the spaces above and outside the conventional narrative structures and medium of television itself.

NOTES

1. Sam to Dean, "Fallen Idols" (5.05).
2. At various times, Sam and Dean pose as Agents Bonham and Copeland (Led Zeppelin and The Police), Fathers Simmons and Frehley (Kiss), Agents DeYoung and Shaw (Styx), Agents Angus and Young (AC/DC), Detectives Bachman and Turner (Bachman-Turner Overdrive), U.S. Marshalls Gibbons and Beard (ZZ Top), Agents Page and Plant (Led Zeppelin), and Agents Greer and Ehart (Kansas—who performs the unofficial *Supernatural* theme song, "Carry On Wayward Son"). For a more comprehensive listing, see the Supernatural Wiki at http://www.supernaturalwiki.com/index.php?title=Pseudonyms.
3. Sam and Dean's last name—Winchester—is also parodied by their alternate-world surnames of Smith and Wesson: they are both the names of firearm manufacturers.
4. Even the names Harry Spengler and Ed Zeddmore are a way of paying tribute to the 1984 Ivan Reitman film *Ghostbusters*, which featured characters Egon Spengler and Winston Zeddmore. This film gets another nod from season five's episode title, "The Real Ghostbusters," as well as in Dean's line, "We came, we saw, we kicked its…" in "Fan Fiction."
5. Marie to Dean, "Fan Fiction" (10.05)
6. A reference to Kristen Stewart, who plays Bella Swan in the *Twilight Saga* films.
7. "Meta Fiction" is part of a trinity of episode titles that refer to fictional practices with fandoms; the other two are "Slash Fiction" (7.06) and "Fan Fiction."
8. *Dr. Sexy, MD* was first mentioned in "The Monster at the End of This Book," by the publisher of the *Supernatural* books, thus creating a reference not only to *Grey's Anatomy* but also to its own history. The joke about why a show about doctors would have a ghost in it is a further meta reference, as Jeffrey Dean Morgan in fact did play a ghost (or at any rate, a character's memory of her dead lover) on *Grey's Anatomy*.
9. Sam, "The French Mistake" (6.15).
10. Dean Winchester, "The Monster at the End of This Book" (4.18).

WORKS CITED

Barnett, Richard-Laurent. "Metatextualities." *L'Esprit Créateur*, vol. 31, no. 2, Summer 1991, pp. 3–4. *Project Muse,* doi: https://doi.org/10.1353/esp.1991.0046.
Dewey, Caitlin. "The Complete History of 'Slender Man,' the Meme That Compelled Two Girls to Stab a Friend." *Washington Post.com*, 27 July 2016, https://www.washingtonpost.com/news/the-intersect/wp/2014/06/03/the-complete-terrifying-history-of-slender-man-the-internet-meme-that-compelled-two-12-year-olds-to-stab-their-friend/?noredirect=on&utm_term=.dc9a4edcff3c.
Fiske, John. *Television Culture*. Routledge, 2011.
"Ghostfacers." *SupernaturalWiki.com*, 14 Sept. 2017, http://www.supernaturalwiki.com/index.php?title=Ghostfacers.
Internet Archive Wayback Machine. Internet Archive, https://web.archive.org/.
Mittell, Jason. *Complex TV: The Poetics of Contemporary Television Storytelling*. NYU Press, 2015.
"Supernatural: Hollywood Babylon." *Internet Movie Database*, http://www.imdb.com/title/tt0964436/?ref_=fn_al_tt_1.
Torrey, KT. "Writing with the Winchesters: Metatextual Wincest and the Provisional Practice of Happy Endings." *Journal of Fandom Studies*, vol. 2, no. 2, 2014, pp. 163–180, doi: 10.1386/jfs.2.2.163_1.

Part Two

"A cruel, cruel, capricious god"

God Is Dead and the Death of the Author
Theorizing Divine Absence in Supernatural Season Five

Kwasu David Tembo

Introduction

Supernatural first aired on the WB Network and now continues its syndication on WB's successor, the CW. Like its predecessors, including *Buffy the Vampire Slayer*, *Angel*, *Charmed*, and *Smallville*, *Supernatural* focuses on the bildungsromans of two young protagonists set against a backdrop of Apocalyptic supernatural action-drama and comedy. Major themes of the series include family, horror and fear, religion and morality, heroism and sacrifice, misogyny, gender and sexuality, identity and transgression, fandom and fan works, specific objects and secondary characters in the show, folklore, mythologies, and theological mysticism. Keith R.A. DeCandido notes in "Not just a pretty face (or two)" that unlike their predecessors, Sam and Dean do not possess any special abilities (ix). Instead, the Winchester Brothers are portrayed as manifestations of quintessential frontier/heartland Americana, two simple, sturdy young men from Kansas whose shared Apocalyptic destiny is thrust upon them as children by God Himself (Garvey 88). For the preponderance of the series' first four seasons, series creator Eric Kripke uses the show as an aesthetico-narratological space within which to explore American urban legends and folklore in the present-day United States, having the Winchester Brothers travel the back roads of America in their 1967 Chevy Impala, fighting paranormal enemies including but not limited to demons, monsters, ghosts, and other mythical beings, typically nocturnally, in haunted houses, cemeteries, and crypts (Abbott). During its fourth season, *Supernatural* the series becomes more focused on Christian mythology. This manifests primarily in an overarching storyline pertaining to the Winchesters' centrality in the conflict between the forces of good and evil in the Apocalypse as detailed in the Bible's Book of Revelation. In season five, the Winchesters discover they are each to serve as the human vessels for Lucifer and the Archangel Michael, to engage in a conflict intended to catalyze Armageddon. In their attempts to avert the End of Days, the brothers discover that God has abdicated and abandoned His throne and, seemingly, His dominion as well, being nowhere to be found by angelic, demonic, and/or mortal seekers. In His absence, the angels, led by the Archangel Zachariah, pursue the Apocalypse and place humanity in antagonistic relationships with both divine and infernal forces of the Judeo-Christian ecumenical and mystical traditions. The Winchesters succeed in their preventative mission, but do so at a high cost. Sam leaps into a supra-dimensional "cage" built for Lucifer, taking the Archangel Michael with him. In the aftermath, Dean, brotherless, is left on Earth to pursue a normal life. A cursory survey of critical attitudes toward the series, many of which are compiled in Supernatural.tv's *In the Hunt: Unauthorized Essays on* Supernatural, reveals that these are surprisingly less varied than one might expect. While there are more academic collections in which incisive scholarly essays about the show and its fandoms appear, such as Robin DeRosa's *Simulation in Media and Culture: Believing the Hype* or Valentina Marescu, Silvia Branea, and Bianca Mitu's *Critical Reflections on Audience and Narrativity*, not to mention scholarly books focused specifically on the show, such as Erika Engstrom and Joseph M. Valenzano III's *Television, Religion, and* Supernatural, or Melissa Edmundson's *The Gothic in* Supernatural, *In the Hunt* is clearly directed at fans. That said, however, in its entirety, the collection offers some broad insights concerning the *Supernatural* diegesis and beyond, especially as pertains to fan engagement.

Trimming the Hedges: Authorial Voices, Grand Narratives and Free Will in the Face of Authorial Presence and Absence

Most pertinent to this analysis is Joseph M. Valenzano III and Erika Engstrom's "Cowboys, Angels, and Demons: American Exceptionalism and the Frontier Myth in the CW's *Supernatural*," which explores the numerous ways "*Supernatural* not only succeeds as an example of a horror show on television but embraces a Catholic version of faith as the hegemonic power in the religious arena" (Valenzano and Engstrom 554). In so doing, the authors examine *Supernatural* as "a curious hybrid of horror, Western, and melodrama," drawing upon folklore and a critique of religious dogma (Abbott xv). Another point they make that will be important to this essay's discussion of the nature of the authorial voice in the series pertains to the fact that Kripke predicated the relationship between the American Monomyth, horror television, and Judeo-Christian eschatology on a decidedly humanist principle; namely, that the trials and hardships the Winchesters endure and overcome are representative of the underlying two-fold philosophy of the series: (1) "there's humanity and a bunch of supernatural sons-of-bitches and humanity will always win" and (2) "humanity trumps all supernatural forces, including the more religious entities like God, gods, angels, demons, and the Devil" (Valenzano and Engstrom 559). The implication here is that *Supernatural* can be regarded as an extended meditation on the onto-existential and psycho-emotional issues and debates concerning the conflict between destiny and free will, divine authorial scripture and/or prophecy contra humanistic authorial agency. It is also important to draw attention to a point made by the authors concerning the philosophical tensions between free will and destiny that form the theoretical nexus of the show, particularly over seasons four and five:

> In *Supernatural*, the Winchesters are told by angels that God—who [...] is [...] revealed to be absent from Heaven—chose the brothers to be primary actors in the Biblical prophecy of Armageddon, even though they still have the free will to avert it. The Winchesters, viewers learn, are not only well known in the "hunting" world (a sub-culture of fellow protectors in *Supernatural*) but are special brothers with a special destiny chosen by God. They, however, go from fulfilling that special destiny to actively working against its fulfillment. We read this evolution as advancing American exceptionalism—in the form of the Winchesters—from its original conception: Rather than a nation appointed by and subservient to God, it has exceeded its mandate and found a means to place God and his angels in the category of an evil Other. The only true force for good, then, is the Winchesters [Valenzano and Engstrom, "Cowboys, Angels, and Demons" 562].

As the Winchesters are divinely appointed supernatural interventionists, it would seem that this conflict between destiny and free will is somewhat illusory. If the Winchesters behave as vigilantes because they are divinely appointed or chosen to do so, then they have both free will *and* divine authorial agency to alter the eschatological narrative concerning the Judeo-Christian Apocalypse. And yet, as this essay will later explore, the alleged disappearance of God does not nullify the forces of destiny, here understood as an ur-Narrative, without the presence or absence of an author, or what Jacques Derrida refers to as archi-writing in *Of Grammatology*, nor prevent His authority from acting upon all individuals named in His own narrative, from God Himself to the Winchesters.

The ostensible absence of God in season five does not undo the power of the Apocalyptic Narrative, attributed to His authorship in written word (scripture), from acting as an onto-existential and psycho-emotional framework within which Sam and Dean must not only navigate and survive, but save from its own foretold destruction. The fact that Sam and Dean succeed in preventing the Apocalypse makes an interesting comment on the nature of authorial agency expressed on and through multiple diegetic levels. If one thinks of God as an aloof author whose authorial voice and agency is not bound by the diegetic framework of the Narrative—that He either created the Narrative in totality in a pre-historic act of authorship or continually writes out the End of Days as they unfold—then His absence from the diegesis of the narrative He oversees is secondary to the authority of the Narrative itself, one which, according to season five, is in a continual process of creation and revision. It represents a kind of "writing" that precedes both the Word and the Scripture. The aesthetic and narratological tropes and leitmotifs concerning the end of history, regardless of what sociopolitical, socioeconomic, or sociocultural symbols used to frame such eschatonic considerations, are a narrative concern that precedes humanity's contemplation of it in the same way that death precedes birth. Valenzano and Engstrom explore this idea through a conversation between Death and Dean in "Two Minutes to Midnight" (5.21). Death attempts to impress upon Dean the notion of the radical insignificance of humanity in view of the vast scales of time and space older powers and forces such as he experiences. Latent in Death's lesson on philosophy and theology is a self-congratulatory explication of his purpose and role in relation to both human and non-human beings alike. There is some ambiguity in Death's statements, noted in his uncertainty as to who is older between him and God. However, the more problematic ambiguity, in terms of authorial agency and omnipotence, pertains to Death's claim that even God will fall to his scythe in time. The questions Death introduces to Dean and, by extension, the audience, are concerned with self-understanding, self-aggrandizement, and the theme of insignificance. Death achieves this anti-paradigmatic doubt by troubling the power of the greatest authority known in the *Supernatural* diegesis, namely the power of God. From his older, comparatively incomprehensible supra-cosmological vantage, "Death sees humans the way humans view bacteria, and refers to earth as 'one little planet in an insignificant solar system, in a galaxy barely out of its diapers'" (Valenzano and Engstrom, "Homilies and Horsemen" 65).

In terms of authorial agency and the Narrative of reality contra free will, Death's comments serve to invite onto-existential questions regarding both the *value* of said Narrative, the sovereignty of its authorial voice, and the narratological agency of the players therein who are instrumental in "writing" said Narrative by *being* in it. Here, Kripke gestures to and interpolates the overarching structure of semi-fixed concepts concerning Judeo-Christian hermeneutics of the Apocalypse, reterritorializes them within the context of contemporary action horror drama television and, in presenting the series' protagonists as divinely appointed agents whose free will makes them both safeguards and impediments for and against the Apocalypse, complicates the dialectical divide of the sovereignty of divine authorship contra the caprices of human will (Derrida 60). The paradox inherent in this idea is that *preserving* the Narrative, namely the unfurling of the Judeo-Christian conception of history from Genesis to Revelation, means simultaneously *allowing* the narrative to conclude. Therefore, the Winchesters' interventions and participation in the Narrative means that prevention and erasure become undifferentiated, ultimately redounding to the same subjugation to not necessarily the authority of the author of the Narrative, God, but rather the Narrative itself.

An example of this interventionist activity can be noted when the Winchesters are made aware in "Sympathy for the Devil" (5.01) that the angels under Zachariah are seeking to bring about the Apocalypse. Throughout the season, they combat and kill these angels in an attempt to prevent either a God-ordained or Angel-ordained Apocalypse. In so doing, they eradicate a supernatural threat to humanity. The very fact that mortals like Sam and Dean are able to kill angels, emissaries of God, means that they are able to undo God's Work by eradicating and erasing entities essential to His Narrative. Therefore, though appointees of God and other divine entities of the Judeo-Christian tradition, Sam and Dean are not only equal to God in this way, but in attempting to use their respective free wills to alter His Narrative, are also better authors than the Author. "By having God play a role in ensuring the destiny of the brothers in their fight against evil," Valenzano and Engstrom argue, "*Supernatural* illustrates the divine ordination that justifies interventionist practices and firmly entrenches a powerful Judeo-Christian deity as directing the actions of the Winchesters [...], albeit one whose plan the brothers ultimately reject" ("Cowboys, Angels, and Demons" 562).

While Valenzano and Engstrom again take up the notion that *Supernatural* explores the Winchesters' intervention in the Narrative of a divine authority, the Judeo-Christian God, and the value and function of beings other than the brothers whose purpose it is to help conclude said narrative, there exists a paucity of theorization concerning the role of authorship in the series, particularly in season five. This essay will now look more closely at the paradoxes of authorial agency and free will expressed in season five by theorizing the paradoxical present-absence of the Authorial voice in *Supernatural* as embodied by God, also known as the writer-prophet Chuck.

Narrative and the Problem of the Authorial Voice

While a similar argument can be made for Metatron, the archangel amanuensis of the Word of God, this essay contends that the most persistent meditation on the nature of Narrative and the problem of the Authorial voice in the series to date is circumscribed almost entirely by the character and portrayal of God. God reflects the familiar profile of the Judeo-Christian God. Within the *Supernatural* diegesis, He is characterized as a powerful primordial being credited with authoring the Narrative of the universe, the human soul, and free will. In view of Death's claim of being able to reap God, the only other being able to match God in terms of authorial agency or, in this case anti-authorial agency, up to and including season five, is Death, greatest of The Four Horsemen of the Apocalypse. In the series, following the revolt and fall of Lucifer and his rebel angels, God left Heaven and sought seclusion on Earth. After thousands of years in isolation, God re-emerges to partially aid in the Apocalypse, disappearing again once it has been averted. As part of His cover, God takes up the name and identity of "Chuck Shurley," thereby dissimulating His presence from His creations, allowing Him to live undisturbed among them, only keeping in contact with Joshua, caretaker of Heaven's gardens, via prophecy. God later takes up the identity, responsibility, and authority of a prophet, further hiding His true power by becoming an author of a marginal book series "Supernatural," which recounts, in exact detail, the entirety of the Winchester brothers' experiences during the show's run as of season five. In this way, these Winchester Gospels act as the *Supernatural* diegesis' Dead Sea Scrolls.

Much like Javier Bardem's portrayal of God in Darren Aronofsky's *Mother!* (2017), in this essay's chosen episodes, Rob Benedict plays God as a tortured artist. Sam and Dean meet Him in "The Monster at the End of This Book" (4.18). They discover that Chuck has seemingly omniscient knowledge of their emotions, fears, loves, mistakes, victories, and destinies, including every detail of their lives up to and including Dean going to Hell in the previous season. Upon learning that Chuck is writing a new Winchester Gospel/ "Supernatural" text, the brothers find Him and reveal themselves to Him. After initially taking them for overly enthusiastic fans of His work, He is convinced of their identities and the philosophical meaning thereof. He profusely apologizes for all the heartache and suffering He has caused them over the entire series and speculates that he may indeed be God. Chuck goes on to reveal that though frustrated with the self-perceived sub-par quality of his authorial output, He never stopped writing, going as far as to even write Himself into His own Narrative. God seemingly completely undermines His own authorial agency by giving the brothers an unpublished manuscript which describes the upcoming Apocalypse.

Two philosophical works that help illustrate the various tensions between a deistic Authorial voice and free will in the face of both divine presence and absence in the series can be found in Friedrich Nietzsche's *The Gay Science* (1882) and Roland Barthes' "The Death of the Author" (1967). Using the parable of a madman seeking God, Nietzsche in *The Gay Science* sets forth one of his most famous existential concepts, "God is dead." The phrase, a synecdoche of Nietzsche's atheism, is a reaction against the concept of a singular Authorial voice with unchallenged authority and insight over and into the lives of human beings, structuring both the psycho-emotional and onto-existential conditions—determining everything from natural phenomena to morals and ethics. When related to the series, Nietzsche's aphorism could easily be taken as Sam and Dean's secretly held personal mantra or motto. In view of all the ill fortune, suffering, loss, and pain the pair endures under the aegis of an absent deistic authority, "God is dead" can be seen to encapsulate their, and by extension all mortal, disappointment and frustration with the caprices and mysteries of gods of all kinds.

In contrast to the Judeo-Christian Narrative, whose eschatology promises paradise and rest for those who lived pure and good lives after the End of Days, and damnation for the evil, Nietzsche encourages humanity to forsake the promise of postmortem otherworldly rewards and embrace their freedom-in-imminence. As opposed to any reliance on God and/or recognition of His Authorial voice as insuperable, Nietzsche's perspectivism, and his analysis of power as the real force and explanation behind people's actions, puts forth a new way of challenging and countering established forms of authority, through which penetrating social critiques could be achieved. This theme of radical imminence latently contains the concept of radical self-reliance. If people cannot rely on God for succor at least, deliverance at most, they have to rely on themselves or those they *choose* to place their faith in. This is why the theme of familial and filial bonds predicated on absolute trust is so recurrent and important in the series. In the end, Sam, Dean, Bobby and their associates understand that they cannot rely on God to write a happy ending for them, one with light and peace as a reward for all their gallantry and struggles, physical and psycho-spiritual alike, at its conclusion. Ultimately, for Nietzsche, it is not God from whom one seeks peace and freedom, but His shadow in the form of His Narrative. Through the parable of the lantern-carrying madman and his untimely news of God's death in Section 125, Nietzsche professes that the desire and act of not simply altering the Narrative, but destroying it altogether, turning the Narrative from being a sculpture glorifying the agency of His Authorial voice into a storied tombstone signifying His radical absence or death, is both the highest deed of free will and a deed that requires time in order to manifest.

In Book Three, Section 108, Nietzsche describes the notion that while God or Gods or any deistic figures must be overcome, their residue, shadow, or trace, manifest in the Narrative of dogma and scripture, must also be overcome: "New battles.—After Buddha was dead, they still showed his shadow in a cave for centuries—a tremendous, gruesome shadow. God is dead; but given the way people are, there may still for millennia be caves in which they show his shadow.—And we—we must still defeat his shadow as well!" (109). In *Supernatural*, the meta-diegetic narrative of "Supernatural" which describes the actions, events, and ultimate fates of those it follows is a deistic shadow that troubles the notion of free will in those it subtends. Later in Section 343, Nietzsche offers the following pithy definition of the meaning behind the proclamation that "God is Dead," stating that "the greatest recent event—that 'God is dead'; that the belief in the Christian God has become unbelievable" (Nietzsche 199). For Sam and Dean, however, the unavailability of God does not negate or make unavailable his power which not only manifests in his Narrative, but in His power made manifest in the power of his creations, angelic *and* demonic power, for instance.

Much in the same way that following the death of God in Nietzschean terms, "having buried the Author, the modern scriptor can thus no longer believe" in His Authorial agency as something unchallenged (Barthes 146). Barthes's "The Death of the Author" argues against the Authorial voice of a text acting as a limit on said text's hermeneutic possibilities. According to Barthes, "as soon as a fact is *narrated* no longer with a view to acting directly on reality but intransitively, that is to say, finally outside of any function other than that of the very practice of the symbol itself, this disconnection occurs, the voice loses its origin, the author enters into his own death, writing begins" (Barthes 142). Therefore, the Author's identity, person, culture, background, historical context, and onto-existential status should not be relied upon to distill meaning from her/his text. While one might argue that reading the experiences and biases of the Author into the text serves in providing a definitive explanation thereof, Barthes argues that it limits the text, circumscribing the vast interpretive avenues available in the text in and around the singularity of an Author, whose absence from the narrative paradoxically acts as an interpretive anchor around which interpretation of the text orbits. Therefore, separating the Author from her/his Work liberates the Work from a type of interpretive tyranny. As a result of such a release, the numerous component pieces that form the bricolage of a text can express their multi-layered meanings more freely than the singular interpretation predicated on the identity of an Author would allow. When related to *Supernatural*, Barthes's claims come up against two interesting paradoxes. First, that God is as present in His absence as He is in His presence. Second, that God does not need to be present for His Narrative not only to sustain itself, but also to sustain its Authority.

Barthes places the interpretative burden and privilege squarely with the reader in this counter-intuitive style of literary criticism, whereby the meaning of the text is dependent on the impressions of the reader, as opposed to the intentions, agendas, or tastes of the Author. Barthes applies this principle in subtle ways, most noticeably by reducing the Author as a locus of creative influence to "scriptor" as a way of disrupting the ostensible contiguousness of agency between the terms "authority" and "author." For Barthes, the scriptor's role is less creative than it is productive, the scriptor producing the work but not explaining it in any absolute way. In keeping the text open, so to speak, its content does not need the being of an Author preceding or exceeding the writing to substantiate its own myriad meanings and interpretations. The most radical implication of this type of textual analysis inheres in the fact that now every work is always-already written and interpreted with each re-reading thereof. In this way, "writing is the destruction of every voice, of every point of origin. Writing is that neutral, composite, oblique space where our subject slips away, the negative where all identity is lost, starting with the very identity of the body writing" (Barthes 142). When applied to Sam and Dean's actions in season five, the central tension at play is one between Authorial agency and creativity versus the reader's Authorial agency in interpreting that which the Author has written. The question the brothers must inevitably face and negotiate is whether their actions and/or interpretation of events—their hermeneutics of their own lives and destinies—be enough to radically alter those events? Or are there *any* phenomenological possibilities that can emerge and be experienced, both as interpreters and creators of events, *outside* the authority of God's Narrative?

"Sympathy for the Devil" deals with the accidental liberation of Lucifer, thus beginning the Apocalypse. Having been saved from death by an unknown force, Sam and Dean seek out information from the prophet Chuck. Aside from revealing that their guardian angel, guide, mentor and friend Castiel has been killed for aiding them, Chuck furnishes the brothers with little else for fear of reprisals from the angels who have him under surveillance, and are working against the brothers to bring about the Apocalypse. Chuck later sends a message to the brothers through a fan of his "Supernatural" series named Becky Rosen, telling them that the angels have lost the sword of the Archangel Michael, a weapon capable of vanquishing Lucifer. He gives them a cryptic clue as to its location, a mystery to which Bobby refers as "Chuck's nonsense" ("Sympathy for the Devil"). Disentangling the clue and racing to find the sword before either demons or angels do, the brothers find Zachariah waiting for them. He reveals that he disguised the information as a prophetic vision in Chuck's mind, intending to lure the brothers out and to him. Zachariah further explains that Dean is in fact the sword, that is, Michael's predestined human vessel. Dean refuses to allow Michael to possess his body despite Zachariah's threats to kill Sam. Zachariah then subsequently tortures Dean while stating that "Michael must defeat the Serpent. It is written." Castiel soon reappears, frightening Zachariah and his angelic guard away, after which he uses sigils to hide the brothers from angelic detection, as well as revealing to the brothers that both they and he were saved by God Himself. At the end of the episode, Nick, a man whose wife and infant child have been murdered by a killer, begins having traumatic nightmares in which he relives the horror of his pain and loss. In one such nightmare, Lucifer appears to him in the form of his deceased wife, speaking to him, manipulating his compromised psycho-emotional state to convince him to acquiesce to him and together face God. Lucifer sums up the man's psychological and emotional pain in a dialectic: "either God is sadistic or doesn't care" and that this is the reason he wants to "find Him—to hold Him accountable for his actions. Just because he created us doesn't mean He can toy with us, like playthings." Nick eventually agrees.

In this episode, the authority of the Authorial voice is seemingly always-already challenged by Rob Benedict's performance as Chuck/God. In contrast to the expected expression of omnipotent supremacy and omniscient dominion, Benedict plays Chuck as skittish, paranoid, stammering, awkward, anxious, and timid—thus latently establishing the series' portrayal of God as deeply "human." Benedict's performance contributes "to the desacrilization of the image of the Author by ceaselessly recommending the abrupt disappointment of expectations of meaning" when encountering terms, concepts, and leitmotifs associated with the Judeo-Christian conception of God (Barthes 144). This characterization of Chuck is sustained by the fact that throughout the series, Kripke seems to be "visibly concerned with the task of inexorably blurring, by an extreme subtilization, the relation between the writer and his characters; by making of the narrator not he who has seen and felt nor even he who is writing, but he who *is going to write*," whereby the notion of Chuck being simultaneously God, His prophet, and a (re)writer of his own Narrative presents the concept of the Judeo-Christian God as one of solipsistic self-narrativization (Barthes 144).

The performativity of God has philosophical bearing on the concept of the Authorial voice. As a writer-prophet, Chuck dissimulates His Authorship, as if to preserve it, and in taking up the identities of both prophet and author, takes up what Barthes describes as an ethnographic responsibility for the narrative whereby "in ethnographic societies the responsibility for a narrative is never assumed by a person but by a mediator, shaman or relator whose 'performance'—the mastery of the narrative code—may possibly be admired but never his 'genius'" (Barthes 142). In this way, *Supernatural* portrays God as an Author, a man of "letters anxious to unite [His] person and [His] work through diaries and memoirs" which jointly comprise the "Supernatural" book series, but more broadly, the diegesis of *Supernatural* itself (Barthes 143). The fact that Chuck is a writer of a narrative in which He appears disguised as His own prophet creates an interesting authorial feedback loop, which suggests that God, in being God, is able to permeate and operate, that is influence, erase, write and re-write, significant aspects of diegetic, that is mortal, reality while still being in it. In this sense, if the text/work is seen as reality, and writing as free will, then Sam and Dean's mission to prevent the Apocalypse represents an attempt at "suppressing the author in the interests of writing (which is [...] to restore the place of the reader)" (Barthes 143). This produces a strange simultaneous effect of both absolute power and weakness. In being under surveillance from the Archangels, God is not only the Author of the Narrative in which both said Archangels and their surveillance appear, but one in which He is also *subject* to it—both His creations *and* the Narrative in which they exist. In this sense, God being under surveillance from His own creations is like an Author being held to account for His narrative by both His consumers *and* His characters.

"The Real Ghostbusters" (5.09), in which Sam and Dean re-encounter Chuck when they attend the first "Supernatural" convention where the brothers are mistaken for LARPing (Live Action Role Playing) attendees in a brilliant and humorous display of metatextual self-awareness, presents the essential paradox underpinning the relationship between God and authorship the fifth season explores. While ultimately authored by Him, the Work, Text, Winchester Gospel, and/or reality is meta-narratologically, that is simultaneously, always-already beyond His control. This episode draws attention to the idea that the authority of Authorial Voice/Word/Text is ultimately unstable and, more accurately, defined as a bricolage constantly (re)created by a vastitude of authorial agents, in this case, the Archangels, fans of "Supernatural" by Chuck Shurley (who function as disciples in the diegesis), and the other mortal characters whose authorial "stylus" is limited to their free will or, at least, their *belief* therein. All of this occurs, is foretold, and limited by and within a meta-narrative, an archi-writing, written out/spoken forth by Chuck/God. Though individuals within the Narrative ostensibly express humanistic courage, perseverance, love, brotherhood, sacrifice, and determination, all of the trials and tribulations, successes and failures that draw out or destroy said qualities are semi-pre-determined by a Character whose characterizations *become* "characters" through the power of divine Authorial agency. Chuck sums up the truth of divine authorship and the ethical and moral conundrums of its essential paradox in "The Monster at the End of This Book" when he says to Sam,

> I write things and they come to life. Yeah, no, I'm definitely a god. A cruel, cruel, capricious god. The things I put you through—The physical beatings alone [...] I killed your father. I burned your mother alive [...] All for what? All for the sake of literary symmetry. I toyed with your lives, your emotions for ... entertainment [...] I am so sorry. I mean, horror is one thing, but to be forced to live bad writing ... if I would have known it was real, I would have done another pass [...] Writing is hard.

Chuck then goes on to confess to the Winchesters, "I wrote myself into it. I wrote myself, at my house ... confronted by my characters," and later, the seeming absoluteness of Authorial agency is expressed after the brothers review one of Chuck's manuscripts which describes their actions, demeanor, and emotions verbatim. One possible way of interpreting Chuck/God's multi-diegeticism, as well as the fact that the Narrative of the End of Days exists and continues to unfold regardless of God's Authorial absence, is that *Supernatural* suggests that God can only "mean" anything, His Authorial voice can only have any agency, if it too is regarded as an aesthetic phenomenon. As both Author and a Character in the Narrative, His "character" also simultaneously writes/destroys the concept of a sovereign, impermeable Author, Authorship, and Authorial agency by showing that

> enunciation is an empty process, functioning perfectly without there being any need for it to be filled with the person of the interlocutors. Linguistically, the author is never more than the instance writing, just as *I* is nothing other than the instance saying *I*: language knows a "subject," not a "person," and this subject, empty outside of the very enunciation which defines it, suffices to make language "hold together," suffices, that is to say, to exhaust it [Barthes 145].

In this way, the sovereignty of the Narrative supersedes that of its Author. In the *Supernatural* diegesis, this means that God's Authorial agency is inherent to His subjection to the authority of His own Narrative. Writing Himself into His own Narrative produces an ostensibly radical reversal of Authorial agency in that "instead of putting [His] life into his novel[s...], [He] made of his very life a work for which his own book[s] [were] the model" (Barthes 144). In this sense, it is not Chuck who imitates God, but rather, that God is "no more than a secondary fragment, derived from" Chuck (Barthes 144).

According to Barthes,

> the Author, when believed in, is always conceived of as the past of his own book: book and author stand automatically on a single line divided into a *before* and an *after*. The Author is thought to *nourish* the book, which is to say that he exists before it, thinks, suffers, lives for it, is in the same relation of antecedence to his work as a father to his child. In complete contrast, the modern scriptor is born simultaneously with the text, is in no way equipped with a being preceding or exceeding the writing, is not subject with the book as predicate; there is no other time than that of the enunciation and every text is eternally written *here and now* [Barthes 145].

When applied to the question of Authorial agency in *Supernatural*, Barthes's insights suggest that the authority of the Judeo-Christian Narrative of the Apocalypse *supersedes* the authority of its Author much in the same way the simulation *precedes* the reality it simulates in Jean Baudrillard's *Simulations*. The Narrative as penned by God/Chuck forming the basis of a diegetic series of texts, "Supernatural," which also manifest as the narrative of the overarching series *Supernatural*, means that the Narrative has replaced the reality of Sam and Dean's life that it simulates in written symbols and signs. The human experience in *Supernatural*, therefore, is a simulation of the Narrative. For Sam and Dean, the Narrative-as-simulacra does not merely mediate their reality, adroitly or deceptively, nor is it based on a reality or obfuscation thereof. The Narrative in *Supernatural* functions in such a way as to reveal that nothing resembling a quintessential understanding of reality as distinct from non-reality is relevant to the viewer's understanding of the character's lives and diegetic existences. In this way, the Narrative "is never that which conceals the truth—it is the truth which conceals that there is none. The simulacrum is true" (Baudrillard, 1).

"The Real Ghostbusters" deals with the Authorial voice in a very literal way. Following a summons via text from Chuck, the brothers are unwittingly invited to a "Supernatural" fan convention by Becky. They are shocked and displeased to see their lives recreated meta-narratologically by the fans attending the convention LARPing as Sam and Dean within the context of a mock hunt orchestrated by the convention organizers. During said hunt, it is revealed that the hotel in which the hunt takes place is indeed actually haunted by the ghosts of scalped orphan children. Together with a pair of Sam and Dean enthusiasts, the brothers burn the bones of the one they believe was responsible for the murders, orphanage caretaker Leticia Gore. Addressing the remainder of the attendees who are prevented from leaving the premises by the supernatural forces therein, Chuck assists the brothers in vanquishing the ghosts, which includes distracting the crowd with an open Q&A session during which He reveals He is writing more "Supernatural" books. At the end of the episode, Becky also reveals that a mystical firearm called the Colt is not where the brothers thought it was.

Ostensibly, this episode focuses predominantly on the notion intimated above, namely that within both the *Supernatural* and "Supernatural" diegeses, fans are equatable with disciples, the series to scripture. Fans of the first "Supernatural" convention, like Jesus' first disciples, are portrayed as obsessive congregants which, on the one hand, serves as a tongue-in-cheek critique of fan culture and the show itself, but also, on the other, as a commentary on God being an unreliable narrator. There are strangely banal examples of the instability of the Authorial voice. For example, Becky calls Sam and Dean to the convention by stealing Chuck's phone. While God is shown to struggle with the Narrative in the season, the fact that God is unable to prevent His phone from being used without His permission speaks to the notion of God as an unreliable narrator and/or an Author with an unimaginable faculty for detail. On the one hand, this can be explained by suggesting that this is exactly what God wants to happen, a "mistake" that results in Dean being bolstered by Demian and Barnes's affirmation of their activity, as well as Becky finding valuable agency in the episode. On the other hand, Chuck is seemingly unaware of certain details of his own Story, namely the location of the Colt. This seeming absentmindedness about the Narrative He creates is compounded when, asked by an attendee where He got the inspiration for writing "Supernatural," Chuck responds, "it just came to me." Later in the episode Chuck is confronted by Sam and Dean who ask a deceptively simple question that encapsulates the question of the ethics of Authorship. The brothers ask, "why are you writing more books? Who gives you the right to our lives?" to which Chuck responds, "An archangel," which invites a vehement opposition to Chuck's cavalier attitude in the form of the rebuke, "no more books! Our lives are not for public consumption." Along with divesting responsibility for the ethical, moral, and philosophical problems that have both literally and figuratively plagued humanity throughout time, Chuck simultaneously trivializes and confesses His relationship with the issues and debates surrounding the problem of evil and an absentee God. He states that the underlying reason for penning the series is "food and shelter" and goes on to say to the brothers, "you know what I do for a living? Do you know? Because I don't. I'm not a good writer, no marketable skills, not some hero who runs off and fights monsters. Until the end of the world, I gotta live and the 'Supernatural' books are all I got. I mean what do you want me to do?"

Not only does this scene draw attention to the notion that above all things, the Judeo-Christian God is a story-teller unsure of His aptitude as such, but also the concept that if *Supernatural* portrays God as absentee father, it also portrays Him as witless Author, an *Architecte sans bleus*. In "The Death of the Author," Barthes states, "[s]ucceeding the Author, the scriptor no longer bears within him passions, humours, feelings, impressions, but rather his immense dictionary from which he draws a writing that can know no halt: life never does more than imitate the book, and the book itself is only a tissue of signs, an imitation that is lost, infinitely deferred" (147). When applied to the problems of Authorial agency represented by Chuck/God, the underlying premise in having God/Author face a room of fans (disciples) of His w/Work ("Supernatural"/Scripture) simultaneously seeking more work from Him, but also subjecting Him to probing and rigorous questioning, is tantamount to the frustrated prayers and supplications of those that suffer His Narrative seeking to hold Him accountable as its Author.

In the season five finale, "Swan Song" (5.22), Chuck begins the episode by narrating the history of the Impala as a metaphor for not only the series *Supernatural*, the "Supernatural" book series, as well as the brothers' lives in both, but also as a literal vessel for what, according to Him, *Supernatural* is about. As part of the plan to avert the Apocalypse, Dean finally and reluctantly agrees for Sam to allow Lucifer to possess him. As a condition, Sam has Dean agree not to attempt to resurrect him and, instead, pursue a normal life. Arriving in Detroit, Sam and Dean confront Lucifer with the rings of The Four Horsemen, a joint key that opens Lucifer's cage, which would allow the brothers to trap him therein. Failing this, Sam offers himself as Lucifer's vessel, hoping to trap him in himself and then throw himself into the cage. While Sam attempts to overcome Lucifer's control after being possessed, the latter proves too powerful, completely suppressing Sam within his own body. Later, Castiel intervenes by informing Dean of the place and time of the final battle between Michael and Lucifer. The following day, in a cemetery in Lawrence, Kansas, Lucifer confronts Michael, the former trying to convince the latter not to fight him, but to join him in overthrowing Heaven and God. Failing to convince Michael, Lucifer kills Castiel for interrupting by trying to banish Michael with holy fire, brutally beating Dean after he explodes Castiel and while Michael is still banished. He pauses at the sight of an old army man figurine inside the Impala discussed by Chuck during his earlier narration. From within his body, Sam recalls his life with Dean, their numerous trials and tribulations, their love, trust, and friendship for one another. Subsequently, Sam is able to take back control of his body, and using the rings, re-open the door to the cage. As he prepares to leap inside, Michael returns, only to be dragged into the cage along with Sam after grappling with him. After the cage is shut, Castiel returns, resurrected by God and elevated to the rank of Seraphim, the highest angelic order in Christian angelology, and proceeds to heal Dean. Castiel then vanishes, returning to Heaven in an attempt to restore order in the wake of Michael's absence. Dean fulfills his brother's wish and attempts to relinquish his life as a hunter altogether. The episode concludes with Chuck smiling after finishing his narration, looking into the camera, and then vanishing.

According to Barthes, "the *explanation* of a work is always sought in the man or woman who produced it, as if it were always in the end, through the more or less transparent allegory of the fiction, the voice of a single person, the *author* 'confiding' in us" (Barthes 143). This can be seen in the fact that throughout "Swan Song," Chuck both narrates *and* writes the episode, even going so far as to break the fourth wall at the end of the episode, smiling and addressing the viewer. As a result, the episode is entirely predicated on the Authorial voice, focusing on Chuck *as* an author, depicted writing, editing, and reading His own work throughout the episode. That Chuck narrates *and* writes this episode simultaneously might suggest that the specific diegetic plane upon which His scenes take place is uncertain as at the conclusion of the episode, He vanishes from His writing desk. Other than this demonstration of supernatural abilities, Chuck is entirely human in His portrayal of the difficulties, breakthroughs, vices, and distractions of authorship. Unlike quintessential depictions of the Judeo-Christian God in both ecumenical and secular literature and art across the centuries which typically portray God as an anthropomorphized manifestation of white heteronormative patriarchal prohibitiveness, Chuck is shown to drink whiskey, avail Himself of the services of prostitutes, and keep both an untidy residence and writing desk. Despite being gifted/burdened with an unrivalled authorial voice, as a writer Chuck is shown to hesitate, to erase with the very same hands He writes with. While Castiel says at the end of the episode that he "doesn't know what God wants [or] if he'll return," Chuck seemingly does not know either.

In short, God, within the *Supernatural* diegesis, is, among other things, a typical, almost caricatural representation of a writer. Kripke subtly disrupts the Authorial agency of God as discrete or sequestered from the Narrative; a Narrative that, despite the remonstrations God faces throughout the season regarding the seemingly unnecessary retention of pain and suffering inherent to the Narrative of the End Times, the suffering, heartache, calamity, and death facilitated, allowed, and even encouraged by *both* His presence and absence as Author, shows a deep sense of understanding and attention to detail. For God, the "Supernatural"/*Supernatural* Narrative/narrative is about free will, faith, loyalty, love, and brotherhood—all of which are concretized in the symbol of the Impala. In a montage highlighting the centrality of the Impala in the Narrative, Chuck makes a comment that seemingly countermands the idea that He is making it up as He goes along when He observes, "the devil doesn't care what car the boys drive" ("Swan Song").

Throughout the season, Kripke maintains a persistent sense of paradox regarding the relationship between Chuck and Authorial agency. Chuck's authorial agency is unavoidably troubled by the fact that Chuck tells Dean he had a vision of the final battlefield despite the Archangels' attempts to prevent it. On the one hand, this means that we have God writing the End/end in a bathrobe, but also on the other, we have Him as a prophet in His own Narrative/narrative. In this sense, He *is* making it up as He goes along, and this paradoxical sense of pre-determined chance is as paradoxical as the free will that constitutes it. The idea that even God cannot control the Narrative based on the idea that the characters interceding in their reality, taking over the narrative in which they appear, must negotiate its veracity against the fact that this confluence of free will and intercession is only permissible because the Author of the Narrative framing their existence always-already not only wrote it, but wrote it in *that* randomly-specific way. Sam/Lucifer draws attention to this ostensibly simple, albeit tremendously complex and pregnant philosophical problem stating, "think about it. Dad made everything. Which means he made me who I am! God wanted the Devil" and later when Michael/Adam accuses Lucifer of pushing their Father away with his actions, he responds, saying, "no one makes Dad do anything. He is doing this to us" ("Swan Song"). As a result, we encounter the same paradox with regard to the idea that "a text is not a line of words releasing a single 'theological' meaning (the 'message' of the Author-God) but a multi-dimensional space in which a variety of writings, none of them original, blend and clash. The text is a tissue of quotations drawn from the innumerable centres" (Barthes 146) of experience highlighted throughout the series. The underlying idea here is that the sum total of said experiences had always-already been written.

The season concludes with an episode that questions the agency of the Authorial voice, its Narrative, changing that Narrative from within it, and its ending. Chuck concludes the episode by saying that "no doubt—endings are hard. But then again ... nothing ever really ends, does it?" a statement which raises the problem of a character (mortal) in God's Narrative ("Supernatural"/ *Supernatural*) trying to prevent it from ending or writing itself out, so to speak ("Swan Song"). Castiel sums up this dilemma before vanishing, telling Dean, "you got what you asked for [...] No Paradise. No Hell. Just more of the same. I mean it, Dean. What would you rather have? Peace or freedom?" From a Barthesean perspective, the underlying concept of Castiel's question is that "to give a text an Author is to impose a limit on that text, to furnish it with a final signified, to close the writing" and that "in the multiplicity of writing, everything is to be *disentangled*, nothing *deciphered*; [...] the space of writing is to be ranged over, not pierced, writing ceaselessly posits meaning ceaselessly to evaporate it, carrying out a systematic exemption of meaning" (Barthes 147). In this way, by refusing the Authorial agency of God in the wake of His death or, in the case of Chuck, absence, "by refusing to assign a 'secret,' an ultimate meaning, to the text (and to the world as text), liberates what may be called an anti-theological activity, an activity that is truly revolutionary since to refuse to fix meaning is, in the end, to refuse God and his hypostases—reason, science law" (Barthes 147).

In terms of the above discussion of the problem of the Author as explored in *Supernatural*, Castiel's line of thinking here is perhaps the most important because it suggests that the real dilemma of Authorship is not the presence or absence of the Author, but the necessity of the Narrative itself. It is, therefore, why this essay maintains that the freedom and peace Castiel is referring to do not pertain to freedom or peace from God, but from the Narrative that circumscribes both Him, the power of His Authorial voice, and the products thereof, namely reality and its history. Hence Chuck's conclusion regarding endings which, during a hyper-emotional season finale, is meant to provide viewers with some measure of succor in the wake of the high drama and heartache they experienced watching it. However, from the perspective of those whose onto-existential and psycho-emotional being is bound to the Narrative, the Narrative is an Apocalypse that never ends.

WORKS CITED

Abbott, Stacey. "Introduction." *TV Goes to Hell: An Unofficial Road Map of Supernatural*, edited by Stacey Abbott and David Lavery, ECW Press, 2011, pp. ix–xvi.
Anderson, R. Lanier. "Friedrich Nietzsche." *The Stanford Encyclopedia of Philosophy*, edited by Edward N. Zalta, 2017, https://plato.stanford.edu/archives/sum2017/entries/nietzsche/.
Barthes, Roland. "The Death of the Author." Image Music Text, by Roland Barthes, translated by Stephen Heath, Fontana, 1977, pp. 142–148.
Baudrillard, Jean. *Simulations*. Translated by Paul Foss, Paul Patton, and Philip Beitchman, Semiotext(e), 1983.
DeCandido, Keith R.A. "Not Just a Pretty Face (or Two)." *In the Hunt: Unauthorized Essays on* Supernatural, edited by Leah Wilson, Benbella Books, 2009, pp. ix–xii.
Derrida, Jacques. *Of Grammatology*. Translated by Gayatri Chakravorty Spivak, The Johns Hopkins UP, 1967.
Garvey, Amy. "'We've Got Work to Do': Sacrifice, Heroism, and Sam and Dean Winchester." *In the Hunt: Unauthorized Essays on* Supernatural, edited by Leah Wilson, Benbella Books, 2009, pp. 87–96.
Nietzsche, Friedrich. *The Gay Science*. Translated by Josefine Nauckhoff, Cambridge UP, 2001.
Valenzano, Joseph M. III, and Erika Engstrom. "Cowboys, Angels, and Demons: American Exceptionalism and the Frontier Myth in the CW's *Supernatural*." *Communication Quarterly*, vol. 62, no. 5, 2014, pp. 552–556.
_____, and _____. "Homilies and Horsemen: Revelation in the CW's *Supernatural*." *Journal of Communication and Religion*, vol. 36, no. 1, 2013, pp. 50–72.

The Author, the Audience and the Almighty
Supernatural's *Chuck Shurley* as Metatextual Mirror

EDEN LEE LACKNER

The first five seasons of the CW television show *Supernatural* culminate in a two-season arc in which Sam and Dean Winchester find themselves dealing with an infestation of angels looking for an absentee God. While the narrative eventually reveals that the missing deity is directly under the Winchesters' noses, masquerading as a vulnerable pulp fiction author-cum-prophet, Chuck Shurley is also a fully metatextual character, specifically standing in for series creator and showrunner Eric Kripke, and more generally standing in for the *Supernatural* writers' room. Chuck also acts as a connection between *Supernatural*'s writers and the audience, doubling the act of watching, as he provides a way for Kripke to represent the show's audience onscreen, allowing the audience to see its fictionalized reflection through the *Supernatural* writers' eyes.

While we identify fiction on a very basic level as a narrative that is not true, that does not mean that it does not contain elements of the truth. In the article "Author's Characters and the Character of the Author: The Typical in Fiction," Tahir Wood explains that

> fiction does not require a complete disidentification of real world from fictional world. The elements of semantic memory that are activated in comprehension have themselves been abstracted from real-world descriptions. In fact we might suggest that the fictional world is a subset of the real world [165].

Regardless of the level of fantasy present in a tale, certain familiar, real-world qualities must be present in order to provide a logical framework in which the story can operate. These qualities may be as basic as the fictional world adhering to the laws of physics, as elaborate as detailed fidelity to the social, political and natural rules of the real world, or as metatextual as an authorial observance of the proper rules of grammar. Indeed, "[t]here [can] never [be] a fictional world that [is] not already dependent on real-world experience for its construction" (165). Further, this dependence on the real world stretches beyond setting or atmosphere. Characters connect with audiences in part because they draw on the foibles and follies of humanity, which are interpreted and represented in the story through the authorial lens. The author provides a fictional world in which he or she places characters to perform this humanity, and as a result, "[t]he author's performative act is such that, while ostensibly telling a story about characters, whose existence precedes the story, the author is in actuality creating them" (160). The life which is represented within a fictional piece of art is thus a reflection of real life, and a "subset of the real world" (165). As a result, *Supernatural*'s Chuck is connected to Kripke's and the writers' room's conceptions of the author as a character category. This link strengthens given that it is based not only on generalized conceptions, but lived experience, as the *Supernatural* writers are able to draw on their own familiarity with writing as both a profession and an identity.

The Author

Even more so than the link between author and character, the link between author and God is a familiar one. The author, creator of his or her own universe, naturally exists in an omniscient and omnipotent position due to the simple fact that the work itself cannot exist without an authorial figure to put pen to paper. Every narrative event and character action comes directly from that creator, closely paralleling Western religious conceptions of the roles of predestination and free will, as well as the relationship between the Christian God and humanity. By virtue of being both creator and showrunner of *Supernatural* through season five, Kripke occupies this authorial space, a deity of his own creation over a fictional universe.

It is no stretch, then, to acknowledge this link between Kripke and Chuck. By virtue of placing an author within the text of *Supernatural*, Kripke and the writers' room immediately invite the connection between their own positioning as creators, and the fictional author embedded in the text. They go one step further, however, by very clearly delineating the parallels between Chuck and Kripke. Kripke, creator of the television show *Supernatural*, showrunner and captain of the writers' room, manufactures this successful media property, alongside which grows a large, enthusiastic, and active fandom. Chuck, creator of the novel series "Supernatural," manufactures a far less successful media property, alongside which grows a small, enthusiastic, and active fandom. The differences in size and level of success act, on a surface level, as a joking self-denigration; a way for Kripke to pop the balloon of Godhood and signal to the viewer that he knows he holds sway over nothing more than a television show, a narrative primarily created for the entertainment of those same viewers, and as a delivery-system for advertising revenue.

Therefore, even as Chuck stands in for the all-powerful author, Kripke undercuts the weight of this relationship by undermining Chuck's authorial abilities. He is a second-rate author with a cult-like fandom. His books sport covers that blend "boys' own" stories with romance novels, including posed, shirtless models who look suspiciously like Fabio ("The Monster at the End of This Book," 4.18). In-universe, Chuck is at once all-powerful and barely notable. His creative output is rejected by the Winchester brothers, and held up for ridicule by the show. In what becomes Chuck's very first on-screen appearance in "The Monster at the End of This Book," Sam and Dean discuss not only their surprise at finding out their lives are being recorded, but also how truly non-notable Chuck's books are. Dean begins, "This is freakin' insane. How's this guy know all this stuff?... Everything is in here. I mean *everything*. From the racist truck, to–to me having sex.... I'm full-frontal in here, dude. How come we haven't heard of him before?" To which Sam replies, "They're pretty obscure. In almost zero circulation, uh, start in '05, publisher put out a couple dozen before going bankrupt. And, uh, the last one, *No Rest for the Wicked*, ends with you goin' to Hell." Here, Dean grapples with the dawning horror that the events of their shared past are fodder for public consumption, including his most intimate, naked moments. Sam, on the other hand, confirms the near total lack of interest of the world at large for the monsters the brothers have confronted, and the contents of Dean's pants. Yet in this short exchange, where Dean struggles with the horror of the non-consensual recording of their past, Sam must confront the terror of a predicted future. If this in-universe author has accurately written down the past, it follows that his record of the future may be equally accurate. Chuck and his novels, therefore, become active threats, occupying a strange, precarious space between world-shakingly important to the brothers themselves and completely irrelevant to the world at large. It is here, before Chuck has even appeared on screen, that Kripke already begins to complicate his portrayal of authorship and audience.

Just as the Winchesters reject any positive associations with Chuck's novels, Chuck also engages in diminishing his creative abilities. In season five, episode nine, "The Real Ghostbusters," when confronted by Sam and Dean after announcing that he will continue to write books about the duo, regardless of their firm, repeated requests that he stop, Chuck sums up his relationship with writing: "I'm not a good writer. I've got no marketable skills. I'm not some hero who can just hit the road and fight monsters, OK? Until the world ends, I gotta live, all right? And the 'Supernatural' books are all I've got. What else do you want me to do?" Once again, the *Supernatural* writers have undercut Chuck's skills, slyly engaging in their own self-denigration. Chuck's acknowledgment of his lack of writerly skills falls in line with the notion of television writers as lesser creators, engaged in the business of entertainment, rather than art, pandering to the lowest common denominator. This exchange, as well as Sam's description of the "Supernatural" book series as a product of a failed publisher, also subtextually traces the trajectory of *Supernatural* as a television series. Beginning its life on the WB Television Network, *Supernatural*'s first season, airing in 2005 (the same year Chuck's books were published), spanned twenty-two episodes (or "a couple dozen") before the WB effectively merged with the United Paramount Network to become the CW Television Network. Additionally, Chuck's assertion that he is not a hero evokes the challenges of successfully launching a creative property; within the Hollywood system, it is not necessarily the generation of content which is a challenge, but rather achieving executive and studio backing which will allow that property to "hit the road" and find an audience. For Chuck, gaining a substantial readership seems beyond his abilities, even as he is compelled to seek one out.

Indeed, this self-denigration continues as Chuck first reveals that he is a prophet, and thus connected to a small fragment of the knowledge of God. He has become the compelled author, a creator not in control of his creations, but rather ruled by their whims, tasked with recording their trajectories rather than piloting their ships. He receives visions from God, but is, essentially, nothing more than a tool. He is merely the pen, not the mind.

The Almighty

Yet, as viewers of the show know, Chuck is more than just an author, more than a prophet. He is God himself, existing within and without the text. This reveal, obliquely shown in season five, episode twenty-two, "Swan Song" and in later seasons fully and clearly confirmed, undercuts the very self-denigration that Kripke and the writers use in characterizing Chuck and representing their relationship to the larger text. It is in this final episode of season five that Chuck moves fully into his role as *Supernatural*'s deity. In the very first opening moments, Kripke and his room of writers elevate Chuck from an in-universe chronicler of the Winchesters' lives to a metatextual narrator, addressing the audience as he begins telling a larger tale that encompasses not just the episodic adventures of Sam and Dean, but a story that stretches beyond them to include framing events that fall outside of the series itself. As the episode begins, Chuck's voice overlays stock footage of a 1960s General Motors car factory, and the moment the hundred thousandth car "rolled off the line" ("Swan Song"). He describes the ceremony that accompanies this moment, but follows up by highlighting a seemingly unimportant successive event: "Three days later, another car rolled off that same line. No one gave two craps about her. But they should've. Because this 1967 Chevrolet Impala would turn out to be the most important car.... No, the most important object in pretty much the whole universe" ("Swan Song"). This particular framing narration underlines the tone of the entire series. The Winchesters are unsung heroes, working in near-secrecy to protect a populace largely ignorant of the supernatural realm. They drive an otherwise unremarkable muscle car which takes on mythical properties, both within the show and the fandom; they have access to and receive help from characters who are similarly hidden in blue collar working positions, and overlooked by those in authority; and once they deal with the supernatural threat of the week, they move on to the next problem with little to no rewards.

In line with this emphasis on the unseen world, Chuck himself exists as a hidden deity. As a God, he has made himself over into an unimportant author, tucked away from public knowledge. Yet he is the character that delineates the boundaries of the Winchesters' story, as after he explains the origins of the Impala, he says, "I guess that's where this story begins. And here is where it ends" ("Swan Song"). More than in any other episode, in "Swan Song" he is the voice that speaks to the audience, bypassing the Winchesters entirely. Indeed, during this opening monologue, he shares with viewers that "Sam and Dean don't know any of this, but if they did, [he] think[s] they'd smile" ("Swan Song"). Chuck understands the boundaries of Sam's and Dean's knowledge of the world around them, and he knows enough to predict their behavior. By acknowledging the world that exists around it, Chuck successfully breaks out of the confines of the show; simultaneously, he expands the events and universe of *Supernatural* even as he expands past the boundaries of the television screen, speaking directly to those watching. At the end of "Swan Song," which acts as Kripke's own exit from the show, Chuck summarizes the thematic thrust of the entire series:

> So what's it all add up to? It's hard to say. But me, I'd say this was a test ... for Sam and Dean. And I think they did all right. Up against good, evil, angels, devils, destiny, and God himself. They made their own choice. They chose family. And, well, isn't that kind of the whole point? No doubt, endings are hard. But then again ... nothing ever really ends, does it?

Here, Chuck touches on the otherworldly threats that make up each episode's central conflict, but highlights the theme that lies at the heart of the show itself. Despite its generic framework, *Supernatural*, at its core, is a family drama. While the main focus is on Sam and Dean's sibling relationship, that familial focus extends outward to the other characters, both biological and non-biological relations. Relationships between the brothers and other hunters are often refigured as familial, as Bobby Singer underlines in season three, episode sixteen, when he says that "family don't end with blood" ("No Rest for the Wicked"). Just as Bobby acts as a surrogate father to the Winchesters even as they struggle with their own father's absences—one of which, after all, begins the trajectory of the entire show, as Dean draws Sam back into the family business after John Winchester's disappearance—so too do the brothers interact with other hunter characters as extended family members. It is fitting, then, that Kripke places God within this framework, as his avatar, as it allows for an explicit father-child dynamic between God and His Angels, and Kripke and his writing team. At the same time, while Chuck delineates the start and end of Kripke's tenure as *Supernatural*'s God, he also opens up the possibility of the show going on without him. Throughout his arc, Chuck intercedes enough to confirm that Sam and Dean are able to continue without active Heavenly intervention, ushering them forward into a future in which God's presence is far less important than their ability to rely on themselves and their larger family of hunters. Endings may be hard, but "nothing ever really ends," whether the initial creator or instigator of events is present or not.

While exploring the divide between the representations of God in Judaism, Islam, Protestantism and Catholicism, and that of secular movies, Andrew Greeley observes that the "God of the film-makers [...] is unfailingly kind, patient, friendly, and appealing. You want to love this God because S/He is so loveable–and so patently on your side" (67). There is an inherent physical appeal in media conceptions of the Almighty, as "God is presented as an attractive Someone who cares about us, indeed cares passionately. This theme is usually presented in a context of secular rather than traditionally religious symbols (save for angels and light) and never in an ecclesiastical context" (71). The God of *Supernatural*, however, does not easily fit into such conceptions of attractiveness. Chuck is not kind, nor patient, rarely friendly, and not particularly appealing. Although Rob Benedict is not inherently unattractive, the writing room, costuming, set design, hair, makeup and Benedict himself work together to present Chuck as a short, untidy, hygienically-impaired and vaguely misanthropic recluse who only begins to break away from his self-imposed creative isolation when Sam and Dean inadvertently pull him into the uncanny world. He does not represent "the pathos of God" (71), a deity who so loves His children that He willingly suffers alongside them, but rather, Chuck suffers *because* of them. His isolation reflects that intersection between secluded author and cloistered hermit; as an author, this separation from humanity allows him to channel his creativity, which the narrative quickly identifies as divine prophecy. As a hermit, his separation is far more profound. He is a God who has turned his back on his creations, mirroring the lack of religious faith present in an increasingly secular world.

Alongside the scripted narrative of "Swan Song," visually, the shifts in wardrobe, makeup, and Benedict's acting choices change how Chuck fits into the larger *Supernatural* text. Chuck's rumpled, dark clothing is replaced by a blindingly white, perfectly pressed shirt and trouser combination; his near-permanent slouch and nervous facial expressions are replaced with a confident bearing—including a straight back and relaxed movements—and self-assured smiles. He *becomes* God at the same moment that he *is revealed* as God, just as the episode's metatextual narration helps to enforce this transformation. Through Chuck, we see Kripke completing the connection between creator and deity. As Chuck records the details of the Winchesters' lives within the television show, he records *and* predicts their narrative trajectories, creating their circumstances in parallel with Kripke's guiding role in the writers' room. Chuck thus exists in a space between the *Supernatural* universe and the real world; he is created by the show's writers in order to create the multi-season arc.

Writing for television already exists in a complicated space. While popular culture tends to romanticize the notion of the solitary author, working away on draft after draft, isolated from distractions until the perfect story comes together—while neatly ignoring the existence of agents, editors and publishers who insist on deadlines and demand product—television writing is an inherently collaborative act. Kripke is not the sole auteur behind each episode of *Supernatural*; as with most television properties, Kripke heads up a larger group of creators who work together on a script, a few taking the lead and receiving writing credits on particular episodes. As the series creator, Kripke therefore receives a creator credit on each episode, whether or not he is specifically involved in the writing of each script, as he will for the duration of the series. While this structure distances Kripke from the content of each episode, it strengthens his positioning as a God-like overseer. *Supernatural's* writers are able to craft stories and scripts that allow room for their own creative flourishes, while adhering to Kripke's larger plan for each season, much as Chuck influences larger events while allowing the other characters to exercise free will through their own choices.

The Audience

Throughout *Supernatural's* exploration of the links between author and God, there is a deliberate folding of the show in on itself, where the show and Chuck's relationship to it is simultaneously creatively significant—to the characters, audience, cast and crew—and thoroughly frivolous—to non-*Supernatural* fans, non-television watchers, and the larger world.

As Andrew Crome explores the use of parody in media representations of the Christian Rapture, he notes that

> [w]e are now unable to imagine what an *actual* apocalypse might be like, other than through images derived from popular culture. We have seen the apocalypse portrayed so many times on film and television that these portrayals have replaced both the biblical text of Revelation and the possibility of imagining any form of apocalypse in the real world [395–6].

For Chuck and *Supernatural*, this portrayal of apocalypse goes one step further. The series does not simply showcase popular notions of the end of the world—including horror tropes, (un)natural disasters, and violent confrontations—but continues to revisit the apocalypse so that it is transmuted from *the* end of the world, to an(other) end of the world. As a result, the apocalypse becomes a dangerous, tragic, and frightening event in the moment, but once Sam and Dean have prevented its occurrence, it becomes one in a series of apocalypses, lessening its power by being merely one of a collection of thwarted end-of-world events. Each world-shattering threat thus becomes part of a chain of episodes, narrative arcs, and seasonal trajectories, creating a series of endings, but never resulting in a true end. Similarly, the Winchester brothers die repeatedly over the course of the series, but the state is never permanent, as they are brought back a multitude of ways, including via demonic deals ("All Hell Breaks Loose: Part 2," 2.22), angelic intervention ("Lazarus Rising," 4.01 and "Swan Song"), Godly intercession ("Dark Side of the Moon," 5.06), and fighting their way out of Purgatory ("We Need to Talk About Kevin," 8.01). This chain of deaths, resurrections, and apocalypses is a necessary part of the lifecycle of a dramatic speculative fiction television show like *Supernatural*: each season encapsulates a high stakes narrative arc, yet in order to maintain an audience and ratings, each new season must raise these stakes and attempt to outdo the previous arcs. In this never-ending cycle of increasing risk is a distancing from each ending. Crome's popularized apocalypse loses not only its Biblical imagery, but its connection to a firm end. Sam and Dean prevent the world from ending so many times that the apocalypse loses both risk and meaning. In a show which deals, even indirectly, with the specter of the Rapture and the promise of Judgment Day, the continual cycle of apocalypse prevention derails both God's power, and the possibility of a clear narrative ending. As Chuck says,

> Endings are hard. Any chapped-ass monkey with a keyboard can poop out a beginning. But endings are impossible. You try to tie up every loose end, but you never can. The fans are always gonna bitch, there's always gonna be holes, and since it's the

ending, it's all supposed to add up to something. I'm telling you, they're a raging pain in the ass ["Swan Song"].

More so than any of Chuck's other dialogue, this passage best encapsulates both his and Kripke's relationship to *Supernatural* as a text. Chuck acknowledges the difficulty inherent in completing a story, as well as recognizing the relationship between the story and its audience. He frames it as an unwinnable proposition, where an imperfect author cannot craft the perfect ending. Although Chuck is God, he is a deity created by an imperfect human, and thus cannot exist in a perfect state. As much as Kripke works to close plot holes and please fans, just like every other piece of art, *Supernatural* can never be an objectively perfect text. Kripke may be the God of the series, manifesting as Chuck, but by virtue of Kripke's humanity, Chuck must always be divinely imperfect.

Beyond this play with the (un)importance of creativity and authorship, however, lies a larger metatextual pool. Chuck's interstitial positioning allows him to simultaneously provide commentary on the show, the in-world narrative, and the *Supernatural* audience. He is the conduit through which the viewers encounter the show's most dedicated fans: a version filtered through the writers' placement as objects of fandom, rather than active participants. It is through Chuck that the audience experiences the in-world version of the *Supernatural* convention, a surprisingly male-dominated version of an exceptionally female space ("The Real Ghostbusters"). Chuck is also how the audience encounters fan fiction—a sly, teasing look at the creative work of fans—and how Becky Rosen, the show's version of an overenthusiastic fan, enters the narrative ("Sympathy for the Devil"). By virtue of being a male character, standing in for a patriarchal version of the Christian God *and* the male show creator and showrunner, Chuck acts as a masculine lens through which Kripke and his writing team filter a distinctly female fandom.

Much has been written on the presentation of (female) fans within the *Supernatural* universe, in both academic circles and media outlets. For instance, in "Sympathy for the Fangirl: Becky Rosen, Fan Identity, and Interactivity in *Supernatural*," Brigid Cherry considers fans' reactions to the show's portrayal of female fandom through the lens of Becky, underlining the intricacies that arise when the show "encodes several trajectories of fans and fandoms, and [...] suggests hierarchies of fan behaviors—almost all other fan trajectories are valued higher than young women's adoration of celebrities" (209). Cherry explores the (im)balance of power between creator and audience, and illustrates that fans' "cultural ownership" (218) of the show allows for a centralization of their textual desires in ways that allow for an increase in interactivity with both the text itself, and its cast and crew. In contrast, Laura Felschow's "'Hey, Check It Out, There's Actually Fans': (Dis)empowerment and (Mis)representation of Cult Fandom in *Supernatural*" notes that the show's representation of fans "has wrested some control back to the side of production and left the fans to either accept it or not" (6.6), arguing for a more hierarchical power structure, in which the fictionalization of fan behavior acknowledges the importance of the audience to the success of the show while simultaneously reminding that audience of its place in the hierarchy. While Cherry, Felschow and many other critics recognize the delicate balance between fans, their textual representations, and the shows' creators, few consider the equally complex place Chuck occupies within this structure.

From the very first mention of Chuck, *Supernatural* aligns him with fans and fandom. In "The Monster at the End of This Book," Sam and Dean encounter Chuck's novels for the first time in a comic book shop while presenting themselves as official, authoritative investigators—aliases which fans of the show are both familiar with and expect during the course of any of their cases. Yet instead of being accepted as such, almost immediately, their disguises are misinterpreted as fannish displays. This scene involves a significant amount of metatexuality, folding the non-fictional with the fictional so that the show at once refers to its genesis as a media property, and creates a fictionalized version of itself in which the "Supernatural" book series does not enjoy even a fraction of the success Kripke has seen from his creation. There is a complex layering where Chuck's books exist within Sam and Dean's world, which in turn exists within Kripke's show. Kripke, as creator and showrunner, is thus positioned as the ultimate source of Sam's, Dean's, *and* Chuck's lives and choices. Even as he is an imperfect human writer, Kripke is also "Supernatural"'s out-of-universe God to Chuck's in-universe God, and therefore, the deity who is a higher power than God himself.

More importantly, however, is how the scene links Sam, Dean, and *Supernatural* itself to Chuck's creative output, and by extension, his fandom. By interpreting Sam and Dean as Live Action Role Players (LARPers)—a type of roleplaying that moves beyond tabletop interactions centered on dice-rolls and collaborative storytelling to a more performative, active model—the clerk refigures them as existing in relation to a second layer of fictionalization: just as Sam and Dean are fictionalized creations of Kripke, so too do they become fictionalized creations of Chuck. As much as Chuck is a creation of Kripke's and therefore completely under his control, he is also the character given full control of the *Supernatural* universe. An absent God he may be, but in terms of *Supernatural*'s mythology, he remains the omnipotent author of Sam and Dean's world.

Sam and Dean therefore shift into a complex, contested space. As viewers of *Supernatural*, the audience is fully aware that Sam and Dean are fictionalized characters, and any appearance of free will is illusory, a function of created conflict and narrative arcs. Yet the presence of Chuck as God draws the metatextual narrative of showrunner and writers' room into the text, manifesting the real-world boundaries within the fictional realm. The Winchester brothers enter a recursive space, at once existing separate from Chuck, and also subject to his creative will. When they confront Chuck for the first time, the entire scene is littered with evidence of this circular relationship, from the moment they introduce themselves:

> SAM: I'm Sam. And that's Dean.
> CHUCK: Sam and Dean don't exist! They're fictional characters! I made them up! They're not real! ["The Monster at the End of This Book"].

Once Chuck is convinced that they are, in fact, the very characters he is writing about, he jumps to what is an absurdly illogical in-universe conclusion, as it requires a significant amount of suspension of disbelief and ego, but it is also the absolutely correct deduction:

> CHUCK: Well, there's only one explanation. Obviously, I'm a God.
> SAM: You're not a God.
> CHUCK: How else do you explain it? I write things, and then they come to life? Yeah, no, I'm definitely a God. A cruel, cruel, capricious God. The things I put you through! The physical beatings alone!

Even when Chuck presents himself as ignorant of his true nature, he possesses extra-textual knowledge that elucidates the narrative for the viewer, even as it confuses the characters themselves. This circular relationship between author-created-author-cum-deity-created-deity resolves itself into a spiral, as the looping does not terminate when it connects back to its starting point; instead, as Kripke reveals the layers of Chuck's identity—transcriptionist, creator, prophet and God—the relationships between Kripke and Chuck, Chuck and the Winchesters, and Chuck and the *Supernatural* universe resolve into a Gordian knot of epic proportions.

Further complicating matters is Chuck's relationship with his fans, or rather, the fact that fans of Chuck's novels exist within the show itself. Chuck, in many ways, is at the center of a fandom which reflects expectations over reality—a heavily male, heavily role-playing population. Given the significant level of involvement by the cast in *Supernatural* conventions, the increasing ability of social media and the internet in general to provide direct conduits between fans and creators, and the simple existence of the trappings of fannishness within the show, the cast and crew of *Supernatural* is not wholly unaware of the makeup of its active fanbase. For instance, Becky—who first appears in "Sympathy for the Devil" is a clear encapsulation of a particular type of female fan. She is overly enthusiastic, willing to suspend her disbelief at a word, and actively creating her own "Supernatural"-inspired romantic fiction. For all that *Supernatural* the show centers on the adventures and relationships of a heavily male cast, the covers of Chuck's novels reflect an aesthetic better found in a female-directed genre: romance. The cover models fit with the type of bodice-ripper covers best fitting the aesthetic of the Harlequin imprint Mills & Boone ("The Monster at the End of This Book"). There is a distinct femaleness embedded within the fandom around Chuck's books, manifested by Becky, and later by the students of season ten, episode five, "Fan Fiction," who stage a musical version of Chuck's novels, yet it is sublimated by distinctly masculine trappings. Sam and Dean's first encounter with Chuck's novels occurs not in a bookstore or library, but rather in a comic book shop, a stereotypically male space. Similarly, when we look at the "Supernatural" convention that Sam and Dean accidentally attend in "The Real Ghostbusters," it is heavily skewed towards male attendees, something which reflects a more traditional and historical model of in-person fandom, but not the actual genesis of *Supernatural*'s real-world fandom, which has been historically heavily-weighted towards female attendees.

Yet despite the traditional masculine thrust of this convention representation, there is also a valorization of queerness embedded within Kripke's fictional version of fandom. Barnes and Demian, a couple not just cosplaying, but LARPing as Sam and Dean at "The Real Ghostbusters" convention, heroically save the Winchesters at the end of the episode, and impart insight regarding the purpose and pleasure of the text to a doubting Dean; as Demian says, "You're wrong, you know.... No offense, but I'm not sure you get what the story's about.... *Our* lives suck. But to be Sam and Dean, to wake up every morning saving the world, to have a brother who would die for you, who wouldn't want that?" Barnes and Demian give Sam and Dean some insight into the worth of their narrative, and their relation to an audience that lies outside of the young heterosexual masculine demographic traditionally coveted by genre shows and their advertisers. Their positioning as queer fans who are the heroes of "The Real Ghostbusters" validates "othered" audiences as important parts of *Supernatural* fandom. Even as Dean is surprised to find out that Barnes and Demian are in a romantic relationship with each other, ultimately, the writers represent the couple as understanding the Winchesters' own sibling relationship in a deeper way than the brothers themselves. Barnes and Demian thus express textual insights that reflect their fuller engagement with Chuck's novels, and the show as a whole.

Becky, on the other hand, exists as both a valued member of fandom who is able to help both Chuck and the Winchesters at crucial junctures, and a figure of ridicule, with persistent romantic notions that disrupt Sam's and Dean's lives. In her appearances before Kripke leaves his position as showrunner, Becky is instrumental in passing along critical information to Sam and Dean ("Sympathy for the Devil" and "The Real Ghostbusters"), resulting in positive gains for the brothers going forward ("Abandon All Hope...," 5.10). As with Barnes and Demian, she demonstrates significant textual knowledge that Sam, Dean, and Chuck himself do not possess. In "The Real Ghostbusters," in the midst of revealing that Bela did not give Lilith the Colt revolver that the brothers are looking for, she admonishes Sam for his lack of knowledge, as she exclaims, "Didn't you read the book?" Further, when Sam confronts Chuck for not passing on this information, Chuck explains that he's "not as big a fan as [Becky] is." Both of these exchanges emphasize the detailed readings performed by *Supernatural*'s audience, surpassing the creators' own recollections. Indeed, one of the largest repositories of *Supernatural* information is *The Supernatural Wiki* (colloquially known as the *Super-wiki*), a fully fan-run internet resource, available to fans and *Supernatural* writers alike for fact-checking purposes. In these in-universe moments, Kripke not only acknowledges the audience, but locates a significant amount of textual understanding in their readings and encyclopaedic cataloguings of each episode via his representation of Becky as an invaluable member of Chuck's fandom.

It is not until Kripke leaves *Supernatural* that Becky shifts fully into a figure of ridicule, forcefully attempting to rewrite Sam's and Dean's trajectories, derailing them in favor of plotlines that support her own wishful thinking, and causing significant harm ("Season Seven, Time for a Wedding!" [7.08]). Before that turning point, however, Becky mixes realism with suspension of disbelief, as she explains, "Yes, I'm a fan, but I really don't appreciate being mocked. I know that 'Supernatural' [is] just a book, okay? I know the difference between fantasy and reality" ("Sympathy for the Devil"). Yet when Chuck tells her that "it's all real," she immediately abandons her skepticism in a delighted shout of, "I knew it!" Bringing her own ideas and insights to her relationships with Chuck, Sam and Dean, throughout Kripke's tenure, Becky grows and changes alongside her fannish enthusiasm. She successfully accepts the intersections of fiction and reality in the *Supernatural* universe, and moves beyond her initial infatuation with Sam in order to enter into a mutual adult relationship with Chuck. This relationship, and Becky's maturation and narrative arc, remain intact until Chuck disappears and Kripke leaves the series. Just as Barnes and Demian help Dean understand the importance of the family business and his relationship with his brother, Becky brings fannish enthusiasm and increasingly deeper readings to Chuck's creations.

Significantly, Chuck's presence in *Supernatural* allows for a detailed layering of author, audience and deity. By situating Chuck as both author and God, Kripke playfully echoes his own positioning in *Supernatural* throughout the first five seasons; just as Chuck disappears at the end of this season, so too does Kripke depart. Chuck is a creator who has abandoned his creations and largely relegates himself to a recording role—Kripke, before stepping down as showrunner, remains the authoritative creator. Yet Chuck is not simply a showrunner avatar, nor just a tongue-in-cheek deconstruction of the relationship between author and product. He disrupts both the Biblical and popular media representations of God, fitting neither the redemptive and suffering God, nor the attractive, loving God. His apocalypse is one of many, de-escalating the end of the world, and placing it alongside difficult, imperfect narrative endings.

Chuck is also a looking-glass through which the audience can see themselves reflected in the eyes of the writers' room: a conduit through which *Supernatural* doubles the action of watching. Instead of a simple transaction, where Kripke and the writers' room create episodes to be viewed by the audience without any other aspect to the creator-viewer transaction, they represent the audience within the show. Barnes, Demian, Becky, and the unnamed convention attendees cluster around Chuck—who, as the author of "Supernatural," is the default center of their fandom—reflecting playful versions of the writers' interpretations of *Supernatural*'s fans. By constructing Chuck's fandom and placing them directly within the narrative, however, the audience simultaneously sees themselves alongside the primary, Winchester-centric narrative, and then reinterprets Kripke and the writers' representation of themselves through the act of watching. As Wood notes, "[t]he mediation between author's and reader's worlds is achieved through characters" (160), and Kripke invites the viewers into his world through Chuck and his fans, going beyond solely representing himself in the text by clearing a space for the viewers. For Dean, this doubling manifests itself as he reads a "Supernatural" novel while existing within a *Supernatural* television episode, as he says, "I'm sitting in a laundromat, reading about myself sitting in a laundromat reading about myself. My head hurts" ("The Monster at the End of This Book"). For the audience, this doubling positions them in a distinctly powerful space: Kripke may be Chuck, and Chuck may be God, and all three may exist simultaneously inside and outside the show, but Kripke positions the audience above all three. *Supernatural*'s viewers possess the powers of interpretation and knowledge gained through detailed reading, placing fans and fandom inside, outside, and *above* the show, shifting them from a receptive audience to a God above both of the show's authorial Gods; in essence, the audience becomes *Supernatural*'s Almighty.

Works Cited

Cherry, Brigid. "Sympathy for the Fangirl: Becky Rosen, Fan Identity, and Interactivity in *Supernatural*." *TV Goes to Hell: An Unofficial Road Map of Supernatural*, edited by Stacey Abbott and David Lavery, ECW, 2011, pp. 203–218.

Crome, Andrew. "Left Behind or Left Below? Parodies of Christian End-Times Fiction in American Popular Culture." *The Journal of American Culture*, vol. 38, no. 4, 2015, pp. 386–400.

Felschow, Laura E. "'Hey, Check It Out, There's Actually Fans': (Dis)empowerment and (Mis)representation of Cult Fandom in *Supernatural*." *Transformative Works and Cul-

tures, vol. 4, 2010, journal.transformativeworks.org/index.php/twc/article/view/134. Accessed 31 August 2019.

Greeley, Andrew. "A God Who Plays It by Ear: 5 Metaphors for God in Recent Films." *Journal of Popular Film and Television*, vol. 19, no. 2, 1991, pp. 67–71.

The Supernatural Wiki. supernaturalwiki.com. Accessed 16 September 2018.

Wood, Tahir. "Author's Characters and the Character of the Author: The Typical in Fiction." *Journal of Literary Semantics*, vol. 40, no. 2, 2011, pp. 159–176.

"You don't have to be a monster. You have a choice"
Supernatural, *Free Will and the Deterministic Concept of Monstrosity*

Annika Gonnermann

> Every age exercises its own evils through literature.
> —Sam Lundwall

Introduction

Demons, shapeshifters, wendigos, pagan gods, witches, reapers, ghosts, werewolves, vampires, djinns, and angels[1]—the world of The CW's *Supernatural* is populated with a rich and terrifying cast of nightmares. Featuring a monster in nearly every episode (*Supernatural*'s by now famous "Monster of the Week" formula), the cult series employs the figure of the monster and its disposal as the central narrative device. In accordance with their family motto "saving people, hunting things," the brothers Dean and Sam Winchester[2] "pursue a never-ending procession of demons and other otherworldly things" (Katz) which they hunt and kill before the monsters in turn murder innocent civilians unaware of the existence of such monsters in the first place.

Regularly addressing controversial topics such as theodicy or the nature of good and evil, *Supernatural* lends itself to cultural analysis with a special focus on the concept of monstrosity. As it turns out in the course of *Supernatural*'s fifteen seasons, the conceptualization of the monster is not as simple as it seems because "Sam and Dean begin hunting with a seemingly clear-cut distinction between humans and monsters, but as the series progresses black-and-white distinctions quickly turn grey" (Ford 28). The series skews the ontological differences between human and monster by having its entire cast constantly cross the boundaries between hunter and hunted: The hunters themselves lose their human soul, angels fraternize with demons, and the King of Hell becomes the most congenial character. *Supernatural* thus employs a unique cast of liminal monsters and liminal humans. This is significant since, in accordance with Jeffrey Jerome Cohen's claim that monsters are to be considered as signifiers of cultural anxieties, the concept of monstrosity functions in *Supernatural* as a cultural cipher. As the series' creator Eric Kripke has stated, monsters "reflect what our culture was afraid of at a particular time" (Kripke quoted in Edmundson 1). *Supernatural* takes up this theory and situates it in a discussion about destiny and free choice, deconstructing the latter in an antithesis to the American Dream. The show is deeply pessimistic about the characters' potential for good and constructs their insistence on choice ("You don't have to be a monster. You have a choice." "Metamorphosis," 4.04) as a cruel fallacy: In fact, *Supernatural* offers a deterministic reading of monstrosity, stressing the element that, despite good intentions, humans will ultimately be bent into monsters by external forces beyond their control.

The Gothic Tradition of Monsters in Supernatural

As a genre of excess, diffusion, and transgression which "undermine[s] physical laws with marvelous beings and fantastic events" (Botting, *Gothic* 6), the Gothic always features monsters that "define and construct the politics of the 'normal'" (Punter and Byron 263). Monsters—etymologically connected to the Latin noun "monstrum," i.e., "divine omen, sign," and the verb "monere," i.e., "to warn" (cf. Foresman and Tobienne 17)—are not only a narrative device to trigger horror or fear, they also do a lot of "cultural work" (Punter and Byron 263). According to Jeffrey Jerome Cohen's "Monster Culture," "the monster's body is a cultural body," meaning that the figure of the monster has to be read against the cultural background of its time of origin. He claims that

> the monster is born [...] as an embodiment of a certain cultural moment—of a time, a feeling, and a place. The monster's body quite literally incorporates fear, desire, anxiety and fantasy [...] giving them life and an uncanny interdependence. The monstrous body is pure culture. A construct and a projection, the monster exists only to be read [4].

Cohen's claim rests on the cultural uniqueness of certain monsters and their close intellectual and metaphorical proximity to a specific point in time. As something "that [...] reveals" (4), the monster expresses a limited number of concepts and fears: In Mary Shelley's *Frankenstein* (1818), for instance, Frankenstein's creation is the personified nightmare of 19th century England in which science seems to run amok (cf. Turney); Robert Louis Stevenson's Mr. Hyde from *The Strange Case of Dr. Jekyll and Mr. Hyde* (1886) can be read as the logical consequence of Darwinism, showing British fin de siècle society that culture and cultivation are mere shells (cf. Poole); and the eponymous vampire from Bram Stoker's *Dracula* (1897) is the emancipation of colonial fears, dreamt up by a British Empire that has itself invaded the world (cf. Arata). In short, Gothic monsters are not a cheap trick to stir horror and fear; on the contrary, they are metaphorical signifiers of a specific culture, embodying anxieties and thus serving as a cipher for cultural studies.

Postmodernity has complicated Cohen's claim that monsters express one specific fear. Nowadays, monsters often do not represent anything at all. As Jerold E. Hogle phrases it, "One danger, to be sure, is that the Gothic as postmodern can become sheer capitalist reproduction of its emptied elements, what Jameson laments as the 'airport paperback categories of the gothic and romance'" (10)—a commodification process which the influential Gothic scholar Fred Botting has termed "Candygothic" (134).[3] Paraphrasing Botting, Catherine Spooner argues that "the production of meaningful terror [is] stymied by the channeling of excess through the path of least resistance" (155), implying that the Gothic has lost its cultural significance. She is alluding to series like *American Horror Story* (2011–), *Penny Dreadful* (2014–2016) or *Once Upon a Time* (2011–2018), which feature iconic Gothic characters such as Frankenstein and his creature, Dr. Jekyll and Mr. Hyde, and Dracula, yet fulfill no warning or mirroring function but "'exploit' the cultural capital of these figures for a postmodern audience that loves its intertextuality. But then: Where is *Supernatural* to be positioned? As Melissa Edmundson has shown, the show is unequivocally indebted to the Gothic mode, its horror subgenre, and its concept of the monstrous other (Abbott, "Rabbit's Feet," 10f.; cf. Jowett 33). Having aired its 300th episode in season fourteen, the series is "part of a longer journey through the horror tradition, building upon what has come before, but taking the genre further and making it darker" (Abbott, "Introduction" xi). This means that on the one hand the series regularly points back to its generic origins as a classic Gothic tale, featuring monsters like witches, vampires, werewolves and ghosts. Whenever the series "draws upon traditional monsters it not only makes those connections explicit but fully recognizes that the audience is aware of the lore too" (Koven and Thorgeirsdottir 187). With episodes such as "Time Is on My Side" (3.15) with its obvious reference to Victor Frankenstein and the crossing of moral and ethical boundaries, or the parody episode "Monster Movie" (4.05) with its mocking of the "airport paperback gothic" Jameson referred to by explicitly recycling "the classic myths of Dracula, Frankenstein, the Mummy, and werewolves" (García 153), *Supernatural* effectively taps the cultural capital of Gothic hallmarks.

On the other hand, the series cannot be suspected of recycling only since it takes up the challenge to create something new. While it is obviously indebted to the American horror movies of the 1970s (cf. Brown 63)[4] and the literary American Gothic, resonating with Charles Brockden Brown, Edgar Allen Poe, William Faulkner or Stephen King (cf. Blake 228), *Supernatural* offers a distinctly new side to the American Gothic by relying heavily on folklore tales. Local myths and tales harbor American anxieties in a typical American setting of haunted houses and sinister forests. Early episodes such as "Wendigo" (1.02), "Hook Man" (1.07), "Bugs" (1.08) or "Route 666" (1.13) provide a clearly discernible American focus on topics such as religious fanaticism, persecution of indigenous people, superstition, and racism (cf. Liebs quoted in Jowett 42) illustrating that "the Winchester brothers encounter all the 'anxiety, darkness, threat [and] paranoia' that the American gothic tradition can throw at them" (Lloyd-Smith quoted in Blake 232). Lorna Jowett therefore even claims that "Dean and Sam's adventures are becoming a new American myth" (43) themselves.

Moreover, *Supernatural* starts to develop its own mythology by incorporating various gods, monsters and beings from cultures all over the globe. In the manner of pastiche, *Supernatural* introduces not only deities from Christianity, Islam, or Norse mythology, as well as various (pagan) religions, but also their foot soldiers: Arab djinns and qareens, Indian crocottas, Hindu rakshasas, Greek lamias and sirens, Peruvian pishtacos, Japanese kitsunes and shojos, Scottish banshees, and Hebrew shedims. The show's full creativity, however, is unleashed when it introduces monsters handcrafted for anxieties permeating the 21st century. The series introduces, for instance, a demon specializing in plane crashes ("Phantom Traveler," 1.04), a Wi-Fi–ghost murdering college students via the Internet ("Halt & Catch Fire," 10.13) or the Tulpa, a ghost animated into being by a website ("Hell House," 1.17), thus addressing the dangers of technology. While these monsters remain only occasional pointers to *Supernatural*'s potential, the show demonstrates its capabilities in seasons seven, eight and ten with the introduction of Leviathans, "prototypical antisocial monsters [lacking] any regard for the human race and implement[ing] a plan to turn [them] into a factory-farm-style food supply" (Stout 12). Originating from the serpentine sea monster of Judeo-Christian mythology, Leviathans are re-constructed in terms of capitalism, thus incorporating growing anxieties about globalization and the power of corporate networks. *Supernatural* fittingly constructs the leader of the Leviathans, Dick Roman, as a billionaire and one of the top 35 successful businessmen in the country. Foreshadowing Donald J. Trump's electoral campaign of 2016, the series even discusses the influence of economy on politics by having Roman attract some conservative political attention: "He's ruthless, but good-looking. I think he'll make a great candidate" ("How to Win Friends and Influence Monsters," 7.09). *Supernatural* then is a unique mixture of both traditional elements and progressive new monsters fitting for a contemporary audience.

Free Will vs. Determinism—How to Escape the Monster Within

When it comes to the concept of monstrosity at the core of *Supernatural*, some scholars have proposed a very absolutist categorization: "Monsters are evil and harmful to others, so the brothers are completely justified in eliminating the various creatures they encounter" (Stout 7). However, this statement is too simple. There is more to the monsters than meets the eye, or, to say it in the words of Linnie Blake, "monsters are never simply monsters" (232). The series introduces an ambiguity of evil, meaning that "the supernatural landscape is not as clear-cut" (Abbott, "Introduction" xii) as both characters and viewers would like to believe at first glance. The show lives off the tension between monstrosity and humanity, calling essentialist notions into question and stressing the positions of both concepts on a continuum. As Lisa Schmidt argues, "Monsters are not *born* as such; through bad luck, accident or intended destiny they may find themselves with something in them that predisposes them to violence and chaos [...] Becoming a monster is an imminent tragedy that can be averted" (169). Accordingly, the show abounds in monsters that were born human but *turned* into monsters due to external circumstances. Across the run of the show, nearly any monster is re-evaluated as a potential victim. Initiating this concept, the episode "In My Time of Dying" (2.01) features a young girl called Tessa, a reaper who has chosen the human form of a young girl to deliver a severely injured Dean the message of his impending death. From her Dean learns about the process of how angry spirits are born:

> REAPER/TESSA: You'll stay here for years. Disembodied, scared, and over the decades it'll probably drive you mad. Maybe you'll even get violent.
> DEAN: What are you saying?
> REAPER: Dean. How do you think angry spirits are born? They can't let go and they can't move on. And you're about to become one. The same thing you hunt.

Finding himself between life and death, Dean is introduced to the "evolution" of angry spirits. Moreover, Tessa prophesies a similar fate for Dean, dissolving the ontological differences between hunter and hunted. According to her, the fate of angry spirits is not only relatable, but also a natural process awaiting potentially anyone after death.

The episode "Roadkill" (2.16) provides a similar example. The brothers try to release Molly McNamara, a young woman oblivious to the fact that she is a ghost. When Sam tries to break the delicate news, he relies on the use of metaphors and choice of words that parallels Tessa's:

> SAM: Spirits [...] are like wounded animals. Lost. In so much pain that they lash out. [...] There's some part of them that's keeping them here. [...] they just hold on too tight. Can't let go. So they're trapped. [...]
> MOLLY: You sound almost sorry for them.
> SAM: Well, they weren't evil people, you know? A lot of them were good. Just, something happened to them. Something they couldn't control.

Both excerpts stress the fundamental helplessness and innocence of angry spirits. Sam and Tessa conceptualize ghosts as trapped, scared, and tortured individuals, i.e., victims of circumstances beyond their control. The metaphysical difference between humans and monsters is thus turned into a gradual continuum devoid of any clear-cut categories. Episodes like these justify Nathan Stout's question: "What if the monster is really a lot like you and me, a genuine member of the moral community?" (8), thus encouraging the audience to consider their own position in relation to the monstrous other.

While "Bloodlust" (2.03) and "Heart" (2.17) construct vampires and werewolves as conceptually close to humans (cf. Calvert 95), the episode "Sin City" (3.04) establishes even demons—entities usually defined by their antithetical position to humanity as victims of circumstances and, in fact, refugees. According to the demon Casey, Hell is a "pit of despair. Why do you think we want to come [to Earth instead]?" The demon Ruby relates another case in point in "Malleus Maleficarum" (3.09):

> DEAN: So all of them–every damn demon–they were all human once?
> RUBY: Every one I've ever met. [...] Most of them have forgotten what it means, or even that they were. That's what happens when you go to Hell, Dean. That's what Hell is—forgetting what you are.

Summing up, the monster in *Supernatural* is a victim. Even demons are reconceptualized as humans who have lost their humanity due to external circumstances beyond their control. The show insists that "the potential for evil, the demonic, lies in all of us" (Stevenson 108) by constantly foregrounding the tragedy-element in monstrosity. This way, *Supernatural* is both progressive (in terms of fully aligning with contemporary ideas about morality) and aware of its roots, meaning that the series harks back to a longer tradition evaluating the Gothic as a textual inquiry into the moral status of a given monster (cf. Shelley's *Frankenstein*).

What meets the eye, though, is the conceptual closeness between monstrosity and choice which results from the fact that monsters are not inherently evil but rather victims of larger-than-life tragedies. As Schmidt claims: "In *Supernatural*, being a monster is not an all-or-nothing proposition but 'a choice.' [The show] insists that free will is both *possible* and *necessary* regardless of *what* you are" (169, emphasis in original). At first glance, this claim seems valid. Throughout the series both protagonists stress the deliberate nature of "coming to the dark side." In "Metamorphosis," the brothers encounter a being called a "rugarou," a carnivore with a genetic predisposition for eating human flesh. While they are fully human until their early thirties, rougarous turn for good (or bad in this case) when they give in to their insatiable hunger and feed on human flesh. *Supernatural* establishes eating human flesh thus as the fundamental threshold between monsters and humans. Not only rugarous are judged accordingly, but also vampires and werewolves as well as wendigos. This form of cannibalism is thus reinforced as the ultimate taboo, distinguishing humans from non-humans. Reluctant to kill someone who has not yet committed a monstrous act, Sam points to a loophole for rugarous, stating that "if they never eat human flesh, they don't fully transform." According to him, all the rugarou Jack needs to do is to never cross the threshold into monstrosity, i.e., to decide to "go vegan" in Dean's words. It seems as if Jack Montgomery had a choice based on his own free will, facing the question of whether to give in to his animalistic instincts or opt for an enlightened notion of self: "You got this dark pit inside you. I know. [...] But that doesn't mean you have to fall into it. You don't have to be a monster. [...] It doesn't matter what you are. [...] It only matters what you do. It's your choice." According to Schmidt, it is episodes like these that offer "variations on the theme of agency" and that allow "for a fresh insistence that acts of free will are the cure for monstrosity" (177), since they advocate an indeterministic reading, arguing for will power and self-control. Schmidt also mentions the characters of the vampire Benny Lafitte and Cyrus Styne as examples, both of whom are monsters according to their genes but who behave differently. Both characters reject their monstrous heritage proposed by genes, family, or tradition and attempt to lead a life free of killing and murder.

The series, however, counteracts this thesis on the power of the will as a means of self-control. In fact, *Supernatural* insists on a grand narrative void of free choice. It negates its protagonists' hopes and suggests that their strategy of re-humanization through free will is a mere fallacy. *Supernatural* is indeed deeply deterministic and thwarts any reading offering a more positive outlook. Coming back to Schmidt's example, the episode "Metamorphosis," one cannot fail to notice that despite Jack's deliberate abstinence, he is forced to transform into a monster: When the hunter Travis attacks Jack's pregnant wife, Jack is coerced into accepting his monstrous self. External actors and the wish to save her and the unborn child force Jack to give in to his genealogical disposition eventually. He kills Travis and feeds on him in a tragic self-fulfilling prophecy situation. Jack has crossed the threshold and cannot be re-incorporated into society. Indeed, *Supernatural*'s canon includes many episodes in which monsters initially recoil from their disposition but are later forced to give in to their monstrosity, stressing the aspect of determinism. In "The Girl Next Door" (7.03), Sam spares the kitsune Amy Pond—a werewolf-like creature with a special taste for the pituitary gland of a human brain—because she has "never killed anyone." Some twenty years later, however, Sam and Amy's paths cross again, when Sam accuses his former friend of having killed humans:

> AMY: No, you don't understand. It's not like that. I'm—I'm not just some murderer. I had to. [I'm feeding on] the dead. I'm a mortician. [...] I quietly take what [my son] Jacob and I need. No one gets hurt. But it can be risky, feeding like that, especially for a kid. Jacob got sick. He was dying, and the only way to fight it off was—
> SAM: He needed fresh meat.

The pattern which "Metamorphosis" introduces to the audience is repeated in "The Girl Next Door." Although Amy has made a conscious choice not to commit murder, she is forced to break the ultimate taboo by external circumstances to save her child. Her free will has been short-circuited by her son's medical condition, forcing her to kill for fresh meat. Despite good intentions, Amy has transformed—reason enough for Dean to finish her off: "No matter how hard you try, you are what you are. You will kill again. [...] Trust me, I'm an expert. Maybe in a year, maybe ten. But eventually, the other shoe will drop. It always does." Dean's prophecy is highly deterministic, denying the potential of reform by prophesying another relapse.

The Kripke-era of *Supernatural* (seasons one to five) is especially haunted by the themes of determinism, fate, and free will. The younger of the two brothers, Sam, desperately wants to believe that free will is an option potentially averting the transformation from human to monster. However, his wish eventually turns out to be mere self-deception. His insistence on choice can be read in terms of self-protection and an ideological clutching at every straw. With Sam being contaminated with demon blood, the two brothers are constantly re-positioned on the continuum "human-monster" themselves. As Blake states, Sam and Dean exist "in human, demonic and vampiric form, being variously inhabited by angels and shapeshifters and manipulated by a range of external agents, from love potions (7.9) to the devil himself (5.4)" (230). Both protagonists are constantly on the brink of losing their human status. For instance, when Dean is turned into a vampire it is only a matter of time until he will give into his hunger for blood. Sam's timely rescue is the only thing saving him from transformation into a monster.

Consequently, Sam summarizes their liminal position by stating, "I'm infected with demon blood. You've been to Hell. Look, I know you want to think of yourself as Joe the Plumber, Dean, but you're not" ("Death Takes a Holiday," 4.15). The brothers "repeatedly blur the boundary between hero, victim, and monster" (Abbott, "Rabbit's Feet" 12), i.e., they can "exist neither as complete monsters nor as total heroes" (Burnell 47). Firmly positioned outside of society due to the absence of a permanent home, bourgeois, i.e., non-hunter friends, or stable partnerships, Sam and Dean's otherness is frequently commented upon by other characters as well. The thief Bela Talbot for instance classifies them as being a "stone's throw away from [...] serial killer[s]" ("Red Sky at Morning," 3.06) while the FBI agent Victor Henriksen frequently refers to the brothers as "monsters" (cf. "Folsom Prison Blues," 2.19). Ultimately, their insistence on choice and their wish to grant mercy to "monsters" who promise personal reform must be read in this light. Sam and Dean cling to an intradiegetic narrative of free will and indeterminism permeating the mythology of the show in order to preserve their own humanity. When the hunter Gordon Walker goes after Sam because of his demonic heritage, Dean insists that Sam's ability to choose will triumph over genes or blood:

> DEAN: Come on, man. I know Sam, okay, better than anyone. He's got more of a conscience than I do, I mean, the guy feels guilty surfing the Internet for porn.
> GORDON: Maybe you're right. But one day he's going to be a monster.
> DEAN: How? Huh? How's a guy like Sam become a monster?
> GORDON: Beats me. But he will ["Hunted," 2.10].

With these words, Dean admits to his double standard: While more than happy to grant his half-demon brother the opportunity for free choice in a desperate attempt to save them both from damnation, he is not as generous with others. Amy is the case in point again. Since she has flaunted their deal breaker, i.e., killed humans, Dean will not allow her to go on. This seems paradoxical, for after all, Sam and Dean have killed dozens of innocent bystanders themselves. For instance, in their quest to fight demons, Sam and Dean willingly accept the death of the human host body in order to send the demon back to Hell. Being possessed by an evil demon, i.e., having lost their agency and potential to alter their fate, the demon victims thus stand as a metaphor for the lack of options once evil has taken control.

Summing up, the brothers are "worse than many of the monsters [they] hunt [...]" (Ford 35). Reading *Supernatural* psychologically, then, Sam and Dean's insistence on the narrative of reform is nothing more than self-protection. Being physically and psychologically "contaminated" and conceptually close to "real" monsters themselves, the brothers are eager to accept theories of free will as exit strategies from their own monstrosity. Choice is their only option in a situation where they need to "run from what's inside" ("When the Levee Breaks," 4.21)—a futile attempt as it turns out.

In *Supernatural* nobody can escape a pre-determined fate. Just as it is the destiny of monsters to degenerate sooner or later, the hunters are equally forlorn in terms of options: They cannot choose their fate. In this regard, two episodes stand out especially, namely "What Is and What Should Never Be" (2.20) and "It's a Terrible Life" (4.17). Both construct an alternative reality in which neither Dean nor Sam work as hunters but lead a more quotidian life composed of 9-to-5-jobs and houses with "white picket fences"—the *Supernatural* symbol for a suburban, middle-class life style antithetical to hunting (cf. Brown). Although robbed of their hunter-knowledge and original sense of self, the brothers distrust the idyll because of the absence of evil. In both realities, the brothers sooner or later find their way back to their "true" hunter-selves irrespective of how much they long for a "normal" life. The notion of fate is introduced explicitly, circumventing any deliberations about free choice, when Dean asks the angel Zachariah why the angels orchestrated an alternative reality in the first place:

> ZACHARIAH: To prove to you that the path you're on is truly in your blood. You're a hunter. Not because your dad made you, not because God called you back from Hell, but because it is what you are. And you love it. You'll find your way to it in the dark every single time and you're miserable without it. Dean, let's be real here. You're good at this.

Although Sam and Dean try to reverse history and alter fate multiple times, both gradually have to accept that it cannot be done. In "In the Beginning" (4.03), Dean is sent back in time to 1973 to prevent the death of his mother. Despite his best efforts, however, he is soon to learn that fate cannot be changed. On the contrary, it is specifically because of Dean and his failed interventions that his mother Mary is forced to accept a demon's deal that will lead to her death and Sam's contamination. The same holds true for Sam's constant attempts to escape his destiny and leave "the family business." In fact, the narrative of *Supernatural* in season one starts as an interruption of Sam's "normal life" as a college student. Although he has decided to lead a different life quite early (cf. the episode "After School Special" [4.13] in which a teacher tells Sam to pursue his own ideals), Sam cannot run from his destiny. All attempts to do so eventually fail.

The ultimate instance of determinism is to be found in the character of the writer Carver Edlund. In "The Monster at the End of This Book" (4.18) the brothers are confronted with what Castiel calls "The Winchester Gospel," i.e., a cheap paperback series called "Supernatural" recounting the lives of the brothers in detail. These books, written by the prophet Chuck, capture every detail of their past, present and future, offering no way out of destiny.

The episode is dominated by Dean's attempts to outsmart fate, trying to do the exact opposite of what was written, only to discover that Chuck's visions prove to be true despite Dean's intentions. *Supernatural* addresses the topic of inevitable fate consciously for the first time in this episode, but the show comes back to it multiple times, showing that evaluated retrospectively, the brothers' attempts turn out to be futile and even result in the opposite outcome from their intentions:

> Sam tried to stop Dean from going to hell, but he did anyway. Dean tried to stop his torment, but instead opened the First Seal. Sam tried to do the right thing and kill Lilith, but he opened the Final Seal. The entire series is about Sam and Dean's quest to stop the inevitable [Kubicek].

Although they try, neither the monsters nor Sam and Dean can run from destiny.

Conclusion

Characters and audience alike have fought their way through a long series of monsters. Starting in season one with the ghost of a young woman, *Supernatural* has offered countless incorporations of fears and anxieties following "a fairly simple formula" (Fathallah 157), celebrated by fans and therefore employed regularly by the creators of the show: After a murder involving a narratively undefined and under-determined evil presence at the beginning, the audience follows Dean and Sam in the identification process of each monster. Or as Dean phrases it, "Well, why don't you figure out what the hell it is, and I'll figure out a way to kill it" ("The Memory Remains," 12.18). Each episode climaxes in the showdown between monster and monster hunter—an often overly dramatic, Hollywoodesque scene with deus ex machina solutions and last-minute rescues in which the brothers triumph over evil—more or less alive and in one piece. Once the supernatural presence has been disposed of, Dean and Sam leave town in their iconic 1967 Chevrolet Impala only to initiate the same narrative circle one week later in a different Mid-American town.

But what strikes the viewer is not the repetitive schema but the show's continued engagement with questions concerning free will and choice that are counteracted time and time again. *Supernatural* insists on determinism and the inevitability of fate, which seems counter-intuitive at first glance. After all, the series is located in the United States of America, a country grown out of Enlightenment principles and the liberal conviction that everybody forges their own destiny. Yet, what might seem paradoxical at first glance is in effect a hallmark of classic American Gothic fiction: "the Gothic, it is frequently reasoned, embodies and gives voice to the dark nightmare that is the underside of 'the American dream.' This formulation is true up to a point, for it reveals the limitations of American faith in social and material progress" (Savoy 167). Linking back to this discourse, the show constructs free will and choice as an illusion (cf. Kubicek). Its deeply pessimistic reading of free will and its insistence on questions of determinism concerning personal fate is thus one of the latest versions of a tradition going back centuries. *Supernatural* renders familiar monsters as desperate creatures, advertising an "understanding that these monsters are, in a way, our victims" (Schmidt 179). By blurring categorical boundaries, *Supernatural* asks for a re-evaluation of the monstrosity within. Or as Friedrich Nietzsche said, "Beware that, when fighting monsters, you yourself do not become a monster…. For when you gaze long into the abyss, the abyss gazes also into you" (qtd. in Frase 146).

Summing up, the figure of the monster is not only culturally relevant for *Supernatural*, giving the series the potential to illuminate for instance the underside of grand narratives, i.e., the American Dream. Additionally, it also carries a vital narrative meaning. Thanks to the monsters, *Supernatural* is still running (cf. Canode 78). It "lacks narrative closure, because there is always something to hunt. Therefore, the brothers' misfortune must continue" as Agata Łuksza phrases it (187). As long as there are monsters—and there always will be—Dean and Sam will have to carry on.

Notes

1. Interestingly enough, "monster" is the umbrella term for what awaits the brothers in each episode. As Shannon Ford correctly observes, "Although there are many important differences among supernatural creatures, Sam and Dean use the generic term 'monster' as shorthand for categorizing all the creatures they hunt" (27), thus reducing them—on the surface—to a narrative device. This reading, however, does not sustain a closer analysis of monstrosity in *Supernatural*. Monsters, as will be proven, are so much more than just "monsters."

2. The name is an allusion to the Winchester rifle and the Model 1873, intrinsically linked to the American frontier and the process of colonialization. Often termed "the gun that won the west" (as it is even advertised today on the Winchester Webpage; cf. also Blake 227), the rifle resonates with American notions of frontier and hunting and serves therefore as a fitting allusion and a distinctly American take on the Gothic.

3. In his essay "Gothic Culture," Botting has also coined the term "Disneygothic," arguing along the same lines as "Candygothic." Botting describes a process of commodification inherent to contemporary Gothic, by listing the example of a planned theme park based on Count Vlad Tepes, allegedly the real-world reference for Bram Stoker's Count Dracula. "Gothic," he writes, "preserves the illusion of darkness, death and sexuality in a world given over to the omnipresence of virtual light and life on screens" (Botting, "Culture" 203).

4. Fans of pop culture derive a great deal of pleasure from tracing all kinds of pop cultural references. In fact, *Supernatural* is crammed with intertextual references: the various cover names for the Winchester identities, for instance, are in no way random but relate to rock stars and movie personalities. Furthermore, many episodes such as "When the Levee Breaks," "Out of the Darkness, Into the Fire" (11.01) or even "Mamma Mia" (12.02) allude to songs from various genres and styles. The same holds true for the episodes; titles such as "It's a Terrible Life" (4.17) and "The Real Ghostbusters" (5.09) hint at popular movies, and

other TV series in America. James Francis argues that "the television, film, music, and nonfiction references help create an intertextual world that connects the series to other pop culture art forms beyond its fourth wall. [...] Viewers are entertained by the show, but simultaneously educated about the world in which they live" (125).

Works Cited

Abbott, Stacey. "Introduction." *TV Goes to Hell: An Unofficial Road Map of Supernatural*, edited by Stacey Abbott and David Lavery, ECW Press, 2011, pp. ix–xvii.
_____. "Rabbit's Feet and Spleen Juice: The Comic Strategies of TV Horror." *TV Goes to Hell: An Unofficial Road Map of Supernatural*, edited by Stacey Abbott and David Lavery, ECW Press, 2011, pp. 3–17.
Arata, Stephen D. "The Occidental Tourist: *Dracula* and the Anxiety of Reverse Colonization." *Victorian Studies* vol. 33, no. 4, 1990, pp. 621–645.
Blake, Linnie. "All Hell Breaks Loose: *Supernatural*, Gothic Neoliberalism and the American Self." *Horror Studies* vol. 6, no. 2, 2015, pp. 225–238.
Botting, Fred. "Candygothic." *The Gothic*, edited by Fred Botting, D.S. Brewer, 2001, pp. 133–151.
_____. *Gothic*. Routledge, 1996.
_____. "Gothic Culture." *The Routledge Companion to Gothic*, edited by Catherine Spooner and Emma McEvoy, Routledge, 2007, pp. 199–213.
Brown, Simon. "Renegades and Wayward Sons: *Supernatural* and the '70s." *TV Goes to Hell: An Unofficial Road Map of Supernatural*, edited by Stacey Abbott and David Lavery, ECW Press, 2011, pp. 60–74.
Burnell, Aaron C. "Rebels, Rogues, and Sworn Brothers: Supernatural and the Shift in 'White Trash' from Monster to Hero." *TV Goes to Hell: An Unofficial Road Map of Supernatural*, edited by Stacey Abbott and David Lavery, ECW Press, 2011, pp. 47–59.
Calvert, Bronwen. "Angels, Demons, and Damsels in Distress: The Representation of Women in *Supernatural*." *TV Goes to Hell: An Unofficial Road Map of Supernatural*, edited by Stacey Abbott and David Lavery, ECW Press, 2011, pp. 90–104.
Canode, Jillian L. "Hunting the American Dream: Why Marx Would Think It´s a Terrible Life." *Supernatural and Philosophy: Metaphysics and Monsters ... for Idjits*, edited by Galen A. Foresman and William Irwin, Wiley-Blackwell, 2013, pp. 74–82.
Cohen, Jeffrey J. "Monster Culture (Seven Theses)." *Monster Theory: Reading Culture*, edited by Jeffrey J. Cohen, U of Minnesota P, 1996, pp. 3–25.
Edmundson, Melissa. "Introduction." *The Gothic Tradition in* Supernatural: *Essays on the Television Series*, edited by Melissa Edmundson, McFarland, 2016, pp. 1–12.
Ford, Shannon B. "Hunters, Warriors, Monsters." *Supernatural and Philosophy: Metaphysics and Monsters ... for Idjits*, edited by Galen A. Foresman and William Irwin, Wiley-Blackwell, 2013, pp. 26–36.
Foresman, Galen A., and Francis Tobienne. "Aristotle's Metaphysics of Monsters and Why We Love *Supernatural*." *Supernatural and Philosophy: Metaphysics and Monsters ... for Idjits*, edited by Galen A. Foresman and William Irwin, Wiley-Blackwell, 2013, pp. 16–25.
Francis, James, Jr. "'That's so gay': Drag, Camp, and the Power of Storytelling in Supernatural." *TV Goes to Hell: An Unofficial Road Map of Supernatural*, edited by Stacey Abbott and David Lavery, ECW Press, 2011, pp. 119–131.
Frase, Peter. *Four Futures: Visions of the World After Capitalism*. Verso, 2016.
García, Alberto N. "Breaking the Mirror: Metafictional Strategies in Supernatural." *TV Goes to Hell: An Unofficial Road Map of Supernatural*, edited by Stacey Abbott and David Lavery, ECW Press, 2011, pp. 146–160.
Hogle, Jerrold E. "Introduction: Modernity and the Proliferation of the Gothic." *The Cambridge Companion to the Modern Gothic*, edited by Jerrold E. Hogle, Cambridge UP, 2014, pp. 3–19.
Jowett, Lorna. "Purgatory with Color TV: Motel Rooms as Liminal Zones in *Supernatural*." *TV Goes to Hell: An Unofficial Road Map of Supernatural*, edited by Stacey Abbott and David Lavery, ECW Press, 2011, pp. 33–46.

Katz, Josh. "'Duck Dynasty' Vs. 'Modern Family': 50 Maps of the U.S. Cultural Divide." *The New York Times* 27 Oct. 2016. www.nytimes.com/interactive/2016/12/26/upshot/duck-dynasty-vs-modern-family-television-maps.html. Accessed 14 March 2018.
Koven, Mikel J., and Gunnella Thorgeirsdottir. "Television Folklore: Rescuing *Supernatural* from the Fakelore Realm." *TV Goes to Hell: An Unofficial Road Map of* Supernatural, edited by Stacey Abbott and David Lavery, ECW Press, 2011, pp. 187–200.
Kubicek, John. "Is There Free Will On *Supernatural*?" 2010. www.buddytv.com/articles/supernatural/is-there-free-will-on-supernat-34313.aspx. Accessed 19 April 2018.
Łuksza, Agata. "Boy Melodrama: Genre Negotiations and Gender-Bending in the *Supernatural* Series." *Text Matters* vol. 6, no. 1, pp. 177–194.
Lundwall, S. J. *Science Fiction*. Grosset & Dunlap, 1978.
Poole, Adrian. "Robert Louis Stevenson." *The Cambridge Companion to English Novelists*, edited by Adrian Poole, Cambridge UP, 2010, pp. 258–271.
Punter, David, and Glennis Byron. *The Gothic*. Blackwell, 2004.
Savoy, Eric. "The Rise of American Gothic." *The Cambridge Companion to Gothic Fiction*, edited by Jerrold E. Hogle, Cambridge UP, 2002, pp. 167–188.
Schmidt, Lisa. "We All Have a Little Monster in Us: Dean Winchester, the Mark of Cain and the New Monster Paradigm." *The Gothic Tradition in* Supernatural: *Essays on the Television Series*, edited by Melissa Edmundson, McFarland, 2016, pp. 167–181.
Shelley, Mary. *Frankenstein: Or the Modern Prometheus*. 1818. Penguin Books, 2003.
Spooner, Catherine. *Contemporary Gothic*. Reaktion Books, 2006.
Stevenson, Gregory. "Apocalyptic War in *Buffy the Vampire Slayer, Angel, Supernatural* and *Battlestar Galactica*." *Small Screen Revelations: Apocalypse in Contemporary Television*, edited by James Aston, Sheffield Phoenix Press, 2013, pp. 96–117.
Stoker, Bram. *Dracula*. 1897. Wordsworth Editions, 1993.
Stout, Nathan. "Are Monsters Members of the Moral Community?" Supernatural *and Philosophy: Metaphysics and Monsters ... for Idjits*, edited by Galen A. Foresman and William Irwin, Wiley-Blackwell, 2013, pp. 7–15.
Turney, Jon. *Frankenstein's Footsteps: Science, Genetics and Popular Culture*. Yale UP, 1998.

Part Three

"Our lives are not
for public consumption"

"Where's the pie?"

Nostalgic and Apocalyptic Foodways in Supernatural

KELLI WILHELM

In *Supernatural*'s season three episode "Bedtime Stories" (3.05), a couple hiking in the woods comes across an idyllic scene of an unassuming blue sided house with white shutters, a pie cooling on the windowsill, and a sweet grandmotherly woman standing out front. As the old woman invites the lost couple inside, the camera zooms in on the pie, and it is clear that the promise of a sweet treat makes their decision. Occurring in an episode featuring fairy tale stories, this is an obvious reference to "Hansel and Gretel." It then comes as no surprise when, two slices into the delicious cherry pie, the couple realize they have been drugged, and the old woman unceremoniously begins to murder the male hiker (the female hiker survives; the subsequent scene shows her recovering in hospital). Although this moment in "Bedtime Stories" seems minor, it demonstrates how food is not only a subtle focus of the series but also how that focus highlights two significant ideas: first, ideal or idyllic sights—grandmother on the porch, pie cooling on the window sill—while undeniably inviting, rarely turn out to be true; and second, food often occupies a dual position as both idealized and dangerous.

Operating under both ideas, pie in this scene helps to present a safe and nostalgic home, but it also reveals a façade of safety while actually functioning to bait the unsuspecting hikers. Occupying such dualities—inciting comfort and revealing untruth—food holds a certain cultural power. Sidney Mintz's highly influential text *Sweetness and Power* speaks to the significant relationship between food and power, and since the advent of food studies and foodways in the 1970s, food has been additionally linked to gender ideologies, exclusion, the body, and fears of industrialism, by scholars across disciplines including Sherrie A. Inness, LuAnne Roth, Susan Bordo, and Eric Schlosser.[1] Roth significantly indicates that classic studies of foodways emphasize food's ability to create community, but following a second wave of food studies in the early 2000s, scholars "moved beyond this positive function of food behavior to consider how food may be employed simultaneously to reinforce hegemonic or patriarchal structures as well as punish, cajole, or otherwise negotiate power relationships" (197).[2]

The incorporation of foodways is suggestive of a collective cultural experience, highlighting values related to gender, domesticity, and the family structure. Mikel J. Koven and Gunnel Thorgeirsdottir argue that series like *Supernatural* consciously incorporate and transform lore and legend in a performance of collected cultural experience which, when recognized, allows scholars to "redraft the imaginary boundaries that define identity in our postmodern worldview" (199). I am examining how *Supernatural*'s foodways proceed to disrupt these values through presentations of American fast food and monstrosity. This essay will therefore first evidence food's traditional or nostalgic relationships to family and the mother figure as well as demonstrate how food begins to suggest shades of untruth in nostalgic versions of these relationships. Second, the essay will explore examples of the American fast food industry and its relationship to a loss of the nostalgic family and a distrust of food. As the two monster-hunting brothers Sam and Dean Winchester confront the Biblical apocalypse, among other disasters, they continually grapple with their definition of family. By repeatedly grounding itself in themes of family, small town America, and 1970s and contemporary popular culture, *Supernatural* locates American traditions, albeit stereotypical ones, at its center. Food, while seemingly incidental to these larger themes, serves an important role in indicating the American cultural values of the show. I will argue that foodways in *Supernatural* are fundamentally a reaction to an early loss of the nuclear family dynamic and domestic sphere, which allows the series to demonstrate a paralleled relationship between food and American familial nostalgias.

These initial examinations are the "pie on the windowsill" portion of the essay and will be logically followed by the "drugged pie" portion. Here I argue that as the series progresses, food becomes untrustworthy and even monstrous, especially in relation to the Leviathan story arc, as it reveals the traditional family to be an unattainable ideal and reflects rumors surrounding the making and eating of American fast food as well as apocalyptic foodways.[3] Expanding upon Michael Newbury's ideas concerning food-apocalypse texts, I use the term apocalyptic foodways to indicate when the intersection between food and culture suggests significant damage to the social order and even the current state of the world (see Newbury's discussion of food's role in filmic depictions of the zombie apocalypse). This latter portion will examine cultural fears related to fast food and the food industry which manifest in *Supernatural* to acutely disrupt nostalgic cultural ideals described in the first portion of this essay and to underscore a concern for what is "natural" as both a central issue of the series and a collective cultural anxiety. *Supernatural*'s progression from food and family to the food apocalypse disrupts the American nostalgia surrounding food and represents an historical trajectory of twentieth and twenty-first century America's equal parts nostalgic and suspicious relationship with food. I use the term food apocalypse not as an apocalypse *of* food—an inability to grow certain foods or obtain certain nutrients from food—but as an apocalypse *by* food, as a zombie apocalypse is caused by the destruction resulting from the presence of zombies.

Pie on the Windowsill: Food Representing Desire

In no way has food become more recognizable in the series than in the form of pie. First appearing in "Scarecrow" (1.11) when Dean orders a slice of pie which he never receives, pie has become a reappearing symbol inextricably linked to the character. Fans of the show speak to the importance of this food item through a fan "super-wiki" page devoted entirely to the show's pie moments, as well as through pie-themed fan and even slash fiction, and multiple memes which include show quotes such as "Love me some pie," "Where's the pie?," and "You don't understand. I need pie." The wiki page describes the pie dilemma: "The running gag relating to Dean's pie love is that Dean rarely gets to eat his pie" ("Pie"). While he is often seen devouring cheeseburgers, sandwiches, donuts, and other unhealthy foods, not eating pie has become recognizable and meaningful for the character. The inaccessibility of a food item which invokes images of domestic Americana and the American "apple-pie life" ("Pilot," 1.01) mirrors the inaccessibility of a traditional familial lifestyle.

The inaccessibility of pie—and thus of an image of traditional family life—draws on a familiar nostalgic American idealism centered on domesticity and the image of a woman cooking—the staple Suzy Homemaker image. This nostalgic idea had come to seem "natural" (Parsecoli 15), and this naturalness is the object of *Supernatural*'s deconstruction, particularly when viewing the repercussions of Mary Winchester's death. Bronwen Calvert, in "Angels, Demons, and Damsels in Distress," emphasizes Mary's "mother in the house" image and argues that female characters in *Supernatural* reveal complexities in the show's dominantly masculine narrative and indicate the brothers' ongoing development (92). Examining episodes featuring Mary, through various narrative methods, during the early seasons reveals such complexities and development. These Mary episodes more specifically display food as crucial to Dean's image of an ideal mother figure and demonstrate a progression towards a disbelief in a domestic ideal. Mary is first seen, outside of the pilot episode and subsequent recaps, in "What Is and What Should Never Be" (2.20). In this episode, an encounter with a djinn creature places Dean in an alternate reality created by his deepest desire come true: that his mother had never died. Having provided Dean with a home and a mother, the show also begins to display food in greater detail. Up to this point, food had made brief cameo appearances—Dean refers to a giant bag of M&Ms as provisions in "Wendigo" (1.02), or Dean orders a slice of pie in "Scarecrow"— but in episode 2.20, the series takes time to focus on food. One scene opens with the camera focused in on a homemade sandwich as Dean lifts it and takes a big bite. With his mouth still full he exclaims, "This is the best sandwich ever," and his mother thanks him as she walks out of the kitchen. He has been "home" less than a day, and his mom has already fulfilled her traditional domestic role and made him a sandwich. For him, food and this lost mother figure are connected; to gain one is to regain another.

However, the nostalgic desire Dean has gained is shown to be faulty in the episode's stereotypical dining scene meant to celebrate Mary's birthday. Dining out, according to Joanne Finkelstein, comes with its own set of rules and meanings. Finkelstein asserts, "in the restaurant, we can find any number of acceptable and convincing images of how social life *should* be, including the desire for happy families" (204, emphasis added). By depicting Dean and his alternate-reality family—including mother, brother, brother's fiancée, and his own girlfriend—dining out in this stereotypical way, complete with a champagne toast, the show allows Dean to fully give in to his desire for a traditional family experience. However, Finkelstein additionally notes that such a dining experience, much like the context of the alternate reality, invites fantasy; "it can be a practice that invites the fanciful, fleeting, and disingenuous" (205). The disingenuity of the fantasy is in fact shown as the dinner ends and a conversation with Sam reveals that in this reality the brothers have no relationship. Therefore, even as Dean is given his greatest desire, the dining experience shows that desire and perhaps even the idealism behind the traditional family image to be faulty. In the show's portrayal of domestic images of food and women, a pattern begins to emerge in which Dean is given a brief moment of the traditional ideal he desires before it is taken away.

While I have connected food thus far in *Supernatural* to a broad cultural nostalgia for family, it also has a connection to very specific memories of Dean's character.[4] Dean's history with his mother and food—particularly pie—is emphasized in a rare memory provided in "Dark Side of the Moon" (5.16). Having been killed at the beginning of the episode, the brothers are shown in Heaven experiencing their favorite memories. For Dean, a childhood memory includes his mother pouring him a glass of milk and making him a sandwich with the crusts cut off. As this scene progresses, Mary has a tense phone conversation with John, and Dean gives her a hug and says, "It's okay Mom, Dad still loves you, I love you too. I will never leave you." Smiling, Mary responds, "You're my little angel. How 'bout some pie?" This scene allows viewers to finally gain insight into Dean's relationship to pie and its connection to his mother. However, it also shows that even when Dean was part of a traditional nuclear family, it was not perfect. His mother responds to this imperfection with pie, and so pie has become both Dean's solution to a lack of family throughout his life and the symbol that family is inaccessible. Reliving this moment in the present also allows Dean to gain some understanding of the memory's significance to his familial desires and his eating habits. Sam stands outside of this memory and reminds Dean that "[w]e should go"—that once again a manifestation of Dean's familial desire is not real. (However, "Mamma Mia" [12.02] reveals that even this memory was false; Mary could not cook, and her pie was store bought.) Similarly, one of Sam's own favorite memories in this episode is of a Thanksgiving with another, stereotypically normal, family. As Sam then tells Dean, "I never got the crusts cut off my pb&j," so for Sam familial nostalgia often takes place outside of his own family or even seemingly outside of reality—indeed, "Just My Imagination" (11.08) focuses on Sam's former "imaginary" friend Sully, who acted as an escape from Sam's imperfect family. Also having never known his mother, prior to her return in season twelve, Sam does not share the same nostalgic affection for traditional images or foods, such as the Impala or pie, instead being more often associated with healthy foods and modern innovations—see for instance "Hell House" (1.17), "Lazarus Rising" (4.01), "The Monster at the End of This Book" (4.18), "Slash Fiction" (7.06), "How to Win Friends and Influence Monsters" (7.09), "Southern Comfort" (8.06), and "As Time Goes By" (8.12), among others.

Dean is perhaps able to examine his own deep-seated relationship to pie and nostalgic familial desires in his relived memory because in the preceding episode, "Dead Men Don't Wear Plaid" (5.15), he is able to see an apparition of nostalgic desire as faulty and eat pie (twice!). The episode centers on Karen Singer, the long dead wife of fellow hunter and the brothers' adopted father figure Bobby Singer. Since recently rising from the dead, Karen has stepped easily back into a traditional housewife role and covered every surface of the house with freshly baked pies. Karen is, like the djinn reality and the heavenly memory, only a pale visage of lost family, but unlike the other memories or visions of nostalgic familial situations the series offers, Dean does not buy into this one, even momentarily. In this instance, Karen is Bobby's dream fulfilled, so Dean stands outside of the vision, the memory, and the dream. He can see that the pie set before him is brought by a pallid, distorted version of the traditional wife/mother/housewife, or as he refers to her, "the American Girl Zombie making cupcakes in your kitchen!" Dean can then eat the pie Karen bakes because he understands the nostalgic vision Karen offers is not real and even that such visions are untrustworthy; in this instance, pie is separate from his own nostalgic desires for mother and family. When Dean's trend of not eating is suddenly broken, it displays a significant change in his character's viewpoint; he is beginning to accept the elusiveness of a traditional family dynamic which pie has always represented.

Dean's acceptance is further shown one season later in "Mommy Dearest" (6.19), which presents the last appearance of Mary Winchester until the season eleven finale, "Alpha and Omega" (11.23), in which she is restored to life; she continues to appear through seasons twelve, thirteen, and fourteen. The episode ends with the final confrontation between the brothers and the season's villain, "the mother of all." The villain appears as a waitress, again representing mothers as servers and providers of food, and tries to explain her motives. In doing so, she literally transforms into an image of Mary and says, "She died to protect you, didn't she? See, you understand a mother's love." The guise of Mary Winchester is used to gain sympathy from the brothers through an all too familiar image of a sacrificial mother. Dean, however, has previously consumed phoenix ash, the one thing that will kill this villain, and merely replies, "Bite me." Acquiescing, she dies by this bite; she dies by a mode of consumption, and Dean, who has in different ways been chasing images of his mother throughout the series, watches this image of her die. It is then not merely a villain or even Mary Winchester who is dying here, but the image of an ideal domestic mother figure dies as well. Earlier in the season, Dean had given up a domestic life, and the image of his dying mother, caused by his own snarky invitation to "bite me," signifies his further relinquishing of a nostalgic image of domesticity.

Drugged Pie: When Food Becomes Monstrous

Throughout *Supernatural*, food, whether it is pie or a bacon cheeseburger, is representative of nostalgia—nostalgia for a mother's domestic affections. Food, however, when nostalgically presented as a key part of the show's false fantasies of family, also aids in displaying the falsity of Dean's nostalgic desires. For instance, "Don't You Forget About Me" (11.12) depicts a family dinner at Sheriff Jody Mills's house. The brothers rave about the food, but even the nostalgic image of this dinner is ruined by an awkward sex talk prompted by Mills's adopted teen daughters and the reality of what family is beyond nostalgic pretense. Homemade pies and mothers in the kitchen, then, comprise one side of America's relationship to food; distrust, uncertainty, and a more distinct disruption of nostalgic ideals characterize the other side. In occupying these opposing positions, food has a complex relationship with truth. Food is a symbol of desired truths, abundance, familial nostalgia, and so on, but also exposes "conflict or emptiness," the truths behind desire. *Supernatural* displays such a complex relationship, and food becomes increasingly untrustworthy, even monstrous.

A monstrous view of food is not a stretch for the series, as monstrous consumption surrounds the Winchester brothers. They hunt vampires, werewolves, rugarus, human cannibals, and wendigos—all creatures that devour humans. Devouring is connected with a fear of destruction (Parasecoli 58), and such fear is obvious for the creatures in the show as their consumption of long pig draws hunter attention. Yet for ordinary, non-cannibal devouring, such fear is rooted in the fast food industry and its effect on American life and families.

Twentieth-century America witnessed the industrialization of food, and throughout the century, fast food franchises exploded onto the American market. Americans' hurried eating habits were criticized as early as the eighteenth century (Smith 219–221). With the later incorporation of the assembly line model and the advent of the drive thru, the fast food industry capitalized on American's eating style (Smith 220–223). According to Ester Reiter, this capitalization significantly changed the American family. Reiter attributes the dissolution of the traditional American family construct to the fast food industry, asserting that "the market has moved into the family" and the "socialization of the domestic sphere" moved the family outside of the home and into fast food restaurants as both workers and consumers (14–15). Essentially, fast food disrupted the nostalgic dinner table scene as food preparation became focused on the public rather than the family at home. In her assertion, Reiter is drawing a significant connection between the construction of the American family and American relationship to and making of food.

Supernatural demonstrates that fast food not only alters the American family but the American relationship to food. Multiple legends and rumors of contamination and conspiracy surround fast or processed foods, suggesting distrust in food. Eric Schlosser explores and perpetuates such rumors related to food's freshness, bacterial contamination and government regulation of the meat packing industry, disgruntled employees, and what is put in food from the addition of manufactured flavors to food tampering (128, 195, 221–222). These fears speak to a widespread suspicion of fast foods which Morgan Spurlock's *Don't Eat This Book* and its companion documentary *Super Size Me* famously investigate (and indulge). Spurlock succinctly conveys the popularized negative image of fast food when he criticizes the "mass-produced, mass marketed, chemically enhanced processed food [of McDonald's]" and refers to McDonald's food as "McFrankenfood" (107, 115). The distrust of food, particularly of fast and processed foods, has become pervasive throughout the late twentieth and early twenty-first centuries, and *Supernatural*'s seventh season, while moving away from the domestic nostalgia represented by food in early seasons, situates itself in this history of fast food fears by presenting the threat of an apocalypse initiated by food.

Such an apocalypse is foreshadowed through a particularly Americana-inflected and yet un-nostalgic dining scene in "How to Win Friends and Influence Monsters" (7.09). The restaurant in which the characters eat, "BIGGERSON'S Sizzling Bar & Grill," promotes itself as an "all you can eat *family* (italics mine) restaurant," and before Sam, Dean, and Bobby even enter, the camera pauses on a full screen image of an advertisement hanging inside the restaurant. Alongside a smiling, busty blonde holding a plated sandwich, the sign reads, "Limited Time Only! New! Try it! You'll love it! Pepperjack Turducken Slammer! From $4.99." While the promotion of a family restaurant incites the nostalgic connection between family and food, the limited time only promotion combats such sentiment with a more realistic fast food allusion. This sign invokes fast food franchise McDonald's through the red and yellow color scheme and the use of the "limited time only" advertising technique which popularized the McRib. As the *Supernatural* trio are seated, Bobby says of the irritated waiter, "I sure hope we don't get Brandon's section," thus invoking the fast food legends involving disgruntled employees. These elements situate the scene in a familiar Americana setting and demonstrate Gillian Crowther's definition of meals as "structured interactions through which we [...] construct our identity" (162). The dining scenes of seasons two and seven construct contrasting identities of both the family structure and the American meal/relationship to food. The food the characters order in the episode first constructs individual identities as Bobby, the older father-figure, orders a heart-smart salad, Sam, always health-conscious, orders the "sidewinder soup and salad combo," and Dean, in masculine loyalty to "guy food" (Inness 24), orders the Turducken (TDK) Slammer. In contrast to the nostalgic dining scene of season two, this one is not part of a memory or a vision but of the show's reality, and subsequently, what the show more subtly presents as American reality. Instead of a big happy family, a large cloth-covered table, and a champagne toast, the episode depicts paper napkins, a markedly rude waiter, and three men, who even Brandon notes have some sort of familial relationship in rudely referring to Bobby as a "creepy uncle." The show allows fast food to represent a family structure outside of the nostalgic ideal therein combating that idealism.

The Biggerson's dining scene also recognizes the fears inherent to the fast food industry by introducing the TDK slammer of which Dean enthusiastically claims, "Oh that is a good sandwich." The sandwich and its consumers introduce plans of season seven's villains the Leviathans to turn humanity into a food source, as the episode reveals just how "good" the sandwich is. In a later scene as Sam begins to take note of Dean's newly "stoned" behavior, the camera pans the restaurant to display all the patrons taking big slow bites of TDK sandwiches with distant, glazed but contented looks. Bobby gives voice to the cultural anxiety reflected here: "There's some funky chicken in the TDK Slammer, ain't there?" Both the image of mindless eating and Bobby's words call to mind the close relationship between fast food and the American image as well as the rumors which such a connection has created.[5] The patrons of Biggerson's subsequently "have little or no individuality"; they are the "slow zombies" which have "been accelerated and intensified as the embodiment of a consumer signified by blindly focused, violent, and apocalyptic eating habits" (Newbury 103–104). *Supernatural* is blatantly playing into twenty-first century cultural fears of fast food as a symbol of as well as its effect on America. The episode, in fact, exploits the contemporary distrust of fast food by making food into a literal weapon against humanity.

Bobby and Sam examine Dean's second sandwich outside the restaurant. The sandwich spontaneously gushes out a stream of gray snot-like goo. The sandwich becomes monstrous in both its effect on mind and body and in its appearance. The ultimate fast food concern of what is really in the food is given a distinct and horrific image; the slammer is the ultimate "McFrankenfood" (Spurlock 115). The season's villain has been creating a food additive which will subdue the human race. A Leviathan at the meat distribution and test center explains, "The food additive which I've introduced into the turducken has a near 100 percent rate of effectiveness. Once the subject tries it, they crave more within a few hours. With the very first dose it starts to work on the DNA slowing the metabolism, causing weight gain, and adapting their emotional range, which makes them perfectly complacent." Significantly, the explanation of the TDK's true purpose is provided while the man stands above a test room containing an American family: mother, father, and son are each obese, and they sit on a couch staring at a television screen and eating turducken sandwiches. The only sounds heard are loud chewing and the murmur of the television. Large, unspeaking, and eating fast food—this is an extreme image of the American family transformed from its traditional nostalgic form by the fast food industry "in the interest of maximizing profit" (Reiter 15). They are "eating without regard to consequence or cultural tradition" (or to the grandmother who appears to have died) which according to Michael Newbury "is all that zombies do" (104). *Supernatural* is extending the "standardization of food" (Kincheloe 3) to human beings both through their eating and in order to make humans become food. Humans then become mindless eaters; they become a form of zombie.

In writing about the relationship between zombie films, the food industry, and the food apocalypse, Michael Newbury asserts, "Zombie films show in particularly striking ways the depth and breadth of cultural penetration that food-crisis thinking has achieved" (111). *Supernatural*'s TDK zombies serve the same purpose, but instead of pointing only "to vaguely conceived corporate, military, medical, or governmental blunders [that unleash] a transformative plague," *Supernatural* places a monster at the head of the corporate food industry and shows that industry purposefully creating zombies (Newbury 100). There is no subtlety about invoking the myth of the evil food corporation. Dick Roman, the human persona taken by the Leviathan leader, represents the food industry and all the distrust of it. He is an American "billionaire ... on the corporate takeover warpath" who ironically claims to "believe in good old American values, like unlimited growth [and] merging—coming out on top" ("There Will Be Blood," 7.22). Of course, the "good old American values" Dick Roman references are not family or freedom, but food, specifically fast food, and its ability to produce unlimited growth in weight and allow Roman to surpass humans at the top of the food chain. Roman is further shown acquiring the generically named SucroCorp, "among the world's leading manufacturers in high fructose corn syrup" ("There Will Be Blood"). SucroCorp invokes "the troubling and seemingly sinister science of artificial flavorings and their tendency to make junk food nearly addictive" (Newbury 94). As the new method of distribution for the zombie-creating food additive, sucrose is efficient and far-reaching. Such a wide distribution indicates that Roman's corporation, like "beef factories[,] are models of waste-not-want-not efficiency"(Spurlock 103). Instead of investigating the food industry, *Supernatural* explodes related fears and thus demonstrates the apocalyptic potential of the pervasiveness of the food industry and the American love of fast food.

Differing from a common zombie apocalyptic narrative, fear in *Supernatural*'s seventh season is displaced from the zombie body and focused upon something nostalgically viewed as safe, causing food to become the monster. Fear of food is shown in Sam and Dean's attempts to avoid the widely present sucrose. In "There Will Be Blood," Dean desperately holds up a packaged pie and asks, "Hey, hey, this one says natural. That means it's safe, right?" Sam responds, "I hate to break it to you, but corn syrup is natural, technically," and holds up their only real options in the store, bananas and water. This food buying scene reveals a prevalent consumer anxiety concerning what is really known about purchased food. The scene complicates the definition of "natural" on multiple levels. In relation to food, "natural" can range from organically grown vegetables to corn syrup, and what is "natural" is additionally being equated to what is "safe." Newbury indicates, "if food apocalypse narratives tend to progress partly by offering compelling tales of corporeal, environmental, and corporate horror, they tend also to insist on the capacity of individuals to recover the natural world that seemingly omnipotent corporations are obscuring" (96). In other words, when the industrial world that society has created becomes monstrous, the natural world becomes the hope for safety. Dean's disappointment in discovering the current manifestation of corporate monstrosity, corn syrup, in his favorite dessert which is advertised as natural suggests that "natural" is not necessarily a symbol for safety, but rather, like the pie of earlier seasons, a façade offering only the appearance of desired safety and comfort. "Natural" is obviously not simply defined in a show titled *Supernatural*. The main characters are constantly facing creatures who mean to displace humans at the top of the food chain, and in the sense that "natural" is normal, they struggle personally with occupying "natural" gender roles and their lack of a socially "natural" home and family.

The Last Bite

Pie and burgers symbolize such struggles as they represent traditional gender roles and a traditional nuclear family dynamic, but the inaccessibility of these traditional and nostalgic norms makes food monstrous for its false representations, and it becomes increasingly monstrous, on an apocalyptic scale, as it comes to act as a weapon representative of food industries. Ironically, the norms for which Dean Winchester is nostalgic are rooted in 1950s, '60s, and '70s Americana, which is also the period of the rise of fast and "convenience food" in America (Inness 163). Therefore, even the food which represents nostalgia carries its own falsities.

Supernatural however does offer hope in its deconstruction of American nostalgia—it simply refuses to make the gesture Newbury criticizes by relying on the natural for hope. Instead, by reveling in food fears, subverting nostalgic ideals of family, and presenting the un-natural and the supernatural, the series is questioning the American notion of naturalness, specifically the "natural" family. Mary making sandwiches or Bobby's undead wife baking pies was too unreal, but so was the test center family eating in front of the television in ignorance of the dead grandmother in the corner. These extremes allow for "real" representations of family presented when Bobby, Sam, and Dean eat at Biggerson's, when Dean cooks for Sam while living in the Bunker, the former Men of Letters site they adopted as a home in season eight,[6] or when Mary reveals she could never bake; all her pies were store bought.

Such unconventional family moments have allowed *Supernatural* to develop its own internal nostalgia represented by the season one and two tagline, "Saving people, hunting things, the family business." The series is grounded in a long-standing family tradition of hunting which is developed throughout the series as the Winchester brothers discover more about their ancestry. Just as the show grounds itself in its own nostalgic desire for family, it is simultaneously grounded in a larger American nostalgia. Viewing the series through foodways displays the gendered relationship to food, a desire for the mother figure as represented with pie, and a distrust of the fast food industry, but while these examples vary, they are not isolated foodways. Rather, the movement from pie and familial desires, to the mistrust of these desires, and to weaponized food and a food-zombie/Leviathan apocalypse, reflects the American relationship to food over the past 65 years as constantly shifting, often between desire and mistrust, but grounded in nostalgia. In deconstructing nostalgic food images and interacting with common food rumors, *Supernatural* indicates that television does not merely incorporate food as a part of everyday life but demonstrates a profound understanding of both the history and complexity of American foodways.

Notes

1. A seminal work in cultural anthropology and food studies, *Sweetness and Power*'s social history of sugar and its economic implications has illuminated larger social, cultural, and economic implications of food, especially as it relates to desire. See Camp 25 for more on the development and definition of foodways, the folkloric study of eating habits and attitudes about food related to a group or culture.

2. Paul Freedman et al. chart an expansive recent global academic history of food in the AHA sponsored text *Food in Time and Place: The American Historical Association Companion to Food History*.

3. Fast Food rumors specifically refer to rumors of contamination in fast food. Patricia A. Turner's *I Heard It Through the Grapevine: Rumor in African-American Culture* provides a well-known explanation of rumor related to folklore study and fast food contamination.

4. For more on the connections between food and memory, see Mintz's *Tasting Food* and Parsecoli.

5. See Kincheloe for more on McDonald's as an American symbol.

6. Dean's cooking remains in line with men's cooking or "men's food" (Innes 24). See "Trial and Error" (8.14), "The Great Escapist" (8.21), "There's No Place Like Home" (10.11), and "Brother's Keeper" (10.23) for examples of Dean's cooking.

Works Cited

Baron, Cynthia, et al. *Appetites and Anxieties*. Wayne State UP, 2013. ebrary.
Bordo, Susan. "Hunger as Ideology." *Eating Culture,* edited by Ron Scapp and Brian Seitz, U of New York P, 1998, pp. 11–35.
Calvert, Bronwen. "Angels, Demons, and Damsels in Distress: The Representation of Women in *Supernatural*." *TV Goes to Hell: An Unconventional Road Map of* Supernatural, edited by Stacey Abbott and David Lavery, ECW Press, 2011, pp. 90–104.
Camp, Charles. *American Foodways: When, Why and How We Eat in America*. August House, Inc., 1989.
Charles, Nickie, and Marion Kerr. *Women, Food, and Families*. Manchester UP, 1988.
Crowther, Gillian. *Eating Culture: An Anthropological Guide to Food*. Toronto UP, 2013.
Finkelstein, Joanne. "Dining Out: The Hyperreality of Appetite." *Eating Culture*, edited by Ron Scapp and Brian Seitz, U of New York P, 1998, pp. 201–215.
Freedman, Paul, et al., editors. *Food in Time and Place: The American Historical Association Companion to Food History*, U of California P, 2014. ProQuest Ebook Central. 15 Sept. 2017.
Inness, Sherrie A. *Dinner Roles: American Women and Culinary Culture*. U of Iowa P, 2001.

Kincheloe, Joe L. *The Sign of the Burger*. Temple UP, 2002.
Koven, Mikel J., and Gunella Thorgeirsdottir. "Televisual Foklore: Rescuing *Supernatural* from the Fakelore Realm." *TV Goes to Hell: An Unofficial Road Map of* Supernatural, edited by Stacey Abbott and David Lavery, ECW Press, 2011, pp. 187–202.
Mintz, Sidney W. *Sweetness and Power: The Place of Sugar in Modern History*. Penguin Books, 1985.
_____. *Tasting Food, Tasting Freedom—Excursions Into Eating, Culture, and the Past*. Boston: Beacon Press, 1996.
Newbury, Michael. "Fast Zombie/Slow Zombie: Food Writing, Horror Movies, and Agribusiness Apocalypse." *American Literary History*, vol. 24, no.1, 2012, pp. 87–114, *Project Muse*. Accessed 19 Mar. 2016.
Parasecoli, Fabio. *Bite Me: Food and Popular Culture*. Berg, 2008.
"Pie." *Supernatural* Wiki: *A Supernatural Canon & Fandom Resource*, http://supernatural.wikia.com/wiki/Pie. Accessed 4 Nov. 2017.
Reiter, Ester. *Making Fast Food: From the Frying Pan Into the Fryer*. McGill-Queen's UP, 1996.
Roth, LuAnne. "Beyond *Communitas*: Cinematic Food Events and the Negotiation of Power, Belonging, and Exclusion." *Folklore/Cinema: Popular Film as Vernacular Culture*, edited by Sharon R. Sherman and Mikel J. Koven. Utah State UP, 2007, pp. 197–220.
Schlosser, Eric. *Fast Food Nation*. Houghton Mifflin Company, 2001.
Smith, Andrew F. *Eating History: Turning Points in the Making of American Cuisine*. Columbia UP, 2009.
Spurlock, Morgan. *Don't Eat This Book: Fast Food and the Super Sizing of America*. G.P Putnam's Sons, 2005.
Turner, Patricia A. *I Heard It Through the Grapevine: Rumor in African-American Culture*. U of California P, 1993.

A Cicatricial Romance

Metanarrative, the Textual Wound and a Grotesque View in Supernatural

LINDA HOWELL

"Everything is in here. I mean everything. From the racist truck to—to me having sex. I'm full-frontal in here, dude."
—Dean Winchester, "The Monster at the End of This Book" [4.18]

"I write things and then they come to life. Yeah, no, I'm definitely a god. A cruel, cruel, capricious god. The things I put you through—The physical beatings alone."
—Chuck Shurley

When it comes to the possibility of interpretations, CW's *Supernatural* represents a tesseract, especially when thinking about the deployment of metanarrative. Unlike most other early 21st century cultural productions, *Supernatural* has experienced, or more appropriately *has caused to be experienced,* an untended and organic evolution of narrative, an evolution that cracks the pavement and creeps up into the borders between the stones. This essay explores the show's metanarrative and wonders if it can be reframed as evidence of a traumatic event, where the invasion of the author-god and its eventual dismantling demonstrate an irreparable textual wound.

There is a phenomenological experience at play in the text of *Supernatural* that continually returns to this wound, attempting in each return to reframe the experience and in each return, rewounding and building layer upon layer of scar tissue around what I would argue is an initial violation that never recovers its original elasticity. The story cannot sustain a metacritical eye on itself and instead it buckles under its own self-knowledge, becoming less and less about story and more about the story of the story. This essay ponders what happens when a text tries to cognitize a self-inflicted wound. And is it self-inflicted? Does the introduction of a meta space, especially in a show like *Supernatural*, portend a previous trauma? Is this the reenactment of an unseen or denied wound? This essay argues that indeed the introduction of meta is an answering volley to an encroachment, an obscene pain the show both confesses and dismisses simultaneously—the pain of the fanspace.

With most trauma, there is a wound, whether it be physical, psychological, or spiritual. In the field of trauma studies, the wound takes on various incarnations. From a literary studies perspective, narrative can act to reframe a wound. In her recapturing of psychoanalytic literary study through the lens of trauma, Cathy Caruth examines major thinkers and their contributions to psychoanalysis (Freud, Lacan, de Man) and reconceptualizes these works to view these potential breaks in the symbolic order as traumatic. In that reconceptualization, Caruth gestures towards this complex system of repetition and deferral as primary modes of coping with the traumatic event. Caruth aligns with another major contributor to this discussion, Geoffrey Hartman, who employs a similar psychoanalytic frame in which literature becomes a place where traumatic events can be seen through the process of symbol and metaphor. However, in the lines of psychoanalytic thought, while the phenomenological is present, the experience of an injury is present, the presumption of event as wound complicates the discussion, as Jeffrey Alexander notes in his critique of what he describes as lay trauma theory.

In his "Toward a Theory of Cultural Trauma," Alexander rejects the psychoanalytic exercise as well as other popular concepts of trauma as "lay trauma theory" (2). His rejection relies on the denial of the initial traumatic event as traumatic, claiming that enlightenment ideals presuppose a natural order to the event whereas Alexander focuses on de-naturalizing events as traumatic. Instead he considers how the cultures and collectives give meaning to traumatic events: "For traumas to emerge at the level of the collectivity, social crises must become cultural crises" (10). In Alexander's reading, the collective and not the event have meaning-making power. Alexander proposes that it is a Weberian "carrier group" that first institutes the message of the trauma, and from there four key components must be constructed in the messaging for the trauma event to become traumatic: the pain, the victim, the effect of the pain, and the responsible party of the injury (12–15).

To examine *Supernatural* as a potential cultural trauma, we must first establish the social groups involved. It is with Alexander's approach that I want to consider how *Supernatural*'s metanarrative becomes a traumatic event and message and how that trauma starts out as a strict patriarchal message, wherein the traditional concept of the single author becomes both victim and victimizer in the continued messaging of the show's self-aware and self-storying moments. Here, we have two primary collectives: writer and fan. One group appears to be an elite group, i.e., the writer who has access and authority, while the other group can be defined as marginal or in literary terms, paratextual. So in this reading, I posit that both viewer and writer are two collectives which end up circling around a singular "pain" that becomes traumatic, and that trauma gets acted and reenacted in *Supernatural*'s text.

This first full-on meta episode, "The Monster at the End of This Book" (4.18), provides an initial bookend balanced against the final bookends of *Supernatural*'s meta, namely the death of Charlie Bradbury in season ten ("Dark Dynasty," 10.21) and the exit of Chuck in season eleven ("Alpha and Omega," 11.23), both of which close out this initial event and the subsequent retellings. In this reading, the text answers the question posed by Alexander by stating what happened as a series of metafictional moves which were both self-aware and self-unaware at the time of their occurrence. These shifts penetrate plot in such a fundamental way that the show must consistently try to recover and redeem this wound by assimilating the meta through the evolution of Chuck to "God" and inclusion of fan figures like Becky Rosen and Charlie Bradbury while simultaneously denying its meta by creating Metatron as narrative foil, a superscript to the superscript, a move which risks implosion.

Bring the Pain

In his four-component litmus test for trauma, Alexander begins by asking the question, "what actually happened?" (12). This question seeks to both objectivize the event and contextualize the subjectivity of how that event gets interpreted and remitted. In other words, he poses the question as definitional so the affect can be cordoned off. This event or action becomes the "nature of the pain" in his reading. For *Supernatural,* the "event" or "pain" that gets messaged into a trauma is the *initial breaking of the fourth wall* that appears in season four's "The Monster at the End of This Book" and gets remessaged (and remassaged) through the show's run.

The most powerful symbol of this textual wound appears in the form of Chuck Shurley, a seemingly peripheral character introduced in the show's fourth season episode "The Monster at the End of This Book," which is the show's second attempt at metafiction. Metafiction is the move that postmodern critiques often note in self-reflexive storytelling, where the story becomes a type of artificial intelligence of itself or a pseudo-metaphysical voice that steps outside its textual landscape to comment on its own geography. Whichever metaphor we may want to use, the point of metafiction is meta, being above and beyond. It can be dangerous ego territory. While *Supernatural* edged into metafiction with its second season episode "Hollywood Babylon" (2.18), the show did not fully commit to a metafictional space until the introduction of Chuck Shurley and the series of books called "Supernatural," which, in the show, represent each episode of the first three seasons.

Chuck enters the scene in a particular and peculiar fashion where his presence is clearly a semi-parodic and self-effacing depiction of the show's creator, Eric Kripke, as a narcissitic and self-indulgent "god." Carver Edlund, which is a portmanteau for writers Jeremy Carver and Ben Edlund, is later revealed to be Chuck Shurley, who authored a series of in-series books called "Supernatural." In her examination of the show's use of metanarrative, Laura Felschow observes, "While this is a relationship referred to in jest, underneath the joke lies a kernel of truth, even more so later on when Chuck is revealed to be a prophet whose 'Winchester Gospel' has earned him protection from the archangels." Felschow reads the power dynamic quite accurately in this episode, where the show co-opts control of the fan image, and as her essay was published during the fifth season, one can see the set up that viewers will eventually experience in later seasons. I would extend her thoughts to cite a simultaneous and subterraneous effect that emerges from this superscript footnote. Like a proto–*The Talking Dead* move, the show opens up a commentary space in the narrative by invoking both fangirl Sera and online fan/critic Simpatico. For those unfamiliar with *The Talking Dead*, it is the post–*Walking Dead* episode metahour hosted by Chris Hardwick and on which producers, writers, actors, and celebrity fans discuss the show and the just-aired episode. *The Talking Dead,* then, provides an authorized space for metacommentary, whereas *Supernatural* created an unspoken space inside its own text. The episode includes a fictional message board, which was a popular form of commentary before social media outlets such as Facebook and Twitter made immediate access to creators possible (and probable).

By acknowledging both message boards and explicitly invoking the world of fan fiction, the show creates a diegetic place. Pairing the inclusion of author with viewer/fan proposes a discourse community that hitherto had been denied by the television community, except in rare cases such as *Star Trek* and *The X-Files*. While the show's in-text fan commentary as well as the gesture toward fan fiction can be viewed parodically, they can also be seen as the first textual "pain." In this episode, there is a series of taboo spaces that get unfolded, and as Lynn Zubernis and Katherine Larsen propose in *Fandom at the Crossroads,* there is the possibility of fans feeling shamed by such exposure, that the show now highlights these activities and presents them back to the fan but also to a larger audience. However, here, I would invoke Alexander and the question we are tending to: what actually happened?

What actually happened was that the show included a series of books called "Supernatural," written by Carver Edlund who, upon investigation, was revealed to be Chuck Shurley, a prophet. The books represent his ability to see what events are about to transpire. They are popular among a small group of devoted readers, who include the publisher, Sera, and selected online fans. Chuck's ability makes him a target for angels who are trying to stop Lilith from opening the seals that will release Lucifer. While the inherent humor of a book series that aligns with each episode provides much needed laughter in an otherwise dark season wherein the brothers are being ripped apart by different fidelities, the violence of this intrusion is understated but frames the show's meta from there on out as a traumatic event tied closely to a particular type of textual invasion, one that is sexualized from its inception by the character of Dean Winchester and is exacerbated by the entrance of Becky Rosen.

The Victim(s)

In his second and third questions, Alexander posits that trauma must also have a named victim and that "[e]ven when the nature of the pain has been crystallized and the identity of the victim established, there remains the highly significant question of the relation of the victim to the wider audience" (14). If what actually happened in *Supernatural* was the violation of plot for metanarrative, then the first victims start in-text and extend outward to encompass two communities, writer and fan. The victims of the pain seem, at first, to be characters, but I will move this argument from the victim as character to the victim as text, where the text becomes the substitute for the author/writer and which masks victimizing the viewer, which comes into full being in later seasons. What had begun as an indulgent narrative move opens up a consistent issue in the storyworld of *Supernatural*, that of the condition of the feminine within (and without) the text. This section could name several victims, but it will focus on two categories: Dean Winchester as text and then Becky Rosen and Charlie Bradbury as fan.

As noted in the previous section, one reading of the metanarrative arc introduced in *Supernatural* is one of trauma, and arguably the first named victim is Dean Winchester. The events in "The Monster at the End of This Book" seem like a fourth wall break in the narrative, but they are in fact simply intrusions that get interpreted as violations, but such violations take on a distinct hue: sexual violation. While Chuck represents a parodic author self-insert, a reader should heed the character of Dean Winchester. As he reclines on the bed in a run-down motel room, he is astounded at how the books describe him having sex and that he is "full frontal." Dean is the first to coherently address, in the show, the metanarrative, and his reaction is one of horror. He experiences the metanarrative as being exposed to an audience, but Dean is neither the voice of the fan nor the voice of the viewer, as we will see in subsequent episodes. Dean Winchester is the voice of the "canon" since his continuing perspective, until season ten's "Fan Fiction" (10.05), is preservative, even conservative.

Dean's response partly defines *Supernatural*'s metafiction as a sexualized and gendered space. It's nonconsensual, voyeuristic, and exhibitionist, and that theme is further exacerbated in the episode by vignettes of meta interaction such as when Sera is more than willing to expose her tattoo to the brothers' gaze or when the text explicitly references slash (same sex pairing) fandom involving incestuous sexual behavior between the brothers. The incest reference stands as a noted point, as I will show, to the finale of Chuck Shurley's meta presence in season eleven when he exits the text with his sister, Amara.

Dean's affect about the metafiction is an insight into the canon's unacknowledged response to an anxiety the text can never fully articulate. Fan practices that involve imposing romance on the text is a genre violence, a superimposition of a traditionally feminized reading onto an often distinctly masculine genre, the road narrative. Additionally, Dean's response highlights his hyper-masculinized persona, a persona that can represent a type of patriarchal conceit, both in terms of characterizing a hero but further in defining who is allowed to tell the story. This struggle over storytelling goes beyond Chuck and Dean, though, in season eight when the character of Metatron is introduced, which I will consider in the next section.

Throughout the first ten seasons, Dean's response to meta undergoes a series of oscillations. In "The Monster at the End of This Book" Dean is immediately and forcefully resistant to the metanarrative, a resistance which continues in later episodes such as when Becky appears in "Sympathy for the Devil" (5.01). However, his affect is augmented in season five's "The Real Ghostbusters" (5.09). Dean scolds Sam and Dean cosplayers for devaluing the Winchesters' experience, but ultimately, in an obvious pathos indulgence, he sees the sentimental value of the convention and fan space when he discovers the cosplayers are a gay couple who found each other through the fandom and that their belief in the Winchesters renews Dean's belief as well. It's a move the text makes again and again, the struggle between resenting the intrusiveness of fandom and appreciating its importance to the very fabric of the show's survival and storytelling.

When Becky reappears in "Season Seven, Time for a Wedding!" (7.08), she returns as a physical threat, not a textual one. She uses dark magic to force Sam into marrying her, which forever demonizes her character for not only Dean but for the text as well. Dean, in fact, warns the newly introduced Garth away from Becky. Becky has one final reference in text, and that's during a season nine episode that focuses on the character of Charlie Bradbury. Dean starts to appreciate the fanspace of *Supernatural* with the introduction of Charlie Bradbury. Interestingly enough, Charlie's introduction is set against Becky Rosen's fan persona. This contention returns in two episodes: season six's "The French Mistake" (6.15) and season seven's "Season Seven, Time for a Wedding!" In "The French Mistake" the story revolves around Sam and Dean being sent to an alternative universe where they are Jared Padalecki and Jensen Ackles, who play Sam and Dean Winchester on a fictional television series called *Supernatural*. Shortly before the episode aired, the producers and cast attended a Paley Television Festival panel where it became clear that for viewers to make meaning they would need a certain level of knowledge about fan practices.

Dean eventually succumbs to the sentimental draw of fandom in the 200th episode, "Fan Fiction." The episode focuses on a monster of the week story in which an all-girl high school is putting on a performance of "Supernatural," but as adapted by the students, and the monster is trying to stop the show. While weak in plot, the episode digs up as many fan references as possible, from same sex relationship readings to metacommentary and critique (e.g., the disappearance of the prized necklace that Sam gave to Dean when they were children and which Dean wore during the first five seasons but threw out during season five in a fit of anger at Sam and which was never addressed in show). The ramification of the episode, or the moral lesson, is that fans are acknowledged and their readings are legitimate, but they are outside the text. It is Dean who delivers the succinct line when encouraging Marie, the director and writer of the play within the play. Marie points out that Dean does not even like the play, to which he responds, "No. Like not at all. But you do, okay." This interchange echoes, in many ways, Dean's evolution in the episode "The Real Ghostbusters," wherein he achieves some resistant level of acceptance, but the parallel also provides a marked change in the sentimentality. Where in season five Dean's acceptance seems contingent on the events of the episode, "Fan Fiction" uses Dean as the voice of the reluctant canon, and his acceptance is more about the show's acceptance of fan intrusion than it is about the character's acceptance.

What starts out as Dean being watched turns into Dean watching. Dean's witnessing of the metanarrative's external effects leads to the rare (and truly theatrical) breaking of the fourth wall in "Fan Fiction" where Jensen Ackles turns to look at the audience in camera, but the episode does more than reference the fandom in detail, it positions Dean as seeing how the story of the Winchesters has impacted the world of these young women. His evolving perspective is aided by the continued presence of Charlie Bradbury, who is arguably the redemptive move the show makes to save the "fangirl" from the horrors it visited on its first incarnation, Becky.

There are inherent problems with this approach, such as the gendering and aging of fandom, which was a problem in the previous "The Real Ghostbusters" episode where the fandom was represented as mostly men with the lone exception of Becky Rosen. The show, much like Dean Winchester, has a binary view of fandom, which is in part why Dean, more than any other character, represents the "text," and in a later section of this essay, I will argue that introducing Metatron is the show's way of intercepting that binariness. The long-running nature of the show also contributes to the generational scaffolding, such as Becky and Charlie representing adult female fans, but in the episode "Fan Fiction," fans are portrayed as adolescent girls.

Becky Winchester (née Rosen) and Charlie Bradbury provide a strange counter-commentary to Chuck's presence and Dean's resistance. These characters, in many ways, suffer the trauma of the text with one being figuratively violated (Becky) and the other being literally violated (Charlie). When Chuck returns in season five he recruits a fan, a superfan named Becky Rosen, to help him assist the Winchesters. Becky's appearance is controversial for a number of reasons. Becky is a "Wincest" (fan fiction that represents the brothers Sam and Dean as sexual lovers) fan and she is prone to invade Sam Winchester's personal space, and in a later episode in season seven, Becky drugs Sam and marries him under those nonconsensual circumstances. The show's ambivalent, and at times malevolent, characterization of Becky produces a certain view of the fan, as useful asset but at the cost of being an imminent sexual threat.

As Coker and Benefiel note, the show's view of fan practices can near the uncomfortable in text, such as what is encompassed by the Becky Rosen character, a character which Charlotte Howell reads through the lens of discipleship and as the "fan avatar" (22). Becky is a lightning rod for academic discourse and fan representation since she is the first clear one-to-one fan brought into an authorized text and kept there for an extended period of time as part of the narrative. She is not simply introduced as spectacle but rather as integral to the plot's progression due to her knowledge of the demon-killing gun in season five's "The Real Ghostbusters." In text, the gun was stolen in a season three episode, but in the books as in the aired episode, the reader/viewer has the dramatic irony perspective of knowing something that the characters do not. But Becky is also hypersexualized in each episode she appears in.

When Becky appears in "Sympathy for the Devil" she is writing a passage for a Sam and Dean fan fiction, a romance which implies a sexual encounter is about to occur between the brothers. Her only other appearance in the episode, when she visits the brothers, includes her immediately invading Sam's space and touching him without consent, lingering long enough that Sam has to ask her to stop. In her next appearance, "The Real Ghostbusters," she is the object of Chuck's affection, a sexual affection, that we later learn of in "Swan Song" (5.22). And her sexual arc reaches its violent zenith in her final onscreen appearance, or final as of the writing of this essay, "Season 7, Time for a Wedding!" Becky's arc takes a decisive turn towards sexual violence when she makes a deal with a crossroads demon to put Sam under a love spell so he would marry her. Becky's invasion of personal space that had been played off as more humorous than violent in season five becomes villainous stalking in season seven.

Appropriately, perhaps, as Becky disappears from the text, the character of Charlie Bradbury enters. Bradbury, as Kristina Busse sees her, represents a rare form of female fan presence, and especially in the hyper-masculinized space of *Supernatural* (111). Bradbury has received critical, academic, and popular acclaim as an unrepentant geekgirl, but her introduction at the moment of Becky's narrative demise offers room for discourse about not only the gendered role of the fan in the show but the sexualized role of the fan. While Becky, through one interpretive lens, presents a dark and obsessive kind of sexuality, Bradbury's sexuality clearly takes both brothers out of the dynamic. Her homosexuality is a key component to her entrance, and through her time in the show, her desire for women constitutes a narrative nexus in many episodes. Her sexuality is not the totality of her characterization, but without it the show may have had a very different character, as Walton notes "she also completely avoids the typical heteronormative role as potential love interest to the Winchesters" (119). Instead of providing a one-to-one replacement analysis, I'd like to consider how sexuality is translated between these characters as an annotation or companion narrative to Dean's perception of the metanarrative as sexual violation, and how Charlie extends the narrative into a fanspace that predicts the show resolution about fandom in "Fan Fiction" and tries to recoup the invasion/penetration narrative into one of companionship and affection.

If we read the initial metanarrative event as a sexualized metaphor, which gets translated into a traumatic experience, then the evolution of Becky from a woman with little heed for boundaries to one who grotesquely violates those boundaries is startling and revelatory. When Charlie enters, though, the "fangirl" gets reinterpreted away from the text, into an almost abstract version of what being a fan entails, which aligns more with Dean Winchester's fan practice such as his love of television shows.

While she is moved away from the text, Charlie still retains the more affectionate qualities of Becky: she provides assistance to the brothers, has passion for the things she loves, etc., but whereas Becky's sole connection to the show was via her "discipleship" (to use Howell's term), Charlie's textual loves exist outside of the show and the metatext of the show within the show. She is a *fan* but not a *fan of*, and that is an important, even crucial, distinction.

Charlie's arc, then, demonstrates a kind of redemption arc for the fangirl. She evolves from hacker/comic con nerd in season eight to prized (and invited) family member in season ten, and one way to read her juxtaposition to Becky is that she does not pose a sexual threat to the brothers. Her textual loves, as noted above, exist far away from the Winchester brothers. They are not replacements or icons for the love of the text. Charlie's fanspace takes dramatically different representation. For example, when she appears in season eight for a "LARPing" episode her fan perspective reveals Dean's love of role play as a fan-like experience ("LARP and the Real Girl," 8.11) and again in "Pac Man Fever" (8.20) her love for Tolkien's *The Hobbit* (1937) is contextualized as a personal narrative. Charlie is given a kind of storyspace that Becky was denied; her fan practices and fan loves are narratively important and organic, and more crucially, they are inside the text in a way that Becky's fan practice was not. Becky was always an imposition, an invasion of the outside-the-text onto the inside-the-text, whereas Charlie's work as fan is an extension of her presence, a fill-in-the-blank narrative that offers depth and does not disrupt her move into the center of the text as a character who belongs in the story world.

Charlie's "official" entrance into the world of hunting comes in the season nine episode, "Slumber Party" (9.04). This episode is one of the show's most intelligent, albeit complex, commentaries on the act of reading and what belongs in the public domain since it is a tongue-in-cheek adaptation of *The Wizard of Oz* (1939). It is both appropriate and ironic that when Charlie returns as a full-fledged hunter in this episode that she invokes Becky's name as the source for her knowledge about the *Supernatural* books. Her citation of Becky is humorous and yet traumatic; the Winchesters' reactions are telling. The brothers cringe at the mention of her name and try to deny her in the moment. This scene is a poignant example of the moment the text denies one fan presence in favor of their replacement. The scene and the episode punctuate Charlie's narrative evolution from fan as character to character as fan; she quite literally falls in love with a character and enters into the text via a magic portal where she begins her journey as a hunter, but it is *another* text.

Yet, for Charlie, the cost of entering the hunting world and the emotional inner circle of the Winchesters is high. When she returns in season ten, she is hardened but also a tad more cynical of the world; she is truly part of the storyscape at this point. And as Charlie begins to own her agency as a copiously integrated character, she becomes vulnerable to the dangers of that world. The price of entering the story, of belonging to the story, and of being respected and valued by the Winchesters is simple and tragic: the story will weaponize that emotional connection against the main characters. Whereas Becky disappears and suffers a metaphorical demise, Charlie's importance to the text requires that her disappearance become a physical demise.

Bradbury's violent death rattled the fandom and critics alike. The Geekiary's Angel Wilson, among others such as Carly Lane at *i09*, noted that Charlie was a lone LGBT+ character and her death was especially felt as a loss of representation, but further the way she died also caught many viewers off guard. This death inflicted yet another wound on the text and on fan representation in the text, which had a fully redemptive arc with Charlie. While Charlie, or an alternative universe version of her, returns in the show's thirteenth season, her original death stands as a hallmark event for women in the show and adds another brutal end to the presence of the female fan.

Becky and Charlie open up the question about why and how this narrative and its accompanying metanarrative takes on such a sinister tone and how it eventually tries to resolve or re-salve the textual wound it has suffered. To answer that question, I'll turn to the final component of Alexander's litmus for a cultural trauma: the responsible party.

The Responsible Parties

The issue of the responsible party produces ambivalence because it goes back and forth throughout the seasons, but arguably the show is ultimately the responsible party. It inflicts wounds on both itself and its fandom. For Alexander the question posed about responsibility is simple: who initially caused the injury? (15). The show, here, answers that question in two ways. First it introduces the metanarrative, but second, and more importantly, it reinforces the dissolving metanarrative by including the character of Metatron, who becomes a meta-meta voice in the story, one that slowly replaces Dean as the dominant narrative critique.

In *Supernatural*, the initial wound, the meta wound, comes in the episode "Hollywood Babylon" where the story is that of a ghost haunting a sound stage for a low-budget horror film. The episode, however, introduces the names of behind-the-scenes players from the show. The cataclysm of this wound does not become readily apparent, though, until the show inserts a self-reflective and self-reflexive metanarrative in season four via its "play within a play" adaptation, the book series "Supernatural." The books and their author, Chuck Shurley, mark the intrusive wound whereby the text becomes a *memento mori*, of sorts, which effectively kills the story but keeps its skull.

The text goes even further into this metaphor in season six when, in "The French Mistake," the show indulges in a sharp self-critique that (a) kills off its creator, Eric Kripke; (b) inserts a layer of misogynistic commentary by way of having every man in the production meeting dismiss Sera Gamble, who was showrunner at the time of the episode, which is an interesting meta-

meta commentary since she would have had to sign off on this interpretation; and (c) pointedly calls out fans for intrusive curiosity in the naming of the episode. The phrase "the French mistake" comes from a metanarrative moment in the film *Blazing Saddles* (1974). The end of this film includes an over-the-top musical number that dissolves the audience's belief in the film's western setting. The musical number shows a room full of dancing men who sing, and one line is about a French mistake, which is clearly a mockery of a popular RPF (real person fiction) fandom that was prevalent at the time in the show's fan paratexts. This episode is a clear mirror to the tenth season "Fan Fiction." Both episodes deliberately include specific paratextual readings, interpretations, and fan practices to highlight them and address them in-text.

From the ashes of the metanarrative, though, a secondary metacommentary emerges in season eight, and that happens with Metatron. In his first episode, "The Great Escapist" (8.21), Metatron declares that "[w]hen you create stories, you become gods, of tiny, intricate dimensions unto themselves. So many worlds! I have read ... as much as it's possible for an angel to read, and I haven't caught up." Metatron's almost fetish-level obsession with storytelling becomes a defining feature of his character and it collides, in part, with the show's struggle with metanarrative as a whole.

Metatron provides an authorial layer to the metanarrative, a voice set forth to contend with the conflicts which arise when a work tries to simultaneously create and critique itself, especially in a continuous cycle. For example, in the appropriately titled "Meta Fiction" (9.18), Metatron ponders, "What makes a story work? Is it the plot, the characters, the text? The subtext? And who gives a story meaning? Is it the writer? Or you? Tonight, I thought I would tell you a little story and let you decide." Again, this tension of how to make meaning and who has the power over that meaning gets addressed again and again in text. And Metatron's contentious attitude toward God, who we later learn is Chuck, feeds this anger. The return to that original wound stresses the trauma, in this reading. The commentary constitutes a rewounding and a rescarring, a cicatrix let's say, that does not get formally resolved until the eleventh season and the resolution of the Chuck Shurley storyline.

The show gives this character an enduring and eternal place in its narrative space. Chuck, in this reading, represents the wound between the external, paratextual space of the show's viewer and the previously internal, fortressed space of the show's text, often referred to as its "canon." Chuck's appearance, then, breaches these two spaces and does so in a metaphorically violent way, as noted in the quotations that frame this entry. When Chuck Shurley returns to the story in the final arc of the eleventh season, he not only provides resolution for Metatron, but he also brings the metanarrative to a sort of conclusion that echoes back to his first episode. In "Don't Call

Me Shurley" (11.20) Chuck's return is highlighted as the return of God. The entire episode revolves around Metatron and Chuck delving into Chuck's absence, becoming a psychoanalytic self-examination of the show and its storytelling. Chuck maintains a kind of disdain for the story which Metatron, now contrite for his actions, challenges. If read through a certain lens, this dialogue is about inheritance. It's an opportunity for the writer to defy the author, which is the nature of the original wound in "The Monster at the End of This Book." But Chuck's appearance goes further to address the implosion the story has experienced from its metanarrative.

Chuck's relationship with Amara purposefully returns the viewer to the incest interpretation that framed the initial metanarrative. Their coming back together is a way to resolve that wound, to rename it and retell it as a non-sexualized family romance. But to do so, Amara must take on the mantle of many figures. She must become Becky's replacement as well as Charlie's; she's sexualized but simultaneously familiarized. She must invade the story as complete apocalypse. She must seduce the canon's primary voice, i.e., Dean Winchester, while invoking all the uncomfortable levels of such seduction, which is why her growth from infant to woman is so important to this reading. We have to see her as a child to make the sexualization even more grotesque and resonant.

Her position as seducer/sister defines her place as the untamed, unattainable female companion to the show and its creators. This reading is poignant when we consider Chuck's line, "I thought if I could show my sister that there was something more than just us, something better than us, then maybe she'd change. Maybe she'd stop … being … her. But … every time I'd build a new world … she'd destroy it." Amara, then, is the apocalyptic narrative because every gift he gave in story, she rejected. If Chuck is the god of the text, then Amara, as his companion, is the first reader, the only reader, the first "fan" who sees herself as having exclusive privilege to the story.

But Amara does not experience what Chuck provides as a gift. Instead, she thinks of it as taking away. In their confrontation in "Alpha and Omega" she states, "In the beginning … it was just you and me, and we were family. I loved you and I thought—I knew … that you loved me." And of course Chuck does, but the show needs to take us back to this moment of reunion to retell the story of the break between fan and text, not as an indulgence of one for the other, not as an unwanted (and sexual) violation, but rather as a partnership. Amara is the complete inclusion of the fangirl without ever having been named as such. Chuck's combative love with his sister threatens the world, threatens complete destruction. It is only when he returns to call her back to his side, as family and as companion, that the world is saved.

That's how *Supernatural* tries to heal its original wound, and it is not only appropriate but almost predicted, that the gift Amara would bestow on the story when she gets her brother back is the mother, a stark and blatant invocation of the original brother narrative—the mother killed, the mother restored. However, this metaphorical gesture makes it clear that one story has died (or is dying) and that another one, similar but not the same, is taking its place. This metanarrative end is palliative in many ways.

Conclusion

There are many ways to read *Supernatural*'s metanarrative. By using Alexander's litmus, I wanted to explore how the metanarrative could frame the experience of a cultural trauma for a fanspace, one that is notoriously combative with itself and with its creators. One could work to employ Alexander's approach beyond the basic components of what constitutes a cultural trauma, especially in analyzing how media, both fan-driven and more traditional critical and entertainment outlets, disseminate the experience of the metatextual *Supernatural*.

As the show completes its run in its fifteenth season in 2019/20, it is important to understand how it has shaped the textual experience for its fandom and viewership, but more so that the show provides an effective (and affective) example of a story that struggles to make sense of its popularity, and even more so its fragile and fragmented relationship with a loyal and long-standing fandom. Its metanarrative is a cicatrix of small wounds that open up its body to the exhilarating and dangerous possibilities of boundaryless storytelling.

WORKS CITED

Alexander, Jeffrey. "Toward a Theory of Cultural Trauma." *Cultural Trauma and Collective Identity*, edited by Jeffery Alexander, Ron Eyerman, Bernard Giesen, Neil J. Smelser, and Piotr Sztompka, U of California P, 2011, pp. 1–30.
Busse, Kristina. "Fan Labor and Feminism: Capitalizing on the Fannish Labor of Love." *Cinema Journal*, vol. 54, no. 3, 2015, pp. 110–115.
Caruth, Cathy. *Unclaimed Experience: Trauma, Narrative, and History*. Johns Hopkins UP, 1996.
Coker, Cait, and Candace Benefiel. "The Hunter Hunted: The Portrayal of the Fan as Predator in *Supernatural*." *Supernatural, Humanity, and the Soul: On the Highway to Hell and Back*, edited by Susan George and Regina Hansen, Palgrave Macmillan, 2014, pp. 97–110.
Felschow, Laura. "'Hey, Check It Out, There's Actually Fans': (Dis)empowerment and (mis)representation of cult fandom in *Supernatural*." *Transformative Works and Cultures* vol 4, 2010, http://journal.transformativeworks.org/index.php/twc/article/view/134.
Hartman, Geoffrey. "On Traumatic Knowledge and Literary Studies." *New Literary History*, vol. 26, no. 3, 1995, pp. 537–563.
Howell, Charlotte. "The Gospel of the Winchesters (and Their Fans): Neoreligious Fan Practices and Narrative in *Supernatural*." *Kinephanos*, vol. 4, no. 1, August 2013, https://www.kinephanos.ca/2013/supernatural/

Larsen, Katherine, and Lynn Zubernis. *Fandom at the Crossroads*. Cambridge Scholars Publishing, 2012.
Walton, Ashley. "'What's Up, Bitches?' Charlie Bradbury as Gothic Heroine." *The Gothic Tradition in* Supernatural, edited by Melissa Edmundson, McFarland & Co., 2016, pp. 114–126.

"I have my version and you have yours"

Folklore, Narrative and the (Re)Telling of Supernatural

Kari Sawden

Supernatural is a show rooted in folklore. Beginning with its earliest episodes, in which a Wendigo, the Hook Man, and Bloody Mary all make appearances, it borrows heavily from contemporary legends and folk beliefs. Furthermore, it is richly textured by the material culture that makes up the tangible objects that have come to represent the show, including various weapons, amulets, flannel, and, of course, the Chevrolet Impala Dean drives. It is also situated within the world of the folk. Hunters are unabashedly presented as blue-collar workers, an identity that is highlighted when the Men of Letters appear in season eight, and it is further heightened with the arrival of the British Men of Letters. All of these elements are contained within increasingly flexible forms of storytelling that find the central characters of Sam and Dean Winchester confronting reinterpreted narratives of their lives through books, fan conventions, alternate realities, and, in the 200th episode, a high school musical production based on their lives. These metanarratives have become a signature of the television show and are linked to postmodern approaches to storytelling that break conventional expectations. However, these multiple tellings of a story and the constant struggle against an all-encompassing and preordained divine narrative are also reflective of folklore.

"Folklore," writes Alan Dundes, "whether oral or written, is characterized by multiple existence and variation" (7). Within the context of popular culture, this variation is frequently recognized as part of the input into the content of the show and its output into the fan communities that create their own art, inspired by what is regarded as the fixed and singular entity of the media product itself. The reinterpretation of folklore within the narrative has drawn the attention of scholars who explore how what is happening in these spaces both is and is not folklore. Mikel J. Koven and Gunella Thorgeirsdottir put forward the concept of "televised folklore" as "an attempt to bridge the folklore/fakelore debate for the representations of folklore within television drama" (190). Michael Dylan Foster and Jeffrey A. Tolbert propose the term "folkloresque" to address this concept. Foster, in his introduction to their edited collection *The Folkloresque: Reframing Folklore in a Popular Culture World*, explains that it is "popular culture's own (emic) perception and performance of folklore" (5). However, these performances in *Supernatural* are not about the monsters and magic alone. Instead, they are about the foundations of folklore itself, which Lynne S. McNeill explains as the informal, frequently person-to-person transmission of knowledge and traditions that allows it to be "malleable, adaptable, changeable, and mostly anonymous" (9). These key characteristics are important to the self-proclaimed Team Free Will. Officially consisting of Sam and Dean Winchester and the angel Castiel, unofficially it extends to encompass family and friends within the show—and even the viewers themselves—who battle against the fate of the fixed and unchanging stories that they encounter.

Throughout the show, freedom emerges as the right to narrative variation. Examining how Sam and Dean and, in later seasons, Castiel contend with the authoritative texts pressed upon them, particularly from Biblical archetypes and the Mark of Cain, as well as by the Men of Letters, reveals how the structure of folk narratives and storytelling support the show's processes of shifting and redefining its own canon. It is further heightened by the continual demonstrations of how supernatural entities, themselves, grapple with the fixed plots to which they do not always conform. Finally, the fan communities have picked up on these themes in their own interactions with *Supernatural* and its folkloresque elements. Reflecting on these components and their development over the first twelve seasons of the show makes apparent how these multiple, sometimes conflicting, stories prove to be the foundations of free will itself.

Power in the Telling

The power to narrate one's own life is a key feature of the ongoing tensions in *Supernatural*. Sam's struggle to define himself outside of the family business of hunting monsters that he was raised in is complicated by his exposure to demon blood that threatens to overwrite his own free will. When that crisis is averted, and the demon who was behind the death of their mother and Sam's girlfriend has been killed, instead of a resolution, the brothers find themselves on the precipice of losing even more agency. In the fourth and fifth seasons they are made aware of the divine narrative that has dictated their lives and even those of their ancestors. They are to be the vessels—the bodies to be possessed so that angels can have earthly form—for the apocalyptic showdown between the angelic brothers Lucifer and Michael. Since angels cannot possess an unwilling person, unlike the show's demons—although the violation of the self and loss of the narrative are found in both willing and unwilling possessions—much of these two seasons focus on the battle over what story or stories will emerge victorious. In "Changing Channels" (5.08), the Archangel Gabriel (who has been hiding on earth indulging in his own folkloric tangent as a trickster) explains the situation to Sam and Dean:

> It's about two brothers that loved each other and betrayed each other. You think you'd be able to relate.... Why do you think you two are the vessels? Think about it. Michael, the big brother, loyal to an absent father. And Lucifer, the little brother, rebellious of Daddy's plan. You were born to this, boys. It's your destiny. It was always you. As it is in Heaven, so it must be on Earth. One brother has to kill the other.... Why do you think I've always taken such an interest in you? Because from the moment Dad flipped on the lights around here, we knew it was all gonna end with you. Always.

The world will end if Sam and Dean give in and sacrifice themselves to the divinely ordained narrative. In structuring the battle in these terms, *Supernatural* makes it clear that the apocalypse is that which destroys these changeable, malleable, and frequently anonymous stories that ordinary people, those looked down upon by the angelic elite, live out. This loss will be the undoing of all things that matter to the Winchesters and all of humanity, whom they represent.

"Power produces reality," writes John Storey; "through discourses it produces 'truths' we live by" (132). At times this power is unwittingly wielded, though it is no less damaging. In the fifth season, the brothers meet a young boy, Jesse, who is revealed to be the antichrist, someone who is half-human and half-demon ("I Believe the Children Are Our Future," 5.06). While he has the potential to be a powerful weapon for Lucifer, when Sam and Dean meet him, his damage is limited to bringing to life the folklore of childhood: the existence of tooth fairies, the dangers of consuming pop rocks and coke, and the overestimated power of itching powder and joy buzzers. Quickly, however, his childhood narratives are stripped away as he is confronted with new truths about his past and potential future. At the end of the episode he shuns the narratives of Heaven, Hell, and hunter and runs away. Yet, while he escapes the stories imposed upon him by others, for all his powers, he cannot reclaim his childhood folklore, and the brothers and audience alike are left to wonder about his survival given the new, harsh truths by which he is now forced to live. And since he has yet to reappear on the show, his narrative remains open.

In one of their most overt encounters with traditional folklore narratives, Sam and Dean find themselves in a community where people are being forced to participate in recreations of fairy tales, with the deadly results expected in this show ("Bedtime Stories," 3.05). The culprit is finally revealed to be the spirit of a young woman, Callie, trapped in a coma. Her intentions are rooted in desperation and pain and not a desire to overpower others. Physically confined to her hospital bed, her spirit latches onto the fairytales her father continues to read out loud to her and finds in them the language through which she can communicate her story. When appearing at the scenes of these folklore reenactments she takes on the visage of Snow White because, like this fairy tale character, she too was poisoned by her wicked stepmother. When she is finally heard and her story believed by her father, both are able to let her go and, unlike with Jesse, Callie's release from childhood narratives is not a burden but a freedom.

As the series progresses, angels, demons, Men of Letters, and gods themselves all participate in power plays that emerge over the claim to a right to dominate and deny discourse and, in so doing, control the narrative by which all others are expected to live. Sam and Dean, consequently, find themselves confronting religious doctrine in an effort to maintain the validity of their lived, or vernacular, experiences, particularly what Leonard Norman Primiano terms vernacular religion. This concept refers to the "personal, private" or lived component of religious experience "as human beings encounter, understand, interpret, and practice it" (42, 44) that makes up much of the brothers' world. Frequently overshadowed by holy texts and accompanying deities, it is these lived narratives that become a means by which the Winchesters survive, while also serving as that for which they fight.

When discussing Sam and Dean's struggle against their pre-ordained destiny in seasons four and five, David Simmons frames it as the brothers "effectively working to subvert the grand narrative that had been set out before them" (141). In this grand narrative, the self must be sacrificed to the text. While the angels recognize the failings of the human Bible, they do not contest the idea of the singular narrative it provides because they have their own, absolute version of divine order and meaning. This theological quandary is not an invention of the show. Adrian Thatcher provides a summation of this issue from a Biblical perspective in *The Savage Text: The Use and Abuse of the Bible,* wherein he explains how Jesus Christ as the Word of God has been replaced by the book as the Word of God: "The Person is replaced by the Proposition: Flesh by Words; the Word of God by written, and much-disputed, text" (4). *Supernatural* is about the flesh that exists beyond the text, as is made evident when the brothers are forced to confront the Winchester Gospel, a series of books detailing their lives as hunters, introduced in "The Monster at the End of This Book" (4.18). The books were published under the pen name of Carver Edlund, but they discover that the writer is Chuck Shurley, who is revealed to be a prophet and, eventually, the Judeo-Christian God. While it is perhaps not surprising that a deity would be multi-layered, the show ensures that Sam and Dean, and by extension humanity, are recognized as being in equal possession of their own complex identities as exhibited, for example, through the various roles they play, such as FBI agents, in order to solve their cases.

At first Chuck's writings seem to be fated texts as Sam and Dean find themselves living out what is written on the page. However, as "The Monster at the End of This Book" reveals by simply allowing the audience to observe the brothers contend with the plot, there is much left out of the text when divorced from the actual experiences of those involved, and the story can be rewritten. The confrontation between Sam and Lilith does not end in the manner expected. In this way, the show reflects the "old folklore maxim" described by Bruce A. Rosenberg: "folklore is what gets left out of the performance when it is transcribed onto paper" (155). And it is what is overlooked by an exclusive focus on the text that gives these characters hope.

Chuck's own recognition of the flaws in the grand narrative emerge in his telling of "Swan Song" (5.22), the final episode of season five. Structured as his closing contribution to the Winchester Gospel, his narrative documents how the brothers save the world. But lest the audience choose to replace one absolute story (the angels') with another (Chuck's reclamation of the plot from them), he repeatedly draws attention to the quiet stories of everyday experience that overpower Lucifer, Michael, and a plot that has been in existence for millennia. They are variations of what Amy Shuman describes in her book *Other People's Stories: Entitlement Claims and the Critique of Empathy* as "small world stories," or those that are seemingly innocuous and made up of coincidental meanings found in everyday life; they "convey the sense that an ordinary connection may have a profound meaning" (93). This idea had been established earlier in the season in "Dark Side of the Moon" (5.16) when Sam and Dean die and end up in Heaven, which is made up of the small but meaningful moments in their lives. Hence, only these things would be powerful enough to save the world. It is not love of God or the grand ideals of humanity or angels that halt the apocalypse, it is the relationship of two brothers and the stories and objects that bind them together. It is a 1967 Chevrolet Impala that, when it rolled off the line, "no one gave two craps about" even though it would become "the most important object in pretty much the whole universe" ("Swan Song"). Lucifer and Michael are thwarted by a seemingly insignificant car filled with etched initials and toy soldiers that hold more power than all of the weapons of Heaven and Hell. Armageddon is subverted because the brothers refuse to be a passive audience but are active in demanding variations to the narrative and the right to create and remember their own.

The realization that there is no singular textual authority fuels much of the angelic plot lines in season six and beyond, particularly for Castiel, the angel who rebelled against Heaven to help the brothers. In doing so he "tore up scripture" as another angel, Balthazar, puts it in "The Third Man" (6.03), but his decisions, and those of the Winchesters, plunge Heaven into chaos. Dundes, in *Holy Writ as Oral Lit: The Bible as Folklore*, explores the multiple variations and narratives found in this sacred text that led him to classify it as folklore. However, since the angels are unable to recognize their sacred narratives through this lens and, thereby, relinquish the need for absolute power, they continue to seek a single narrative, and leader, to follow. Castiel, in attempting to take a role in Heaven's battle during season six, finds himself turning to storytelling to make sense of his situation and find help. In a desperate prayer for God's guidance, he engages in the telling of his experiences ("The Man Who Would Be King," 6.20), taking on the authorial position for himself while grappling with the fear he has made the wrong choice. "Let me tell you my story" he says. "Let me tell you everything."

Throughout the episode Castiel tells of the decisions that brought him to the desperate point where he has deceived the Winchesters; made deals with Crowley, the king of hell; and is about to open Purgatory to use the power of its souls to defeat his enemies. In despair, he asks God for a sign to tell him if he is doing the right thing, plot guidance from the master narrator: "You have to tell me. You have to give me a sign. Give me a sign. Because if you don't, I'm gonna ju—I'm gonna do whatever I—whatever I must." This prayer reveals his angelic need for the grand narrative from God to replace his current one. When it does not come, he rejects the flawed, mutable, and vernacular lives of Sam and Dean and the help they offer and, instead, takes on the mantle of God in an attempt to save Heaven.

In season eight, Castiel is yet again forced to contend with an angelic agenda rooted in narrative control. In a confrontation with the angel Naomi, who has been manipulating him throughout the season, he tells her that angels were supposed to be the shepherds, not murderers, of humanity. "Not always, angel" is Naomi's response, and she reveals how Castiel, "the famous spanner in the works," has been defective and, consequently, reprogrammed repeatedly when he rebels ("The Great Escapist," 8.21). It is at this same time that Metatron, the scribe of God, is introduced and with whom Castiel falls into the same pattern of seeking out a unifying story that can right the wrongs. Combined with the textual authority of the angel tablet, Castiel turns to this figure so closely connected to divine narrative to help him fix his mistakes.

Metatron, a lover of stories, at first appears to be a better ally. After all, he recognizes that storytelling is "the true flower of free will—at least as you've [humanity] mastered it so far" that grants the title of god to those who create stories, even if it is only of tiny, intimate dimensions ("The Great Escapist"). However, the hierarchy still stands and, therefore, the people and their vernacular suffer. While Metatron loves all stories, as a scribe and an angel, he cannot see them as anything other than fiction. Sam castigates him when they first meet because while he reads about suffering, he never connects it to actual people and their lives. He still wants authorial distance; he does not want the messiness of the stories when they bleed off the page. After all, this suffering is because, as he notes in "Meta Fiction" (9.18), God published the first draft. What exists now is flawed and broken, a narrative that has the potential to be great, but is far removed from greatness in its current incarnation. It is only at the end of season eleven, when he has been stripped of his grace, that he is able to redeem himself by challenging Chuck's narrative—God's grand story. In "Don't Call Me Shurley" (11.20), Metatron and Chuck work through the story that the latter has constructed, and Metatron forces him to confront the flaws in his idealized version and his desperate need for it to be his story alone and not that of his sister, Amara, the darkness who threatens to destroy all things. Yet, at the end of this season, as in the fifth, the importance of small, personal stories is reinforced. In a quiet moment as they wait for the end of the world, Chuck and the witch Rowena, mother of Crowley, bond through the sharing of memories of their children. These vernacular narratives set up what follows, not a resolution through violent confrontation but a conversation between siblings who find, beyond simplified stories of good and evil, a need for family that echoes the countless situations Sam and Dean have faced due to the same connection.

With the reaffirmed absence of Chuck once again, after he departs with Amara, the struggle for narrative authority takes a more human turn. Sam and Dean, themselves legacies of the secret society the Men of Letters established to combat the supernatural but situated as more elite and intellectually motivated than the hunters, find themselves contending with the arrival of the British division, which drives much of the plot of season twelve. Mimicking the derogatory language of the angels who sought narrative control, the representatives of this foreign contingent disregard American hunters as apes ("Mamma Mia," 12.02) in comparison to themselves and their superior knowledge and precision. While they do not engage in possession like angels and demons, their intent of diminishing the vernacular and establishing a strict adherence to their script is summarized in their approach: "assimilate or eliminate" ("The British Invasion," 12.17). Theirs is a singular narrative of good and evil, and there is no space for the realities, and accompanying complexities, of the lived. In "American Nightmare" (12.04), Sam and Dean let a psychic go, recognizing that her reasons for harming others were not inherent evilness but the contextual situation she found herself in. However, the British Men of Letters kill her, reducing her to a mess that needs to be cleaned up. This approach is emphasized a few episodes later when, in "First Blood" (12.09), it is made clear that they view it as unprofessional to leave survivors. The reality of this worldview is enacted through the brainwashing of Mary Winchester, Sam and Dean's mother who was brought back to life by Amara, stripping her of her own narrative and her connection to the family and friends that make up her vernacular experiences. In challenging this approach, Sam and Dean once again demonstrate that for whatever suffering will arise from refusing to submit to the British Men of Letters, a multiplicity of narratives is essential because anything else becomes a prison.

This theme of imprisonment plays out all through the show, and literal prisons are frequently interplayed with textual ones. The body becomes a site of confinement during possession, angelic or demonic, as the possessed lose control of themselves. Sam's dying body, in season nine, becomes inhabited by the angel Gadreel, a fact that is kept from him by his brother out of fear of Sam rejecting the angel and subsequently dying. While the original agreement was for Gadreel to remain undetected as he healed Sam, he increasingly takes control of Sam's narrative, leading to the death of the prophet Kevin Tran and the fracturing of the relationship between the brothers. As Sam regains full control over his body (and narrative), Dean finds himself losing control of his when he cannot repair the rift in his relationship with his brother. He ends up turning to another story of a brotherly betrayal when he takes on the Mark of Cain. In doing so, he further plays into the religious script that had defined angelic expectations of the Winchesters: brother against brother. In this case, he finds that this text, literally engraved in his flesh, is overwriting his own stories to the point that he becomes a demon.

Regardless of their status in the supernatural hierarchy, all entities from gods to hunters contend with the ways they are confined through their own actions or those of others. The Mark of Cain not only entraps Dean, but also serves as an actual lock on the prison that Chuck created to contain his sister in another narrative of sibling conflict. Gadreel, after escaping his literal confinement, remains haunted by a single story that defines him: he let Satan into the Garden of Eden. All of his actions are an attempt to have control over his own story and be seen as more than his failure. In "Celebrating the Life of Asa Fox" (12.06), the hunter Bucky is punished for his accidental killing, and subsequent coverup of said killing, of his friend and fellow hunter, Asa Fox, by having his story reduced to one single narrative. This is his prison, the hunter Alicia explains, because they will "tell everyone, every hunter we meet. They're gonna know your name, Bucky, know what you did." Her brother goes on to add: "This is the story everyone's gonna tell about you. Forever."

A Monster on the Page

The master narrative that Sam and Dean frequently contend with is that of good versus evil framed by angels and demons; yet, even before they become aware of this celestial battle, it is reflected in their own narrative as hunters: monsters are bad. Adherence to this concept leads their father to burden Dean with the knowledge that because of Sam's exposure to demon blood he will have to save him or kill him ("Hunted," 2.10). These terms are absolute. The pitting of brother against brother began early, foreshadowing the divine story they battle against, but also another one they have to dismantle. Their own experiences with (and sometimes becoming) the possessed, monsters, ghosts, and other entities open up their awareness of the potential multiplicity of these creatures and complicate the plot that their father had provided them and that had guided their lives as hunters.

At first glance, *Supernatural* appears to be creating definitive versions of monsters. In discussing the potential for the show to wander into the territory of fakelore, Koven and Thorgeirsdottir observe that:

> *Supernatural*'s monsters *are* artificial fusions of many folkloric and popular culture variants; the problem here is that, by this fusion, the series could be seen to suggest its version is the "real" one. Each week's monster, in addition to being recognized as having its own folkloric tradition, including variant texts across time and space, is concretized into an actual creature the Winchesters can fight [192].

Yet, while frequently the origins of the monsters and their weaknesses are revealed by sifting through sources to find the "right" version, the multiple variations that also define folklore are found in the brothers' individual encounters with beings who do not follow the script. In season two's episode "Bloodlust" (2.03), Sam and Dean meet Lenore, a vampire who is trying not to hurt people. She proves that she is able to resist human blood and, therefore, the brothers let her go, taking her side against another hunter. At the end of this episode, Dean is left to wish they had never taken the job because, as he asks, "What if we killed things that didn't deserve killing?" And while the brothers try to understand the circumstances they were raised in that shape their perspectives, they are still left with the knowledge that their entire narrative is shifting. Lenore turns up again in season six, having failed to keep her own right to self-determination. In "Mommy Dearest" (6.19) she reveals that the overwhelming influence of Eve, the mother of all monsters, has caused her to kill again. Eve takes control of Lenore's desires and own narrative with her grand, absolute vision for her children. Echoing the possessions of humans in other episodes, and foreshadowing Mary's brainwashing, Lenore finds herself losing her own body and mind, and she asks for death rather than to relinquish her free will and truly become a monster.

Sam and Dean struggle to accept these variations throughout the show. Sam is confused by Dean's trust in the vampire Benny Lafitte, who helped Dean escape Purgatory. He is another monster who eschews the grand narrative that seeks to define him but struggles to find his place in a world that is not constructed for his experiences and will not accept these divergences from the preordained script. In the end, he chooses to return to Purgatory to save Sam, in a subversion of expectation not uncommon in this show, and to stay there where the story is pure and he finds meaning ("Taxi Driver," 8.19). As with Lenore, the desire for one's own variation on the story is not always successful, and it is always a struggle.

One of the reoccurring examples of the individual monster redefined is that of the werewolf. Throughout *Supernatural*, these creatures have defied binaries of good and evil, human and monster, while also demonstrating that there are multiple ways of doing so. Madison, in "Heart" (2.17) chooses to die once she realizes that she is a werewolf and that there is no way to keep herself from harming others when in her transformed state. Kate kills her friend ("Bitten," 8.04) and even her sister ("Paper Moon," 10.04), both werewolves like her, in order to prevent them from attacking, turning, or killing humans. However, she does not shun the world but continues to find ways to exist within it. She only asks that the brothers let her define her own path, as long as she remains monster in name alone and not action.

Werewolves return in "Sharp Teeth" (9.12), an episode that follows Garth, a hunter who is revealed to have become a werewolf. This episode focuses on the Winchesters as they struggle to understand his new identity as, once again, the singular narrative ascribed to such a being is contested. However, the damage of an all-encompassing story is enhanced with the revelation that the werewolves who have taken Garth in are, themselves, fundamentalists, drawing on their own literal and definitive reading of a sacred text to justify further death and destruction. Yet, while Lenore ultimately dies, Kate must destroy her loved ones, and Benny finds peace only by returning to Purgatory, the end of this episode finds Garth victorious in maintaining his own life and freeing himself from any external plots that sought to dominate him, at least for the time being. It does not mean that all werewolves are good but that variation is possible. If angels can be dicks and demons can help save the world, then vampires and werewolves can be more than creatures to be hunted and killed. After all, as Sam tells Olivia, a shapeshifter he encounters in "Ask Jeeves" (10.06), "Being a monster is a choice."

Stories of Our Own Making

In their contributions to *TV Goes to Hell: An Unofficial Road Map of Supernatural*, both Brigid Cherry and Alberto N. García recognize that this is a show that openly dialogues with its audience. The relationship between it and the viewer is complicated by the inclusion of fans within the plot itself that provides multiple variations on the brothers' lives. These fans, much like those who watch the show, are not content, as Henry Jenkins writes in his influential work *Textual Poachers: Television Fans & Participatory Culture*, to participate in the common model of cultural consumption that demands the reader be a "passive recipient of authorial meaning" (25). Instead, the Winchesters find themselves confronted with variations of their experiences told and reinterpreted through fan conventions, cosplay, and fan fiction. While they struggle with having their lives violated by the intrusion of fans (Graham 143), as the show progresses, they come to terms with them as they themselves become more aware of the multiple potential narratives of monsters and angels and continue their own attack on the master one.

Much like Dundes, Stephen Prickett argues in *Origins of Narrative: The Romantic Appropriation of the Bible*, that "the Bible is better described in terms of an on-going tradition of interpretation than as a specific individual work" (xi). Throughout *Supernatural*, Sam and Dean engage in this tradition, challenging set interpretations as they struggle to extricate themselves from these plots. So when fans of the show participate in dismantling the official *Supernatural* stories through their own creativity, they are only doing what the brothers have taught them to do: resist grand narratives. They are embracing the "real power of audience members," which Jay Mechling argues is "to resist, rewrite and withdraw" (285). In their book *Fangasm: Supernatural Fangirls*, Katherine Larsen and Lynn S. Zubernis expand on this theme, noting how some scholars have approached fandom as "a site of resistance" that allows them to both control and fix narratives according to their own personal needs (15). The acknowledgment of fan culture within the show itself reflects an awareness of this reality, and the brothers' ongoing fight for multiple narratives further encourages fan participation.

Jenkins asserts that "[f]rom the perspective of dominant taste, fans appear to be frighteningly out of control, undisciplined and unrepentant, rogue readers" (18). In this way, they parallel the uncivilized American hunters Sam and Dean Winchester, and sometimes even the monsters they encounter. Fans are rebelling against the gods of creation and the proper order of things found in the show, which serves as their Bible, in order to claim new stories. In doing so, the desire is not to end the master narrative but to rip it from its pedestal, to reframe it as one of many, and to have it be recognized that all stories are important, even if their value is known only to a few and they seem uncivilized or inappropriate to others. It is the vernacular, the lived experiences that fans bring with them to the show that makes the stories meaningful. *Supernatural* creates a narrative space wherein characters work through their traumas and demand their own stories, thereby granting the audience this same right. Larsen and Zubernis highlight this when they explore the interplay between fan lives and those within the show:

> We're all the narrators of our own life stories, figuring out who we are in the telling. It turns out that it's even more effective to rewrite our stories as fiction. Dealing with past hurts or broken relationships or just trying to figure out who you are for real? Writing a fictional story of Sam and Dean Winchester enduring something similar—and coming out on the other side—can help the writer come out on the other side of herself [47].

By watching the show itself grapple with fandom, fans gain a better understanding of their own place in the *Supernatural* world, and they are also given the same warnings as characters in the show: you have the right to your story but not to impose it upon others. In "Season Seven, Time for a Wedding!" (7.08), the character of Becky Rosen, an extreme super-fan of the "Supernatural" books, gives Sam a potion so he will fall in love with and marry her. Her crime is not in enjoying the series but in demanding her narrative supersede others. She wants to possess Sam and control his story. This stands in stark contrast to the cosplayers in "The Real Ghostbusters" (5.09), who explain to Sam and Dean what the books are about (to them): "In real life, he sells stereo equipment; I fix copiers. Our lives suck. But to be Sam and Dean, to wake up every morning and save the world, to have a brother who would die for you. Well, who wouldn't want that?" In allowing their narratives to be flexible, the writers of the show, through the Winchester brothers, are able to provide the fans with a starting off point for their own vision of what this could all mean.

In the 200th episode of *Supernatural*, "Fan Fiction" (10.05), the role of fandom takes center stage as Sam and Dean investigate disappearances at a high school where a "Supernatural" musical is being staged. While her play is based on the books, Marie, the student creator behind the production, has taken creative license. Choosing this as the 200th episode is a strong statement about the relationship of the show to its fans, heightened by its resolution. By the end of the episode Dean comes to terms with Marie's interpretation of his life, telling her that "I have my version and you have yours." Furthermore, Sam and Dean are reintroduced to important moments and objects that have defined their journey: being on the road; the amulet (or Samulet); the overarching motto of saving people, hunting things, the family business; and the people they have encountered along the way. There are gifts to be found in the creative output of the ordinary person, i.e., fan. The final blessing upon fandom comes from an appearance by Chuck who, when asked by Marie what he thought of her production, responds with a kindly: "Not bad."

Conclusion

Supernatural is filled with folklore. Its plots involve mythical beings and the folk who hunt them. But, more importantly, it is a show about the telling of stories and the preservation of variation that defines the field of folklore. Its great battles often revolve around grand narratives that dismantle personal stories and any possibility for there to be multiple narrators. Throughout the first twelve seasons the audience is witness to, and a welcome participant in, acts of resistance that claim the right of all to have and tell stories. It also roots these narratives in the frequently overlooked but deeply powerful vernacular.

Each person, their experiences, and their stories matter, even when—especially when—not recognized by the official systems or individuals in power. In "The French Mistake" (6.15), Dean declares that "where we're from, people don't know who we are, but you know what, we matter to that world." Sam picks up on this idea in "The Memory Remains" (12.18) as he and Dean discuss their legacy:

> DEAN: What do you think our legacy's gonna be? When we're gone, I mean, after all the stuff we've done, you think folks will remember us, you know, like, a hundred years from now?
> SAM: No.
> DEAN: Oh, that's nice.
> SAM: Well, I mean, guys like us, we're not exactly the type of people they write about in history books, you know? But the people we saved, they're our legacy. And they'll remember us, and then, I guess, we'll eventually fade away too. That's fine because we left the world better than we found it, you know.

Dean's response is to carve his initials into the table they are sitting at before passing the knife to Sam to do the same, mirroring those found in the Impala. In this exchange, they both dismiss the eternal narratives etched in stone, choosing instead to make their own mark, for however long it lasts. The important stories, after all, are not eternal. The ones that matter most are those that are embodied, changeable, often anonymous, and freely lived.

WORKS CITED

Cherry, Brigid. "Sympathy for the Fangirl: Becky Rosen, Fan Identity, and Interactivity in *Supernatural*." *TV Goes to Hell: An Unofficial Road Map of* Supernatural, edited by Stacey Abbott and David Lavery. ECW P, 2011, pp. 203–218.

Dundes, Alan. *Holy Writ as Oral Lit: The Bible as Folklore*. Rowman & Littlefield, 1999.

Foster, Michael Dylan. "Introduction: The Challenge of the Folkloresque." *The Folkloresque:*

Reframing Folklore in a Popular Culture World, edited by Michael Dylan Foster and Jeffrey A. Tolbert, Utah State UP, 2016, pp. 3–33.

García, Alberto N. "Breaking the Mirror: Metafictional Strategies in *Supernatural*." *TV Goes to Hell: An Unofficial Road Map of* Supernatural, edited by Stacey Abbott and David Lavery, ECW P, 2011, pp. 146–160.

Graham, Anissa M. "A New Kind of Pandering: *Supernatural* and the World of Fanfiction." *Fan Culture: Essays on Participatory Fandom in the 21st Century*, edited by Kristin M. Barton and Jonathan Malcolm. Lampley: McFarland & Co, 2013, pp. 131–145.

Jenkins, Henry. *Textual Poachers: Television Fans & Participatory Culture*. Routledge, 1992.

Koven, Mikel J., and Gunnella Thorgeirsdottir. "Televisual Folklore: Rescuing *Supernatural* from the Fakelore Realm." *TV Goes to Hell: An Unofficial Road Map of* Supernatural, edited by Stacey Abbott and David Lavery, ECW P, 2011, pp. 187–200.

Larsen, Katherine, and Lynn S. Zubernis. *Fangasm: Supernatural Fangirls*. U of Iowa P, 2013.

McNeill, Lynne S. *Folklore Rules: A Fun, Quick, and Useful Introduction to the Field of Academic Folklore Studies*. Utah State UP, 2013.

Mechling, Jay. "On Sharing Folklore and American Identity in a Multicultural Society." *Western Folklore* vol. 52, no. 2/4, 1993, pp. 271–289.

Prickett, Stephen. *Origins of Narrative: The Romantic Appropriation of the Bible*. Cambridge UP, 1996.

Primiano, Leonard Norman. "Vernacular Religion and the Search for Method in Religious Folklife." *Western Folklore* vol. 54, no. 1, 1995, pp. 37–54.

Rosenberg, Bruce A. "The Message of the American Folk Sermon." *Oral-Formulaic Theory: A Folklore Casebook*, edited by John Miles Foley, Garland Publishing, 1990, pp. 137–168.

Shuman, Amy. *Other People's Stories: Entitlement Claims and the Critique of Empathy*. U of Illinois P, 2010.

Simmons, David. "'There's a Ton of Lore on Unicorns Too': Postmodernist Micro-Narratives and *Supernatural*." *TV Goes to Hell: An Unofficial Road Map of* Supernatural, edited by Stacey Abbott and David Lavery, ECW P, 2011, pp. 132–145.

Storey, John. *Cultural Theory and Popular Culture: An Introduction, 6th Ed*. Pearson, 2012.

Thatcher, Adrian. *The Savage Text: The Use and Abuse of the Bible*. Wiley-Blackwell, 2008.

Part Four

Breaking Out of the Box

"Why are you the boy who hates Christmas?"
"A Very Supernatural Christmas" as Nostalgic Holiday Special

Kevin J. Wetmore, Jr.

Supernatural is well known for going meta, and especially well known for "Easter eggs," both in the form of references to other work by the actors, writers and crew, and for calling attention to the medium itself (Macklem 39). Television haunts *Supernatural*, framing several of the episodes. "Hollywood Babylon" (2.18) was the first. "A Very Supernatural Christmas" (3.08) (hereafter "AVSC") was the second. "AVSC" is, in a sense, an anti-holiday special, showing the worst of Christmas in some respects, but it does so by employing the tropes and structure of television Christmas specials of the seventies and eighties. It evokes nostalgia for those old enough to remember watching those specials on television in the era before cable. The show telegraphs its intent from the very beginning with the use of the special CBS bumper ident indicating that the following program was a "CBS Special Presentation."

Series creator Eric Kripke, in his introductory commentary to "AVSC" on the DVD, gleefully posits the idea that this episode would be an inversion of a holiday special: "We want to deliver the most violent, brutal, anti-holiday holiday episode ever." In order to create an anti-holiday holiday special, however, one must follow the structure and format of a holiday special. "In the first few minutes of the episode, we kill Santa," Kripke joyfully announces, which is true. But the killing of "Santa," actually a grandfather pretending to be Santa, signifies that this holiday special will be a very *Supernatural* one. The irony is, as this essay proposes to demonstrate, that despite all the anti-holiday,

151

152 Part Four: Breaking Out of the Box

Santa-killing brutality, the show results in being a rather sweet nostalgic narrative about the true meaning of Christmas, which all Christmas specials, of course, must be. By parodying the Christmas special, "AVSC" becomes one itself.

Nostalgia comes from the ancient Greek words "nostos" (to return home) and "algos" (pain). Coined in 1688 by the Swiss medical student Johannes Hofer, the term refers to a complex longing for the past familiar, while also recognizing the distance from that past and finding that distance or the longing itself painful (Routledge 4). Bittersweet would be another word, describing the experience as both happy and painful. To encounter reminders of the distant past brings both the delight of the memory, and the ache of the distance. "AVSC" becomes an exercise in meta-nostalgia as well, exploring Sam and Dean's own Christmas memories while also recreating (for the viewer of a certain age) the experience of watching a Christmas special about people whose Christmas experiences teach them the true meaning of Christmas.

Two elements from the opening of "AVSC" frame the episode as a nostalgic Christmas special. The first is the reproduction of the CBS Special Presentation ident. The "A CBS Special Presentation" logo preceded all specials aimed at children that ran on CBS November through January and at Easter time from 1973 to 1991. These include Peanuts (*A Charlie Brown Thanksgiving, A Charlie Brown Christmas, It's the Easter Beagle Charlie Brown*) and Rankin/Bass animated specials (*Santa Claus Is Coming to Town, Rudolph the Red-Nosed Reindeer, The Year Without a Santa Claus, The Little Drummer Boy, Jack Frost, The Easter Bunny Is Coming to Town*, and dozens of others, although the ones listed here were the staples). Each special was introduced with the spinning logo that featured the text, "A CBS Special Presentation" which was accompanied by a brief piece of music consisting of drums and horns. This music was composed by Morton Stevens and taken from music created originally for the television series *Hawaii 5-0*. The introduction consisted of six seconds of drumming followed by six notes from horns, matched to a technicolor visual of the spinning words "A CBS Special Presentation," that were centered and legible by the time the brass notes began to play (Humuhumu). To be a child in the late seventies was to immediately recognize that ident and all that it stood for. In a time before cable television and non-stop broadcasting, the CBS special presentation ident marked something singular was about to occur, something that could only be viewed once a year.

In his DVD introduction to the episode, Kripke acknowledges how much work went into locating and securing permission for the CBS Special Presentation bumper introduction. He says it was important to him to have that opening. While he does not detail why it was so important to him, it seems safe to assume both the desire to have this established and nostalgic marker precede his own anti-holiday holiday special, evoking that sense of singular distinctiveness that appeals to Gen X, as well as to frame "AVSC" as this kind of holiday special. Because *Supernatural* does not air on CBS, that part of the ident had to be removed. But Kripke secured permission for the music and the spinning text "A Special Presentation" to play before the show. (I must confess, the first time I saw the episode when it aired in 2007, that ident, more than anything else, did have the intended effect on me, and I was giddy for much of the opening of the show because of it.)

The ident cuts to a pre-credit Christmas scene, set in Seattle, in which "Grandpa" and "Stevie" discuss Santa. Grandpa dresses up as Santa, and Stevie spies on him putting out presents. After checking a noise in the fireplace, "Santa" is dragged screaming up the chimney. "Santa?" Stevie asks as a bloody boot falls out of the chimney. This entire sequence is designed, per Kripke's glee above, to undercut the traditional uplifting imagery of the Christmas special—older relatives pretending to be Santa, children in awe and wonder at the appearance of old Saint Nick, and the chimney as Santa's entrance and egress from the house. Instead, Stevie sees his grandfather-as-Santa get murdered and possibly dismembered in the chimney. Cue the sleigh bells.

Cut to the text "A Very Supernatural Christmas," which received its own special title card complete with sleigh bells ringing, snow, Christmas lights, and a Santa hat on the "A" in "Supernatural." This title is the second element that frames the episode as a specific type of Christmas special. "A Very Supernatural Christmas" is a direct reference to the made-for-TV movie *A Very Brady Christmas* (1988), coincidentally also a CBS Christmas special. In *A Very Brady Christmas*, set 14 years after the original series, the parents reunite the children for Christmas, solving all of their domestic and career problems. That television movie, the most popular of its year, was in and of itself a form of nostalgia. The Bradys are a non-traditional, blended family who faced minor, suburban problems—a high phone bill, sibling rivalry, arguments over bathroom use, and unrequited crushes, among other American, white, middle-class issues. *A Very Brady Christmas* sees the family facing adult, suburban problems: marital discord, challenges at work and in relationships, the two youngest face issues related to college, one wanting to drop out to pursue his passion for race cars and the other not wanting to come home for Christmas but go skiing with friends instead. This Christmas special, designed to continue the Brady vibe with the children now grown up, continues the original series' ideal of knowledgeable parents helping their children solve issues. The name, too—"A Very [blank] Christmas"—has now fallen into pop culture trope territory, with the sequel to the nineties film version of the Bradys called *A Very Brady Sequel* (1996), and marketed with the tagline, "The more everything changes, the more they stay the same," not only a comment on the Bradys but also a call for nostalgia if there ever was one. The world had changed in the quarter century since the original show, but the Bradys can still be counted on to be exactly the same. There is a painful return to home in watching the show and its children, so to speak.

Families and the relationships between parents and children are central to Christmas specials, and John Winchester is no Mike and Carol Brady. In fact, holiday specials usually offer three things: they center on family or a family-like group overcoming adversity during the holidays; they teach the "true meaning" of the holiday (although often this was distinctly unrelated to the actual Christian meaning of these holidays) to someone who often did not believe in or like Christmas, often linked to the previous element (the learning of the true meaning of the holiday ends the family crisis); and finally they explain the origin of traditions. All of these, of course, happen in "AVSC."

"AVSC" also fulfills the tropes of Christmas horror, as distinguished from a holiday special, as defined by Dave Canfield, while simultaneously parodying those tropes. Canfield notes that in Christmas horror narratives, family is often "broken." Canfield calls them "unholy families," in opposition to the birth of Jesus creating the "Holy Family" (223–4). The Winchesters certainly qualify as a broken family, from the often-absent dad to the tensions between Sam and Dean themselves from childhood to present. "A Very Supernatural Christmas" is exactly what the title promises, not just an anti-holiday holiday special, but an anti–Brady, Brady-inspired holiday show in which because of absent parents, the children must learn the true meaning of Christmas and develop their own traditions on their own, without even an Alice to help out (although, given his family-but-not-family status, and position as mentor close to the kids who "cleans up" after them, Bobby Singer can be seen as the "Alice" of *Supernatural*).

Not only is the family broken, it is often in danger in the Christmas special. Canfield cannily observes:

> Mainstream Christmas narratives almost always revolve around threats to the family (*It's a Wonderful Life* [1943]), the usurpation of the true meaning of Christmas by consumerism and other forces (*A Charlie Brown Christmas* [1965]), or the need to cling to a worldview that embraces the possibility of the supernatural in a cynical world (*Miracle on 34th Street* [1947]). Why should Christmas horror be any different? [223].

Christmas specials revolve around either family or created family (a circle of people who come together and then function as a family—see the Peanuts gang specials or the individuals who join Santa, such as Hermie the Dentist Elf, Yukon Cornelius and eventually even the Abominable Snowman, in *Rudolph the Red Nosed Reindeer* for examples of non-biological families centered on Christmas). The Winchesters are both a real family and a created one. They are part of a larger family of hunters, Bobby being the most obvious as surrogate father and non-biological family member. Christmas is not a respite from the horror, it is just another workday for the Winchesters, both in the distant past and the current moment.

The episode alternates between the present-day investigations into the murders around Christmas and the past events in Broken Bow, Nebraska on Christmas Eve, 1991, with each timeline reflecting upon the other for the purpose of demonstrating why Sam does not care for Christmas and how he comes to know its true meaning. In this case, we see multiple families in crisis: both those whose loved ones are being killed at Christmas time that the Winchesters seek to help and also the Winchesters themselves, in both the past and the present, for different reasons. "AVSC" uses the Christmas murders to show the Winchesters overcoming adversity in the manner of a Christmas special.

After Stevie's grandfather has been massacred in a chimney and we get the meta credits, the episode shifts to Ypsilanti, Michigan in the present day, a year after the Seattle slayings. In their guise as FBI agents, the Winchesters interview a woman whose husband has gone missing. Sam finds the husband's tooth in their fireplace, suggesting that the man met the same fate as grandpa.

Sam theorizes Krampus might be to blame, or an "Evil Santa" or "the anti–Clause," and explains there is "all kinds of lore" about Santa's brother. Coincidentally, Bobby theorizes both Winchesters might be morons (again, positioning him as the "Alice" figure, as likely to mock the kids as help them). Dean responds, "Santa doesn't have a brother. There is no Santa." To which Sam rejoins, "Yeah, I know. You're the one who told me that in the first place, remember?" A moment of tension follows which sets the stage for the exploration of the past Christmas issues between the Winchesters. This moment shows Sam's own resentfulness towards Dean (and his father) for depriving him of a traditional childhood, yet paradoxically providing one of the most normal moments of their childhood: the older brother spoiling Santa for the younger sibling.

The two go to "Santa's Village" to investigate and they discover how sad and rundown it is. It is at this location that Dean decides the Winchesters should celebrate Christmas:

> DEAN: It's a Christmas miracle. Hey, speaking of, we should have one this year.
> SAM: Have one what?
> DEAN: A Christmas.
> SAM: No thanks.
> DEAN: No, we'll get a tree, a little Boston Market, just like when we were little.
> SAM: Dean, those weren't exactly Hallmark memories for me, you know.
> DEAN: What are you talking about? We had some great Christmases!
> SAM: Whose childhood are you talking about?

156 Part Four: Breaking Out of the Box

From this conversation, carried on in a rundown Santa's Village with broken reindeer and a drunk Santa (and if that is not literalizing a metaphor about Sam's perception of Christmas, nothing is), we may discern a few things. Sam does not like Christmas, and his memories of it are not happy ones. Dean has very different memories of Christmas, shaped by his experiences as the older brother and the one closer to their father, and with possible memories of Christmas with his mother before her death. Neither one understands or appreciates the other's experience of Christmas. The Winchesters no longer regularly celebrate Christmas, otherwise why would Dean say they should have one this year, unless for the past several years they have not had one. Lastly, Sam lacks the Christmas spirit. He is the family member in crisis, like Charlie Brown, Kris Kringle or George Bailey. He no longer values Christmas and does not know its true meaning.

This crisis is further demonstrated by the flashback which follows. The text on the screen informs the viewer that we are witnessing "Broken Bow, Nebraska, Christmas Eve, 1991." Thus, the Winchesters are in the heartland of America, on Christmas Eve, a time traditionally spent at home with the family (home for the holidays being a major theme in holiday films and television specials, from *Home for the Holidays* [1995] to *Home Alone* [1990] to *Planes, Trains and Automobiles* [1987]—one should be home with family for the major holidays, especially Christmas, according to these narratives). The Winchester boys, Dean almost a teenager, Sam younger, are in a hotel room, alone. John is not with them. Sam wraps a present—a gift for the absent father. Dean tells him their dad will be "home" for Christmas, in the hotel room with them soon. Already, Sam is losing his innocence, implied in the earlier exchange about learning there is no Santa. "I'm old enough," young Sam tells Dean, "you can tell me the truth." The truth that is implied might be that there is no Santa, but also the truth about their frequently absent father.

What is remarkable about this moment is that the cut from Santa's Village to the past begins by showing the hotel room television displaying the Rankin/Bass CBS special *Santa Claus Is Coming to Town*. In 1991, Sam and Dean are watching a Christmas special from 1970 in which a baby is delivered to Sombertown, where the municipal authority, Burgermeister Meisterburger, orders it taken to the "Orphans' Asylum." Instead, the baby is whisked away to an elf family named Kringle who raise the child, named Kris, to become Santa Claus. Kris must evade the Winter Warlock, an evil wizard, whom he eventually defeats by giving him a toy. Kris is determined to deliver toys to the children of Sombertown year-round, as asked. Soon requests are coming in from all over the world, and Kris Kringle announces he will deliver toys only once a year, deciding to do so on Christmas Eve as it is "a night of profound love." The narrator, a postman voiced by Fred Astaire, explains that people who don't like Christmas miss the point—the job of Santa Claus is "to take a little bit of that unhappiness away." If we all try to be more like Santa, and give to others instead of thinking of ourselves, the world would be a better place, the narrator reminds the viewers, forming yet another parallel with the Winchesters decades later, as they are essentially orphans (like Kris Kringle) abandoned by their father at the holidays as they sit in a hotel room spending their lives thinking about how to help others in trouble. In short, it is a story about a young man, facing adversaries both mortal and supernatural, in order to make people, especially children, happy. Sam watches a Christmas special, one of those CBS special presentations, about how Santa became Santa, and how the point of Christmas is to take unhappiness out of the world. Instead, this Christmas above all, it seems, unhappiness is being put into Sam's life and changing his attitude towards Christmas.

Cut back to the present and Sam and Dean choose to follow Santa, who is a suspect and walks with a limp (apparent evidence that he might be Krampus), back to his trailer. They break in, ready to take down the anti–Claus and instead discover Santa with a bong, many beers and porn on the television. To cover for their mistake, Dean begins singing "Silent Night," encouraging Sam to do the same, so "Santa," who is drunk and high, will assume they are carolers. Like the first scene, which Kripke is so proud of, this scene takes many of the elements of Christmas (Santa, carols, etc.) and undercuts them. After Sam once again expresses his disappointment and disgust with Christmas, Dean asks him, "why are you the boy who hates Christmas?" Sam responds that their family history has rendered him unable to celebrate the holiday, as he sees nothing to celebrate.

The episode demonstrates that the family crises continue, as a young boy hears noises on the roof, sees whatever it is that has come down the chimney, and loudly proclaims, "Santa, you're early!" The being drags the boy's father out of the bedroom in his bag, eats a cookie, and drags the father up the chimney and out of the house. Thus, yet another family has a crisis now because the Winchesters have been unable to solve the problem. This time, however, Sam recognizes that the victims all had a particular wreath, which he and Dean track to the shop from which it came and then to the woman who made the wreaths.

While other types of wreath exist, the Christmas wreath is holiday décor that is rooted in specific meaning. The evergreen used to make Christmas wreaths is supposed to suggest eternal life, and the circular shape suggests God, who is without beginning or end (Mosteller 167). Various other associations may be attached, but the original imagery is pagan transformed into a profound Christian message. These wreaths, however, are being made by pagan gods who use them to mark the homes where sacrifice will take place. What is meant to suggest eternal life becomes a death sentence.

The irony is that Sam's realization sparks a happy Christmas memory in Dean—a wreath made entirely of beer cans that their father had stolen from a liquor store. On the one hand, Dean's fondness of the memory displays both his lowbrow taste and his own corruption of Christmas, while on the other hand, it demonstrates his ability to make a virtue out of the situation: if that was the only Christmas decoration they had, he would treasure it as if it were a Martha Stewart tree. In his own odd way, Dean understands the true meaning of Christmas in a manner that Sam does not.

Sam is confused by Dean's sudden excitement over the possibility of celebrating Christmas:

> SAM: I don't get it. You haven't talked about Christmas in years.
> DEAN: Well, yeah. But this is my last year.
> SAM: I know. That's why I can't.
> DEAN: What do you mean?
> SAM: I mean, I can't sit around drinking eggnog, pretending everything's okay, when I know next Christmas, you'll be dead. I just can't.

Dean wants a nice Christmas, as this will be his last one; Sam cannot have a nice Christmas because he knows this will be Dean's last one. Whereas Dean wants to use Christmas to take away some of the unhappiness in the Winchester's world, Sam is incapable.

The episode flashes back to 1991 again. Dean comes back to the hotel room with their Christmas dinner: fast food. "Are monsters real?" Sam asks Dean. "Monsters are real," Dean tells him, "Dad fights them. He's fighting them right now. Almost everything is real." "Is Santa real?" asks Sam. "No," Dean tells him with finality. Oddly, this is Dean's present to Sam: telling him the truth about reality. Not only that there is no Santa, but that there are monsters. They have not been abandoned by a reckless father—John Winchester is a hero who follows Kris Kringle's advice—put the needs of others ahead of yours and the world will be a better place. Sam is unhappy that the good in the world (Santa) is fake, yet the bad (monsters) is real. He cries himself to sleep because of his now lost innocence.

Returning to the present, Sam explains the pagan origins of most Christmas traditions (thus tying into the trope of explaining the sources of tradition). Dean says Christmas is Jesus's birthday. "No," counters Sam, "Jesus's birthday was probably in the fall. It was actually the winter solstice festival that was co-opted by the church and renamed Christmas. But I mean the yule log, the tree, even Santa's red suit that's all remnants of Pagan worship." In other words, Sam sees Christmas as simply being a repackaged reboot of pagan traditions. In doing so, Sam (and "AVSC") play into the larger phenomenon of holiday specials disconnecting the holidays from their religious roots. What is remarkable about all these holiday specials for Christmas and

Easter is the almost complete absence of Christianity. Only *A Charlie Brown Christmas* and *The Little Drummer Boy* directly acknowledge the holiday's origin in the birth of Christ, through Linus's speech to Charlie Brown about the true meaning of Christmas in the former and the eponymous Little Drummer Boy seeking to give a gift to the Christ child in the latter. *Santa Claus Is Coming to Town* obliquely acknowledges the birth of Christ with the suggestion that knowledge of that event is why Kris Kringle chose to make that night the one he delivers presents. In *A Charlie Brown Christmas*, on the other hand, Linus directly quotes Luke 2: 8–14 regarding the birth of Christ, but the true meaning of Christmas is when all the children come together and transform Charlie Brown's sad tree into a beautiful tree, which has nothing to do with Jesus Christ or his birth. If anything, it is a celebration of the power of both the individual (Charlie Brown) and the community (the other kids) to transform something sad and lowly into something magical; which, in fairness, is part of the Christmas message as well, from the birth in a stable to the baby in a manger who then receives gifts from foreign kings. *It's the Easter Beagle, Charlie Brown* has absolutely nothing to do with the crucifixion and resurrection of Jesus Christ. Likewise, "AVSC" has nothing to do with the Christian nature of Christmas. Jesus is derided by the pagan gods Sam and Dean fight as a sort of Johnny-come-lately that ruined everything for them.

The Winchesters invade the house of Edward and Madge Carrigan, pagan gods disguised as "Ozzie and Harriet," as Dean puts it. Bobby has told them sharpened evergreen stakes can kill the gods, but the boys are knocked out as they explore the house. They wake up as the Carrigans plan to sacrifice them, noting they only need the sacrifice of a few people a year to keep themselves alive. Most interestingly, Canfield asserts that Christmas is about "divinity entering the world," through the birth of Christ (233). "AVSC" posits that divinity is already in the world in the form of the pagan gods, rendering Jesus and the Christian God unnecessary, even on Christmas.

The final flash back to 1991 features Sam waking up to find presents for himself in the room. Dean tells him their dad was there while Sam was asleep, John Winchester now taking the place of Santa as the bringer of presents and the symbol of what is good in the world; after all, that is what he is to Dean. Sam opens the gifts—a Barbie doll and a baton—and realizes they are not from John. Dean stole them from a nearby house. Although disappointed, Sam recognizes that Dean was attempting, *in loco parentis*, to give Sam a real Christmas. Sam does not want the stolen presents but gives Dean the present he was wrapping for their father during the first flashback. Given that the third element of Christmas specials is explaining the origins of traditions, here is the moment when "AVSC" does precisely that. "So that's why we do that," echoes through holiday specials in response to the explanations given.

Santa Claus Is Coming to Town, *Rudolph the Red-Nosed Reindeer*, and *The Easter Bunny Is Coming to Town*, for example, all explain the origins of their respective holiday traditions, from Santa's suit and why he leaves things in stockings to why the Easter Bunny dyes eggs and then hides them. "AVSC" does the same, explaining the origin of the "Samulet" that Dean wears, which was originally a gift Sam had planned to give to his father, having gotten it from Bobby, but that he gave to Dean, since Dean had always been there for him in ways their father had not. Dean may have held John up as a Santa figure; Sam sees Dean as trying his best to actually decrease the unhappiness in the world, at least Sam's world.

The pagan gods are defeated and killed, but that is the least important aspect of the episode. Instead, the focus is on the aftermath. The Winchesters return to their motel, the current room clearly echoing the room in Broken Bow. The brothers stay in "The Thomas Kinkade Suite," named after the American painter, which is also a reference to Jared Padalecki's role as Kinkade in *The Christmas Cottage* (2008), itself an inspirational movie about Kinkade's creation of the eponymous painting in his youth. This reference is yet another meta echo of the Christmas special. Dean enters the room, which Sam has decorated for Christmas. Sam gives him rather potent eggnog. They give each other gifts: porno mags and shaving cream for Sam from Dean and motor oil and candy bars for Dean from Sam. This is no gift of the magi; nothing is sacrificed in order to procure gifts. They both went down to the convenience store and purchased what they thought might be useful, appreciated gifts. The gifts themselves are not important; that they are exchanged is. The decorations, eggnog, gift exchange and other tropes of family Christmases serve to demonstrate that Sam has learned the true meaning of Christmas: celebrating with family, even if they will not be there next year; giving of one's self instead of holding on to old grudges, and simply holding on to happiness while one can. Christmas horror, asserts Canfield, like mainstream Christmas specials, features "characters who need reminders of why [...] spiritual redemption matters" (239). Charlie Brown, the Winter Warlock, George Bailey, and Sam Winchester all need to be reminded of the importance of the holiday in their own personal salvation from the darkness in their lives.

The show ends in cliché: "Have Yourself a Merry Little Christmas" begins to play as snow begins to fall. Like a Christmas special or Thomas Kinkade painting, all is sweetly, cloyingly well in the world, and the family crisis is resolved in time for Christmas Day itself. As the camera pulls back out of the window, we see "Baby," Dean's Impala that is the symbol of home for the brothers and whose name then becomes a Christmas pun. The baby being celebrated is not the Christ child just born, but the rekindled Christmas feeling in both brothers as symbolized by the car that serves as their home and as symbol of the larger family to which they belong. Dean may be bound for Hell soon, and all is not well in the world, but Christmas has been restored as an important part of the Winchesters' lives. The episode has used every trope and cliché of Christmas specials to show the miracle in Ypsilanti—Sam Winchester appreciates Christmas again, and we now know why things are the way they are. After the inevitable defeat of the monsters, the brothers demonstrate how they have learned the true meaning of Christmas in an ironic gift exchange ("Skin mags!" and "Fuel for me; fuel for my baby!"), and the value of family. By deconstructing the tropes of holiday specials, signaled by the opening homage to CBS holiday specials and the referential title, carrying through the deployment of those tropes through the episode, and the use of *Santa Claus Is Coming to Town* in the flashback sequences, *Supernatural* both celebrates holiday specials nostalgically (if cynically) and uses them to comment on its own family narrative, finding the Winchesters flawed, but deserving of a Brady-worthy ending. No Mike Brady is needed, however. John Winchester was a hero, but also an absent father. Instead, the Winchester boys solve their own problems and in doing so, save Christmas. Turns out the anti-holiday holiday special is quite pro-holiday in spite of itself.

Works Cited

Canfield, David. "Silent Night, Holy Sh*t: Holy Terror and the Dark Side of the Nativity: Christmas Horror on Film and Television." *Yuletide Terror: Christmas Horror on Film and Television*, edited by Paul Corupe and Kier-La Janisse, Spectacular Optical, 2017, pp. 223–239.
Humuhumu. "Jungle Drums Are Calling You ... to Watch a CBS Special Presentation." *Critiki*. 7 January 2007. https://news.critiki.com/2007/01/07/jungle-drums-are-calling-you-to-watch-a-cbs-special-presentation. Accessed October 20, 2017.
Macklem, Lisa. "I See What You Did There: SPN and the Fourth Wall." *Fan Phenomena: Supernatural*, edited by Lynn Zubernis and Katherine Larsen, Intellect, 2014, pp. 34–44.
Mosteller, Angie. *Christmas*. Itasca Books, 2008.
Routledge, Clay. *Nostalgia*. Routledge, 2016.
Santa Claus Is Coming to Town. Directed by Arthur Rankin, Jr., and Jules Bass. CBS, 1970.
A Very Brady Christmas. Directed by Peter Baldwin. CBS, 1988.

Strap In for the Scariest Hour in the History of Television
"Ghostfacers" as Parody of Paranormal Investigative Show

Kevin J. Wetmore, Jr.

Ghost Hunters, A Haunting, Ghost Adventures, Paranormal State, School Spirits, Most Haunted, My Ghost Story, Celebrity Ghost Stories, The Haunted, The Haunted Collector, and *The World's Scariest Places* are among the dozens of television programs in which paranormal investigators go to an allegedly haunted site and search for evidence of the survival of the human personality[1] after death. These shows follow roughly the same structure to the same ends: no definitive proof of the unearthly, but many events that seem to suggest a presence.

To this list we must add the pilot for *Ghostfacers*, a paranormal investigative show featuring primary team members Ed Zeddmore and Harry Spengler (formerly of Hell Hounds) and their team of "Ghostfacers" (they "face the ghosts when others will not," according to the show's theme song, hence the name). Tangentially, their surnames are also obviously a tribute to Winston and Egon, respectively, of the *Ghostbusters* (1984), setting up an echo of a comedy about inept paranormal investigators who happen to discover real supernatural activity. Frequently the investigations of Harry and Ed reference, copy or even parody the techniques and approaches of the Ghostbusters, who are also graceless and maladroit in their investigations and ghost fighting. The pilot also features secondary team members Kenny Spruce, Maggie Zeddmore, Alan Corbett, Sam and Dean Winchester (technically not really team members but appropriated as such by Ed and Harry when they make their pilot episode). In the pilot, which also features an introduction from Ed and Harry, the team investigates Morton House, which every four years, on February 29, becomes the most haunted house in America. While the pilot begins by following the structure of the shows listed above, that structure is obliterated when actual ghosts obviously manifest on camera, and Corbett and Sam are kidnapped by a spirit, with the former subsequently killed by that spirit and becoming a ghost himself.

"Ghostfacers" (3.13) forms an intertext with the above-mentioned shows, deconstructing them, following their structures, tropes and motifs, and satirizing the claims they seem to make about the paranormal and supernatural. It does so by not being an episode of *Supernatural*, but by being the pilot of *Ghostfacers*, making Harry and Ed the protagonists, with Dean and Sam only showing up later in the episode as supporting characters. It is clear from the prologue addressed to Hollywood fat cats that these people are un-self-aware, incompetent, inept, and a parody of what they aspire to. In constructing the Ghostfacers as bungling and maladroit and echoing the elements of ghost hunting shows, the episode becomes a meta statement on ghost hunting shows.

Like most ghost hunting shows, the episode is shot on handheld cameras, computer cameras, with the team's cameras strategically placed to record the actions of both ghosts and those who face them. Ed and Harry inadvertently reveal the amateur incompetence of the team through their own un-self-aware statements such as "We're two lone wolves" "And two lone wolves need, uh… other wolves," their unprofessional set up (the Ghostfacers' headquarters is Ed's parents' garage, into which Ed's father accidentally almost drives during the first phase of the investigation, and echoing the converted firehouse of the Ghostbusters), their ignorance of the reality of the paranormal, and their cowardice when confronted with it. The result is that the team is skewered as much for the tropes of ghost hunting shows as for their failures to adhere to them. Ghostfacers play at being ghost hunters, the show says, and by implication, so do the *Ghost Hunters*. Sam and Dean are the real deal.

The episode explores several issues related to this type of reality programming, asking if such shows are not inherently exploitive, as Ed and Harry clearly use Corbett's death to promote their show. It mocks such shows as *Ghost Hunters*, in which professional plumbers are also amateur paranormal investigators, or *Paranormal State*, in which college students take time off from classes to investigate the paranormal. Ed and Harry work at Kinko's, and so must wait until six to start ghost hunting, but they're practically management and can do what they want. Spruce we know works at a driving range, driving the vehicle that gathers up the golf balls down range. These are not trained professionals. At best they are self-taught hobbyists.

Furthermore, everything is evidence of the reality of the paranormal in these shows, and everything is presented therefore not in a scientific light but a spooky one. Every noise, every event is considered as having a possible paranormal source. In "Ghostfacers" this aspect is brought to the fore immediately. The strategy session which opens the pilot is interrupted by a mysterious noise. The team wonders if it is some sort of supernatural entity, but it is revealed to be merely Ed's father opening the garage door, thereby spoiling any illusion that the Ghostfacers' headquarters is an actual office with arcane mysteries contained inside. Every mundane thing is considered to be possibly supernatural in origin, until it is conclusively proven that it isn't. The episode takes this to an extreme, by showing the Ghostfacers treating everything as potentially paranormal, but when confronted with the reality of ghosts, the Ghostfacers have no desire to actually face them. This is the episode in which metatext and intertext are used to comment on our obsession with the paranormal in a show about the paranormal.

Several documentary-type shows from the seventies, eighties and nineties featured occasional segments of ghost investigation, from *In Search Of* and *That's Incredible* through *Unsolved Mysteries*. The twenty-first century, however, has seen an explosion of shows solely dedicated to the investigation of the paranormal, especially hauntings. Sharon A. Hill argues that "[t]he popularity of the 21st century ghost hunter can be directly linked to two television programs: *Most Haunted* in the U.K. (2002) and *Ghost Hunters* in the U.S. (2004)" (52). She refers to the groups that appear in these shows as "Amateur Research and Investigation Groups" or ARIGs (2). The complaint of such groups is that ARIGs are not taken seriously by scientists (Hill 24). The complaint of scientists is that ARIGs neither engage in scientific research, nor follow any scientific method in investigating alleged paranormal activity. These groups pretend to engage in unbiased investigation, but, as noted above, every episode at best remains inconclusive after offering several events and phenomena as distinctly and obviously paranormal in origin.

The rise of these groups and shows can be tied to a post–9/11 resurgence in belief in the paranormal and supernatural. Mike Hale sees in this brand of reality television "a nation's resurgent interest in things it can't see (or easily defend itself against)." I would further argue such shows tie in to the cultural trend of the "amateur expert"—one need no formal training to develop expertise in something. Opinion matters as much as fact or analysis in our culture, and so plumbers or Kinko's employees are just as qualified as trained experts to investigate ghosts, so long as they can afford the equipment. Lastly, I have argued elsewhere, however, that there exist multiple reasons for the explosion of ghost shows and ghost hunters after 9/11. While ghosts represent that which we cannot "defend against," ghosts also represent the idea that death is not the end, and that something of those who perish lives on after them (Wetmore 156). These shows offer violent, malevolent ghosts (Freeman Daggett) but also caring, protecting ghosts (Alan Corbett), all being investigated by professional amateur experts.

These teams are also all indicative of a rejection of educated elitists in favor of proletarian self-proclaimed expertise:

> And the teams themselves play the part of working-class heroes, from the plumbers of "Ghost Hunters" to the burly Texas brothers of "Ghost Lab" to the public-school students of "Paranormal State." They've created a new career—the paranormal investigator—that requires neither good looks nor any discernible skill beyond the ability to walk through an old building waving a flashlight [Hale].

To these ranks we might add the Ghostfacers. Their names are working class: given names such as Ed, Harry, and Maggie, as well as the two team members who use their surnames: Corbett and Spruce (rather than Alan and Kenny, and meaning "Little Crow" in the case of the former and a kind of tree in the case of the latter—hardly aristocratic sounding individuals). Their equipment is cobbled together—not state of the art investigatory gear, but cheap cameras, computers and things rigged together based on what they have seen on television.

Supernatural plays against this construction of the shows: Sam and Dean are the real working-class heroes. They know the reality they are up against, whereas the Ghostfacers developed their understanding from the great educational sources of television and the internet. The Ghostfacers themselves, especially Ed and Harry, have been seeking validation through an internet presence and then through seeking their own television program. The original appearance of Ed and Harry set the stage for the satire of ghost hunting and *Ghost Hunters* here. "Hell House" (1.17) introduced Harry and Ed as amateur ghost hunters who believe footage of an actual ghost would lead to "our ticket to the big time. Fame, money, sex. With girls," as Ed tells Harry. Their motives are laid bare. They reveal that most of their knowledge comes from the internet and popular culture. When confronted with the reality of a ghost, Harry freaks out. Ed asks him, "W.W.B.D.?" to which Harry responds, "What would Buffy do? I know, but Ed, she's stronger than me." Another seemingly inside joke here is that two ghost hunters on a television show who want to be television ghost hunters are taking as their guide a fictional television show about a high school vampire hunter. The fact that they model themselves after Buffy instead of the more masculine reality television show ghost hunters is also a comment on their own masculinity, which will reach full fruition later in the episode and will be analyzed, below.

Supernatural appears to satirize the idea that ghost hunting is a path to fame and fortune: the paranormal investigator as pop celebrity who does not actually know or understand how the world of the supernatural really works, and who would freak out if they actually did encounter something genuinely paranormal. Like the *Ghost Hunters*, Ed and Harry will be validated if they can be seen on television, which, with the internet, is the circular confirmation of their own authentic status as ghost hunters (and yet their model is not *Ghost Hunters* but the fictitious *Buffy the Vampire Slayer*). *Supernatural* rejects this model, despite being on television itself. The show seems to suggest that it takes the supernatural more seriously than "reality" television programs. Indeed, the repetition of the "Ghostfacers" theme song at the end of the episode, now over the show *Supernatural*, not the show within the show, indicates that Sam and Dean are the true "ghost facers": they actually do what the song claims Harry, Ed and crew do. This point is echoed later in the episode when Spruce films Dean looking for Sam in the Morton House and asks him why Sam said he only had a few months left. "I'm not going to whine about my problem to some [explicative] reality show. I'm going to do my [explicative] job," Dean responds. The others may be in it for television, fame and fortune. To Dean, however, this is a [explicative] job, part of a family business, in fact, which furthers his working class bona fides.

Spruce, tangentially, is both a comic character and another Easter egg. Spruce states he is "Fifteen-sixteenths Jew, one sixteenth Cherokee," thus tying the Ghostfacers to the trope of the Native American haunting of American land. In Algonquin mythology, Spruce trees mark "where a warrior fell fighting the white man" (Raven 19–20). Even his character serves to satirize the paranormal investigation show: "Everyone knows that ghosts are associated with ancient burial grounds" of Native Americans, observes Hill in her critique of such programs (177). Second only to abandoned hospitals, prisons and asylums, Native American sites and burial sites are classic pop culture haunting locales. Jay Anson, for example, not satisfied with the murder of the DeFeo family at the Amityville house, further notes in *The Amityville Horror* that the house was built on the site where Shinnecock Native Americans would leave their sick, dying and insane, believing the land to be demon-haunted. Spruce frequently is the one behind the camera, but also defines himself as a "shamanologist," another made-up thing that sounds much more impressive than it actually is. Like the other Ghostfacers, he claims a status that he has not actually earned or developed in any manner.

Interestingly, "Hell House" and "Ghostfacers" have a number of overlaps or echoes. Both feature investigations of abandoned homes that are allegedly haunted. Both sites are haunted by malevolent male specters that are not what they first seem to be, although to be fair, that is *Supernatural*'s modus operandi (or indeed that of any investigative show in which a mystery must be solved by the characters within an hour of television: the first two monsters that the brothers Winchester suspect may be involved in any given episode are discovered to be wrong; then they figure out what it really is). In the case of "Hell House" the malevolent male ghost is actually a Tulpa, an apparition created because people believe it exists. In the case of "Ghostfacers," the initial ghosts seen are just death echoes. The real monster, Freeman Daggett, is a powerful and angry spirit with powers beyond those of the average ghost, including the ability to kill or teleport living humans. In other words, the first paranormal encounters in "Ghostfacers" are of the harmless variety. At best in a ghost hunting show, the hunters might encounter what the Winchesters call a death echo (although never a fully visible apparition, nothing so obvious). Behind the death echoes is a much more directed, intelligent, malevolent entity. We might tangentially note that ghost hunting shows frequently gender the behavior of the alleged entities. Female ghosts are in mourning: forlorn, melancholy, and expressing loss and remorse. Male spirits tend to be malevolent, malicious, and vengeful. Occasionally malevolent female spirits are seen, but the gender construction of female-as-brokenhearted and male-as-vicious tends to dominate these shows. While *Supernatural* tends to be equal opportunity in terms of the genders of spirits—any entity that has remained too long will be angry and violent, regardless of gender—in this case the specific angry male spirit ties into the trope of the reality shows. Freeman Daggett is easily the equal of any of the alleged malevolent male ghosts occupying the structures investigated by the *Ghost Hunters*.

Equally important to the ARIGs is the use of ghost hunting technology. The primary purpose of The Atlantic Paranormal Society (AKA TAPS, the official moniker of *Ghost Hunters*) is "to validate what its 'clients' are experiencing by using a wide array of ghost-detecting technologies" (O'Hara 73). The "clients" have already phenomenologically experienced something in the locale. The purpose of the Ghost Hunters is to then use technology to prove the client is not crazy because something really is happening. Through recordings, meters and other means of measuring energy, temperature and other quantifiable elements, attempts to connect to anything using E.V.P. (Electronic Voice Phenomena) and other such assessable qualities, ghost hunters seek to prove the reality of a haunting. The Ghostfacers aim to do this in the Morton house, as their goal is to create a television program. Sam and Dean's use of such equipment is not to prove to an external audience the reality of their experience but rather to locate spirits and entities themselves. Ghostfacers seek external validation through their equipment use. The Winchesters do not. However, as the episode clearly demonstrates, one does not need technology to validate a haunting. As Johnson did, dismissing Bishop Berkeley's arguments by kicking a stone and stating, "I refute it thus," Freeman Daggett kidnaps and kills Corbett: is that proof enough of his reality for you? All the technology they brought neither proves the existence of ghosts nor protects the Ghostfacers from them. Indeed, the actual tools of "hunting" as defined by *Supernatural* come in far handier in the episode. When Dean and Spruce are trapped behind a door, Dean yells through the door to Ed, "Hey, Ed, listen to me. There's some salt in my duffel. Make a circle and get inside." A simple circle of salt is more valuable than all the technology, a point further made by Ed's own senselessness when he thinks, a confused expression on his face, and then asks Dean in response, "Get inside your duffle bag?" "In the salt, you idiot," comes Dean's correction. The show is with Dean on this one. Ed is an idiot, and the leader of the Ghostfacers clearly has no idea how to actually face a ghost, a point made again and again in the show.

The rest of this essay will be a close reading of the structure of the episode in order to consider how *Supernatural* uses the structure and elements of the ARIG show to satirize such shows. The episode begins with a video prologue, Harry and Ed in tuxedos sitting in chairs in front of a fireplace, pretending (poorly) at sophistication. "If you received this tape you must be some sort of bigwig network executive. Well today is your lucky day, mister," proclaims Ed. "Because the unsolicited pilot you are about to watch is the bold new future of 'reality tv,'" finishes Harry, demonstrating that the Ghostfacers have no idea how television shows are pitched and made. Their arrogance fails to mask their incompetence but seems to come from their belief that because the images from the Morton House so clearly demonstrate the reality of the paranormal that networks would leap to have the show. They fail to recognize that most people would believe the tape a fake anyway, as technology could (and indeed did) also produce all the effects. They also fail to recognize that their show itself, while following the tropes of the ghost show, fails at the most important one, which is the need for ambiguity and uncertainty, as I shall detail below. A show that demonstrates the reality of the supernatural would be rejected in favor of one that at best hints at it and allows viewers to make up their own minds. Simulated hauntings are preferred to real ones, since the fear and danger generated by a real haunting are not present at a simulated one. The latter are fun; the former are scary and dangerous. Ironically, the *Ghostfacers* pilot is too scary for television, mostly through Corbett's supernatural death, which is far more violent and graphic than anything depicted in paranormal reality shows, which allude to past violence, but never feature actual death, and through its overt depiction of ghosts that clearly prove the survival of the human personality after death. Paradoxically, the overt presence of ghosts is also anathema to series television, which requires an open-ended answer at the end of every episode as to whether or not ghosts actually exist. Once the existence of the paranormal is proven, the show doesn't need to exist anymore. Reality television ghost hunting is a tease, not a certainty, and the Ghostfacers violate that rule as well. Paranormal television presents orbs, shadows moving at the edge of the screen, odd recordings and things heard at a distance which can then be interpreted as possible evidence of a haunting. A giant spectral janitor that kills people does not fly in such a milieu.

Instead of the typical *Supernatural* opening, the viewer sees the opening credits of *Ghostfacers*, the unsolicited pilot, which resembles the typical credit sequence of the variety of ghost hunting shows on television. The word "Ghostfacers" is spelled out in a creepy, gothic font, with a stylized skull forming the letter "o" in ghost. What follows is a montage of shots from the pilot episode itself (one of the ways *Supernatural* rewards repeated viewing is recognizing the credit shots from the episode that follows when viewed subsequently). Shots freeze on individuals, and text of the team member's name is shown next to their image: Ed, Harry, Spruce, Maggie, Corbett, Sam and Dean. The shots of Ed and Harry are hardly flattering, further mocking the two characters, as even though they were presumably overseeing the editing of the episode they could not even select images that made them look good (or even not terrified) in the credits. Sam and Dean are clearly very angry in their ID shots, not happy to be on film, presented without their consent (yet another problem for the Ghostfacers, who apparently are as inept at television production as they are at ghost hunting). Indeed, Dean gives the camera a pixelated middle finger in his credit shot, which also marks this as not a typical episode of *Supernatural*. As will be discussed below, we learn the Winchesters actually employ a great deal of profanity, which must be bleeped, yet another tip of the hat to ghost hunting shows, in which the bleeped profanity seems to give credence to the "reality" of the experience and the sincerity and working class status of the investigators: these are regular guys who use profanity when encountering the strange or scary. Interestingly, Corbett and Spruce are identified by their last names, instead of Alan and Kenny, their given names. Everyone else is on a first name basis. The credits end, as all ghost hunting show credits do, with a shot of the team all standing with their equipment, arms folded, looking tough and professional, except for Harry, who can't decide whether to fold his arms or put them on his hips.

The theme song, likewise, verges on the ludicrous. It is a pop metal-esque song about the Ghostfacers who assert, as their name suggests, that they will face ghosts when others will not do so, even if that means staying in the kitchen when it gets hot. The song amusingly lists things the Ghostfacers will face: nightmare: dread, the dead, even the faceless. Interestingly, right before Sam and Dean appear, the lyrics suggest that if one has a supernatural encounter, then these Ghostfacers are who you are going to call. The double reference in the lyrics is to both the show *Supernatural*, into which the Ghostfacers have fallen, and *Ghostbusters*, yet another reference to the most famous film about inept ghost hunters. In short, even the theme song of the show-within-the-show is an ironic series of meta references.

The structure of the show proceeds from the structure of ghost hunting shows. Mike Hale offers a summary of the formula of these shows:

> On each show a team—they have names like the Atlantic Paranormal Society, the Everyday Paranormal Team and the Penn State Paranormal Research Society—descends on some purportedly haunted location, often a large, decrepit structure, like

an abandoned hospital or factory. They venture inside with the tools of their trade: K2 meters to detect electromagnetic fields, parabolic dishes to capture the faintest noises, night-vision lenses to penetrate the darkness. Everything is bathed in sickly green light, and people say "Oh my God!" and "Did you hear that?" a lot. Shadows move from left to right (or right to left). Eventually someone yells that something is touching him, everyone runs like a frightened child and the camera flails about. The team members then gather for a post-mortem in which they catalog the bumps and shadows and congratulate one another on their bravery.

This description could also be a summary of the Ghostfacers' investigation into the Morton House, from the opening in which information is given about Morton House, a "large, decrepit structure" to the end in which the Ghostfacers mock Dean and Sam while celebrating their "triumph" in the Morton House investigation, despite the death of Alan Corbett. The structure of the ghost-hunting show "has become ritualized to the point of self-parody," states Hale. "Ghostfacers" is that parody.

The show-within-the-show reveals its own five act structure through title cards dividing the investigation of the Morton House into five phases which follow the standard format of ghost hunting shows. Phase I is "The Homework," which on all ghost hunting shows is the introduction to the investigation. The history of the site to be investigated is given, along with any theories about what entity or entities might be present. The convention is that the viewing audience is briefed as the team is briefed on camera; we all learn about the nature of the haunting simultaneously. In the case of the Morton House, the team shares information about the site. Every leap year, on February 29, the house becomes "the most haunted house in America," a claim itself that sounds ghost hunting show-worthy. It is also revealed, none too subtly, during "The Homework" that Corbett has a crush on Ed. Despite the awkwardness of the moment, Ed attempts to present this investigation as seriously and professionally as possible, that is until, as mentioned above, his father opens the garage door trying to drive the car in, emphasizing both the amateur status of the Ghostfacers, but also their own ineptness, further underlined by the fact that Ed still lives at home with his parents.

"Phase II: Infiltration" starts the actual on-site investigation, which begins with the team cutting through the chain link fence covered in "No Trespassing" signs. When asked if they have permission to investigate (something every television ARIG would have gotten, otherwise the episode would never air), Ed responds, "Permits? That's a pretty good idea for next time." As they prepare to enter the house, however, the first sinister thing happens: a black car drives past slowly, blasting "We're an American Band" by Grand Funk Railroad, before tearing off. Regular viewers immediately recognize the arrival of the Winchesters, scoping out the Morton House before their investigation begins.

Another trope of the ghost hunting show occurs here and several more times in the rest of the episode; not seen in any other episode of *Supernatural* is the use of a series of images of the house as photographic negatives, each one marked with a percussive beat, as a bumper or transition into the next scene. Such bumpers are used for emphasis of the sinister and otherworldly nature of the home, provide a transition to the next sequence, and unnerve the viewer. By doing so here, the episode emphasizes its commitment to the elements of the ghost hunting show being satirized.

There follows a montage of the 'Facers (as they call themselves) setting up the equipment, a standard trope of the ghost hunting show. Identified cameras are placed through the house; these will not only film any visible spirits, they will also record most of the actual content of the show. The montage ends with text on the screen with a time and location stamp (again, standard practice for such shows): "Morton House Base Camp. 10:41 p.m." Doing so continues the verisimilitude of the ghost hunting show within the episode of *Supernatural* but also serves a practical purpose: if the Morton House becomes "the most haunted house in America" on February 29, then this archetypal graphic also provides a countdown to midnight and the moment when the show will switch from goofy to dangerously serious.

"Phase III: Face Time!" marks the start of the actual investigation. "Morton House 10:51 p.m. Team 1: Ed and Corbett" reads the onscreen graphic, again in perfect imitation of ghost hunting shows. Ed attempts E.V.P. in the house, walking around with a recorder, saying, "Hello? I am speaking to the restless spirits of the Morton House. Are there any entity or entities present? Can you give us a sign?" In the typical ghost hunting show, we would either at this moment or later in the episode hear playback of the recording which would have a distorted sound not audible on the camera recording. This sound would be played multiple times and one of the amateur experts would tell us they believe the sound is (insert ominous but meaningless word here), spoken by one of the entities. Alternately, when Ed asks for a sign, a noise would be heard from somewhere in the house. Again, no definitive signs would be given, just a hint of something somewhere else.

The first sign that this is not a ghost hunting show occurs when the monitor showing Ed's camera frizzes, as if there is a distortion of the signal. This camera frizz will become the marker that something is about to happen in the Morton House. Spruce thinks there is just a problem with the equipment, which is ironic, because in a genre in which everything is taken as evidence of the presence of the paranormal, the one thing that actually *is* such evidence is taken as a routine problem with the equipment. Spruce misses the one genuine moment of paranormal activity during the E.V.P. session, further comment by the show that ghost hunters such as this have no idea what they are actually doing.

Indeed, for the next few moments in the house, the utter incompetence of the Ghostfacers is repeatedly demonstrated. Harry tries to kick a door open and fails. Spruce says dryly, "Turn the knob." Harry does, and the door opens easily. His attempt at macho bravado feats of strength is proven unnecessary and physically impossible for him. This is followed by yet another trope of the ghost show—a team member freaks out at something and runs. We are shown their camera POV, shaky and incomprehensible during the run, the kinetic visuals emphasizing the confusion and panic. Ordinarily, the team member who panicked explains that he saw something, or something touched her. In this case it is Harry who runs from a room screaming, "Oh my God! Oh my God! Oh my God!" (a common refrain, heard on everything from *The Blair Witch Project* to *Ghost Hunters*). Then comes the reveal of what made him panic: as Spruce puts it, "It's just a rat, dude." Harry hates rats.

The group then panics again when someone enters the room. It is Sam and Dean, claiming to be police and demanding that everyone show ID and leave. Except Ed and Harry recognize them: "You're those [beeped] from Texas!" Tangentially, this is perhaps one of the best and most meta elements of the episode. Characters swear as they would in real life and as in ghost hunting shows, the obscenities have both a sound over them and the Ghostfacers skull placed over the mouth of the person saying the obscenity. Unlike regular episodes of *Supernatural*, this adds to the verisimilitude of the ghost hunting show, as they are able to use obscenities as they ordinarily would (yet another marker of working-class status), and they are "removed in post" for broadcast. As a result, Sam and Dean swear like sailors in this episode, suggesting that in the "real" episodes of *Supernatural* they might, as well, reminding the viewer that both *Ghostfacers* and *Supernatural* are artificial products of television, subject to mores and the regulations of the Federal Communications Commission.

The Ghostfacers claim that they were "here first," as Ed calls Dean "chisel chest," yet another comment about comparative masculinities. Dean pushes him against the wall and threatens them that they have to leave before midnight. "We have to spend the night. It's for a TV show!" Ed insists. Sam looks right at the camera and the Winchesters realize the reality of the reality show being filmed. "Great. Perfect," sighs Sam in disbelief. It seems clear the viewer is meant to share the Winchesters' disregard (bordering on contempt) for the Ghostfacers.

Sam shares with them his research, which was much more detailed than the information given by Ed during Phase One. Sam explains the history of the Morton House and how many fatalities have occurred in it on February 29. "These look legit," says Ed upon seeing the newspaper accounts. Not only is it apparent Ed did not do very much research, the small amount he did do seems to have glossed over the danger of the place. It is yet another example of incompetence from the 'Facers.

The first apparition is then witnessed by team two, Maggie and Harry, who record the phantasm. Sam and Dean realize what they saw was a death echo, a simple replaying of the moment of death. The 'Facers are excited because they have evidence of the supernatural. The Winchesters, always the counterpoint, attempt to discern what is really happening, as death echoes usually only repeat at the place of death or where the body is. The 'Facers play at being paranormal investigators; the Winchesters are monster hunters: the contrast is obvious.

Corbett, excited to find more proof for Ed, wanders off on his own and employs yet another trope of the ghost show: low light/night vision cameras that display everything in a green light. Corbett turns his on, and suddenly a figure is visible behind him, grabbing him just before a cut to commercial. Whereas the night vision camera effect is used to create atmosphere in a ghost hunting show, here it is used to great effect to reveal the actual entity: Freeman Daggett, who takes Corbett. As the rest of the group realizes that Corbett is missing and calls his name, the onscreen text changes from "Morton House 11:59" to "Morton House 12:00," signaling the start of February 29. This moment marks the shift from a show focused on the 'Facers to a show focused on the Winchesters.

Dean explains to the others the house is on "a supernatural lockdown. This is no death echo, this is a bad mother and it wants us." The Ghostfacers do not even know what a death echo is, but they are beginning to understand the reality of the situation. The Morton House is "our Grand Canyon," they are told. After two more different death echoes, Sam disappears as Corbett did, resulting in Dean and the 'Facers needing to work together to find their missing associates.

A moment is repeated by Maggie and Spruce. In each case Sam or Dean asks why they keep filming and would they not feel better putting down the camera and helping. And in each case, Maggie and Spruce both admit they feel better experiencing the events through a viewfinder or monitor. Again, the repetition of this moment drives the point home: ghost hunting shows revel in the slightest brush of the possibility of the supernatural—a shadow seen in a corner, noise on a recording that could be an example of E.V.P.— but only when filtered and cleaned up. Ghost hunting shows not only mediate the experience of the supernatural, they also leave it ambiguous while generously interpreting even the most mundane event as "possibly" supernatural in origin. Confronted with very obvious manifestations of the supernatural, both Maggie and Spruce prefer to experience it indirectly (even though they share a physical space with it), but to continue the mediated experience.

O'Hara notes, after Baudrillard, a simulated and real haunting produce the same effect: terror in those who experience it (80). But the terror is a manifestly simulated one in the case of ghost hunting shows. Watching at home, one is not in the haunted location, one does not directly experience the phenomena shown or narrated, and yet one can receive a vicarious, visceral thrill through the viewing experience. One can see and hear what may be the supernatural without experiencing any danger or facing a genuinely frightening experience one's self. On the show itself, the danger is also nonexistent. While the individual hunters may run screaming, while a camera may whip around while a voice yells, "What was that? What was that!!??," nobody dies on an episode of *Ghost Hunters* who wasn't already dead when the episode began. O'Hara observes that "[m]ost of these shows conclude with no conclusion at all, thereby beginning and ending with uncertainty" (80). In this episode of *Supernatural*, that uncertainty is wiped away for the Ghostfacers, who are suddenly faced with a very real, very dangerous, indeed very deadly ghost. What ghost hunting shows play at, the world of *Supernatural* reveals to be real.

Corbett and Sam both wake up in a room sitting at a table, tied to their chairs. Around the table are three corpses. On the table is a decaying and rotten cake. Lesley Gore's "It's My Party," from her album *I'll Cry If I Want To* (a title derived from the song's chorus, which consists of the song title and the album title combined), plays, but the record skips, so all that is heard is the repeated chorus of the song. Freeman Daggett proceeds to kill Corbett by thrusting a spike through his throat from behind. Daggett then approaches Sam, and the show seems to suggest the same is about to happen to him. Instead, Daggett places a conical birthday hat on his head. It is an oddly comic moment in a decreasingly silly episode.

The team then sees Corbett's death echo and realizes he is dead. The best-known line (one that *Supernatural* itself has had fun with in a variety of ways) comes when Harry attempts to convince Ed to wake Corbett out of his death echo so he can pass on: "Ed, you've got to go be gay for that poor, dead intern." Ed speaks comfortingly to Corbett, expressing his admiration and love. It is a rare redeeming moment for Ed where despite the homophobia passing as humor, his expression of concern for the man crushing on him wakes Corbett out of the death echo.

Yet this moment also serves as the culmination of yet another trope of ghost hunting shows. In her analysis of masculinity in paranormal reality television, Karen J. Renner argues effectively that:

> men have not only dominated ghost-hunting reality television but have transformed it into a hypermasculine arena through a variety of behaviors: proclaiming and proving physical toughness; treating fear as "girlish"; physically sacrificing themselves, soldier-like, for the greater good; declaring a desire to seek out truth and justice

regardless of danger; substantiating emotion and intuition with evidence; heftily pronouncing their heterosexuality [...] [203].

What is this description if not a summary of the Winchesters, especially Dean? The "hypermasculine arena" of the Morton House pits the manhood of Dean Winchester against Freeman Daggett (a very manly and thus worthy opponent) and Ed Zeddmore, who is obviously lacking in every area. He is afraid, out for himself, of questionable sexuality (at least according to pop culture codes: why would a gay man like you unless you yourself were also gay?) and neither physically nor emotionally "tough." The episode repeatedly contrasts the masculinity of the Winchesters with the lack of masculinity of the Ghostfacers. Even Sam, the more sensitive and feminine of the brothers, is disgusted by the weakness, fear and lack of sense or masculine behavior of Ed and Harry. Ironically, it is the sole gay character who is shown to embody the hypermasculinity most: he is unafraid, exploring the house alone in order to find evidence to make Ed happy; he sacrifices himself to save the group. It is he, not Dean, who defeats Daggett. It is he who is literally killed and yet still keeps going as a ghost. In this way, the show not only fulfills the trope of paranormal reality television as masculine proving ground, it then effectively undercuts that trope by playing against stereotypes while also reinforcing them.

As a result of both investigation and the events that propel the narrative forward, the group, in true paranormal reality television investigatory fashion, is able to discern that Freeman Daggett was a paranoid survivalist and hospital janitor who took bodies from the morgue to come to his birthday party since he had no living friends, and he held his party in a bomb shelter in the basement, where he also committed suicide, returning every February 29 to kill anyone in his house. The mystery is solved and now can be dealt with.

Sam is freed from the shelter in the basement, but Daggett goes on the attack. He is briefly stopped by being shot with rock salt, but it is clear he means to kill the Winchesters and the 'Facers. The spirit of Corbett then grabs the ghost of Daggett and drags him presumably into the light where he will no longer be able to haunt the Morton House. Time for one more trope as we see the team leave the house with a voiceover from the team leader: "The Ghostfacers were forced to face something far scarier than ghosts. They had to face themselves." Tiresome clichés in voiceovers seem to also be a paranormal investigation program trope.

We return to the prologue setting of Ed and Harry in chairs by the fire. They salute Corbett. "As far as we're concerned," Harry says, "you aren't an intern any more. You have more than earned full Ghostfacer status. Plus, it would be cool to have a ghost on the team." The show ends with a tribute to Corbett and a brief clip of him, and then the camera pulls back to reveal that the show we just saw was being played on a monitor for Sam and Dean to watch. The big reveal is that the whole episode was already fully edited and being presented to the Winchesters as members of the Ghostfacers. At this moment, the actual credits for *Supernatural* begin to run under the scene, the first time in the show's history they run at the end, not the beginning.

"What do you think?" they ask the Winchesters, who respond that it was "not half bad," and that they admire how the show honors Corbett's memory "while grossly exploiting his death," which forms the final tongue-in-cheek critique of ghost hunting shows. *Supernatural* plays at tragedy as a fictional narrative show. Ghost hunting shows exploit real deaths, real tragedies. The alleged hauntings are by murdered people, unhappy lovers, the sick, insane or institutionalized, children who died—the more historical and gruesome the death of the person or persons haunting the better.

The ending of this episode involves Sam and Dean leaving an electromagnet in a satchel which goes off when the Ghostfacers open it, thereby erasing and destroying all evidence that the Morton House was genuinely haunted. The world is not ready to know, insist the Winchesters, yet, as noted above, they did not need to do so. No one would believe the video, assuming it was fake. The real reason they erased the material was that they wanted no evidence that they (the Winchesters) exist. As they roar off to the Ghostfacers theme, the world (and the world of the show) has been restored to normal.

"Ghostfacers" marks the second meta episode, using the tropes of ghost hunting shows to critique and satirize such shows through comparison and contrast with *Supernatural* itself. The episode is self-aware in the sense that it plays with the construction of television itself and is revealed, in the end, to be a television show that the protagonists of the actual show watch, enjoy, and then erase forever. They do so in order to keep their own existence a secret. They are able to do so because of the ineptness of the ghost hunters who made the show, who also serve to parody the "professional amateur ghost hunter"—plumber (or Kinko's employee) by day, paranormal investigator on nights and weekends. In doing so, *Supernatural* also indicates its own lack of exploitation, while still being able to deliver scares and warm moments despite being fictional. Finally, by contrasting the uncertainty of the ghost hunting shows with the certainty of the entities like Freeman Daggett that the Winchesters face, it constructs ghost hunting shows as fundamentally ridiculous and just as constructed as fictional narrative shows. Just slightly less scary.

NOTE

1. One of the seminal texts of ghost hunting, F.W.H. Myers's 1903 *Human Personality and Its Survival of Bodily Death*, articulated the idea of the personality continuing after death, and so the phrase has been used in other "ghost hunting texts" such as Richard Matheson's

Hell House (1971). The designation "personality" indicates that there is an intelligence and a purpose in the haunting. Something sentient survives which Myers and those who came after wanted to distinguish from the Christian concept of the soul.

Works Cited

Anson, Jay. *The Amityville Horror*. Pocket Star Books, 1977.
Hale, Mike. "Consigning Reality to Ghosts" *New York Times*, 10 December 2009. https://www.nytimes.com/2009/12/13/arts/television/13paranormal.html. Accessed 20 April 2018.
Hill, Sharon A. *Scientifical Americans: The Culture of Amateur Paranormal Researchers*. McFarland, 2017.
O'Hara, Jessica. "Making Their Presence Known: TV's Ghost-Hunter Phenomenon in a 'Post-' World." *The Philosophy of Horror*, edited by Thomas Fahy, The UP of Kentucky, 2010, pp. 72–86.
Raven, Rory. *Haunted Providence: Tales from the Smallest State*. The History Press, 2008.
Renner, Karen J. "Negotiations of Masculinity in American Ghost-hunting Reality Television." *Horror Studies* vol. 4, no. 2, 2013, pp. 201–229.
Wetmore, Kevin J., Jr. *Post–9/11 Horror in American Cinema*. Continuum, 2012.

Not All Monsters Are Universal

Gothic Parody in "Monster Movie"

Khara Lukancic

In the "Monster Movie" (4.05) episode of *Supernatural*, Sam and Dean arrive to investigate an unexplainable murder in a Pennsylvania town where witnesses are describing creatures akin to Universal monsters from the classic horror films of the 1930s and 1940s (in order to differentiate between the monsters from the Universal movies of the '30s and '40s and *Supernatural* monsters, from here on out the Universal movie monsters will be identified as "classic monsters"). Sam and Dean's challenge is to identify the creature mimicking classic monsters because in the world of *Supernatural*, the creatures as depicted in Universal's *Dracula* (1931), *The Mummy* (1932), and *The Wolf Man* (1941) are not real. Rather, vampires are vicious creatures with animalistic impulses, and werewolves devour human hearts. In other words, they are not creatures wearing fancy prop house costumes such as medallions and black capes or having cute, black button noses.

"Monster Movie" acts as a monster-of-the-week episode, breaking from the major story arc of the season, which is the impending Biblical apocalypse. The aesthetic and narrative conventions of *Supernatural* are broken in the "Monster Movie" episode via simulation of a black and white horror movie from Universal Studio's classic monster era. Everything in the episode from the editing techniques to the sound design refers to these classic monster movies. The first scene ends with an iris out focused on the Impala. This beginning scene features the Winchester brothers discussing the case as they pass the Pennsylvania state sign on the highway. As they pass by the sign, lightning flashes and it briefly reads "Transylvania." Dean expresses excitement about the case being simple, calling it a "straight-forward, black and white case." The episode transitions from the climax to the last scene via another iris out. After the shapeshifting monster is defeated, we cut to Dean and Sam saying goodbye to the heroine of the episode, Jamie, and having one last moment of brotherly banter. In addition to the two bookended iris outs, the most frequently implemented editing technique is the optical wipe, mimicking the aesthetics of the Universal films.

The soundtrack throughout the episode also refers to classic monster movies. The music is symphonic, and the main theme of the episode is a romantic piece written for violin. "Monster Movie" is very self-aware, as are all of the episodes written by Ben Edlund; this self-awareness is apparent from the beginning of the episode when, while the brothers are driving and discussing the case, Dean comments, "the radio around here sucks!" The diegetic music playing on the radio mimics the music of the films the episode is actively reconstructing.

"Monster Movie" invokes elements of Gothic parody to break the expected conventions of the show and to alert the audience to more extreme broken boundaries on the horizon. Some of the conventions include the episode being in black and white instead of color, known creatures such as vampires taking on characteristics beyond the mythology of the show and instead conforming to the traits of classic monsters, in addition to the monster being gender fluid. This essay explores "Monster Movie" in terms of the Gothic, humanism, and Gothic parody. Indeed, this meta, monster-of-the-week episode echoes overall themes of the series. "Monster Movie" functions as a Gothic narrative and engages humanist questions commonly visited throughout the series. The episode evokes these themes by reconstructing elements of classic monster movies, thereby acting as Gothic parody.

The Gothic

The pilot (1.01) episode of *Supernatural* establishes the series within a Gothic narrative. The episode reunites estranged brothers Sam and Dean Winchester, brothers who hunt monsters. Throughout the series, they travel throughout the country, in a Chevrolet Impala, hopping from town to town to battle the forces of evil. The pilot episode introduces us to the series' first monster-of-the week—a woman in white—a ghost preying on unfaithful men as revenge for misdeeds enacted upon her in life. The woman in white from the pilot is a seductive feminine ghost who manipulates men into cheating so that she can punish them for their error. In the introduction to their edited volume on the Gothic, Sharon Rose Yang and Kathleen Healey explore the controversial nature of defining the Gothic, given the range of what it includes:

> Haunted castles, mansions, monasteries, and graveyards replete with hidden chambers, passages, dungeons or attics; nature that is sublime and overwhelming (forests,

cataracts, cliffs, storms) and sometimes hostile; persecuted heroines and disinherited or unjustly exiled heroes; corrupt persecuting villains, usually representing some form of social authority in family, Church, or state (with an occasional perverse combination of any of those three); Byronic overachievers in forbidden knowledge (magical or scientific); seductive females; various assortments of supernatural or unnatural beings, monstrosities of the "natural" world in the form of vampires, werewolves, ghosts, demons, sorcerers/witches, and so on [3].

Indeed, throughout the course of the series, *Supernatural* has checked off each from the list.

In *The Horror Genre: From Beelzebub to Blair Witch*, Paul Wells says that the Gothic "takes up the super-structure of myth and the process of fairytale and configures them in a form which is a direct reaction to the age of Enlightenment, adopting a fervently anti-rationalist stance" (38). Gothic elements include examples of Todorov's marvelous featuring monsters and ghosts that commonly appear within castles. As L. Andrew Cooper notes, "[A] Gothic fiction is a fiction that primarily represents fear, the fearful, and the abject, even if the representation is comic" (6). More to the point, the Gothic is concerned with the occult over the rational.

Two well-known examples of the Gothic are Bram Stoker's *Dracula* (1897) and Mary Shelley's *Frankenstein* (1818). Dracula acts as an "invocation of the supernatural" as its plot describes a vampire preying on women as he moves from Transylvania to England (Wells 47). Tod Browning's film version of *Dracula* (1931) "engage[s] with the monster in a way that demonstrates what Stuart Rosenthal has described as 'situations of moral and sexual frustration'" (Wells 45). Various other adaptations of Dracula demonstrate the cultural fears of the European other.

Gothic narratives are concerned with replacing occult interests with religious belief and fidelity. Traditional Gothic stories show that the dangers of the supernatural—ghosts, vampires, and disturbing the natural order—bring death and destruction. The savior is religion; for example, crosses and holy water are strong weapons against Dracula. Indeed, these weapons are also usually quite formidable in the *Supernatural* universe as well.

In his study of the impacts of Gothic horror on modern culture, Cooper explores the relationship between supernatural fiction and real ideology. Cooper says, "Gothic novels typically situate their supernatural events within a Christian context. According to Coleridge, blending elements of 'false' superstition with 'true' religion blurs the line between the absurdity of the one and the authenticity of the other" (44). Dracula subverts the natural order as he lives as the immoral undead. He gains sustenance by drinking blood. The weapons against him are religious ones: crosses, holy water, and the symbol of crucifixion, wooden stakes.

On the other hand, the plot of *Frankenstein* does not describe an undead creature who preys on victims via exsanguination. In film adaptations of *Frankenstein*, Dr. Victor Frankenstein combines pieces of human remains to create the monster. He obtains the human remains by grave digging. Wells notes, "Frankenstein's curiosity extends beyond finding out the laws of nature, however, and becomes an aspiration to create his own law. It is in this transgression [...] that Frankenstein violates not merely scientific convention but the work of God" (47).

Likewise, *Frankenstein* also occurs within a Christian context, foregrounded by its quoting of Adam's words to God in *Paradise Lost* (1667) in its epigraph. Dr. Frankenstein makes his creature monstrous by creating it outside the natural law. Andrew Smith explores the relationship between real life scientific advancement and supernatural narratives during the Romantic period, noting that "[t]he novel's suggestion that 'life' can be introduced by an external agent such as electricity indicated that the inert coarse physical materiality of the body could be re-animated through a definitively secular experiment" (315). The success of this experiment that bypasses religious ideas of creation is punished: the resultant creature becomes demonized and Victor suffers a horrible fate.

The narratives of *Supernatural* express the marvelous just as do those of *Dracula* and *Frankenstein*. In a study of the function of Dean's car within the show, Thomas Knowles makes a unique maneuver by linking the Gothic castle and the 1967 Chevrolet Impala. In "The Automobile as Moving Castle," Knowles states, "*Supernatural* certainly ticks many of the boxes of a 'shopping-list' approach to the Gothic, but Gothic purists might be tempted to deny *Supernatural* a generic classification as such because of its seeming lack of that central Gothic component: the castle" (25). He argues that the Impala acts as the Winchester's surrogate castle as it "provides a safe haven and bulwark against the threatening outside world for Sam and Dean, and it is quite literally the vehicle that delivers the brothers both from and into danger" (25). However, the Gothic castle typically functions antithetically to this; as Knowles notes, "the Impala might also be said to reverse the traditional role of the castle. In Sam and Dean's world, drawing upon the Gothic tradition, the four-walled house is the last place the brothers would turn for safety" (26). He identifies the Impala as both the Winchester's safe haven as well as their transport to danger.

Humanism

Unlike what the Gothic attempts, the project of humanism concerns itself with the benefit of human society and the cultivation of rational thought and intellectualism. In his study providing an introduction to the philosophy of humanism, Jim Herrick surveys its key tenets. Herrick describes contemporary humanism as "a belief system that calls upon reason and values to enable us to develop our lives and societies [...] [and] is a position which thinking individuals can reach as a personal conviction and an individual way of life" (1). In contrast with various religious belief systems, humanism does not have the goal of serving a higher being out of faith; instead "humanism puts the person in the center" (Lutz and Lux 4).

This paradigm emphasizes that living a moral life does not require a religious context. Similar to Jim Herrick, Paul Kurtz discusses the basics of secular humanism; in *What Is Secular Humanism?* Kurtz notes, "to do something because of God's commandments, fear of punishment, or hope for reward in the afterlife, is hardly moral; rather, it may impede the development of a mature inner sense of empathy" (40–41). Correspondingly, Herrick suggests that human morality results from our innate social nature. "[T]he codes of behavior in society come from our social agreements, our social construct of morals that benefit us all. Without the ability to empathize with the distress of others morality does not operate effectively" (Herrick 2). Humanism is therefore not religious and may be followed by people who are atheists or agnostics. It is important to note that "[a]theism alone is not humanism [...] [h]umanism is atheism/agnosticism with values" (Herrick 2). Humanistic actions are taken in response to the current moment, not in anticipation of an afterlife, for secular humanists do not believe in an afterlife.

As humanism values the scientific method as a basis of inquiry, humanists incorporate a characteristic of skepticism. Herrick says, "[c]omplete skeptics will ask how they can know what they see around them. We receive knowledge of the external world by our senses, our sight, our hearing, our touch" (12). That constant skepticism predisposes the humanist towards atheism or agnosticism.

One cannot consider *Supernatural* to be a completely humanist television show. In fact, it would be a struggle to consider *Supernatural* humanist at all on its surface, as the show involves the paranormal. However, there are nuances of humanism that permeate the series. The pilot of *Supernatural* gives audiences the tag line that pervades the entire series. The phrase encompasses the brothers' modus operandi: "saving people, hunting things, the family business." This line takes the Winchesters' hunting lifestyle and identifies it as an act of communitarianism. They hunt monsters and evil creatures to keep society safe, an inherently humanistic undertaking. Indeed, throughout the series the brothers continually sacrifice themselves to save human society from armies of monsters and impending apocalypses.

The Winchesters' decision to dedicate their lives to fighting forces of evil does not result from a fear of religious wrath or a wish to gain admittance to a glorified afterlife: they do it in response to human suffering. When demons terrorize a town, the Winchesters save them as an act of empathy. They do it because they have the skill set to deal with the monsters and they want to keep society safe.

Additionally, the humanist enterprise is present most strongly within Dean. The tension between the humanist and the religious crescendos in season four. Leading up to this point, we accept Dean as the good, righteous, dutiful brother; while Sam acts as the evil, monstrous, and resistant brother. Dean personifies the righteous brother, as he is the brother who always followed their father's orders. As he is purely human, Dean personifies normality. Dean will always sacrifice himself for the benefit of his family and human society.

Sam, on the other hand, assumes characteristics that identify him as other and a bit monstrous. Early in the series, we learn that when Sam was a baby the yellow-eyed demon fed Sam some of his blood. In adulthood, Sam develops psychic abilities from the demon blood in his system and eventually turns to drinking demon blood to become a stronger psychic and to exorcise demons with his mind instead of needing Ruby's demon-killing knife or an incantation. Sam continually questioned and rebelled against their father and rejected the Winchester lifestyle (the family business) by leaving the family and going to school in an attempt to have a normal life.

Early in season four, in the episode "Lazarus Rising" (4.01), Dean discovers that he was resurrected from Hell by an angel, but he refuses to believe it. He responds that angels do not exist because the Winchesters have never interacted with one. Not taking the existence of angels as fact based on faith or Biblical references alone also represents an act of humanism. Later, Dean becomes horrified when he discovers that not only does Sam believe in angels, God, and Heaven; but that Sam prays to God. These elements set up the idea that the good, righteous son acts upon humanistic tenets that require rationality and facts, while the monstrous, rebellious son ascribes to faith. When Sam learns that Dean was saved by an angel, he believes it immediately; he accepts it on blind faith.

In *The Demon-Haunted World*, Carl Sagan warns against "no one representing the public interest [...] even grasp[ing] the issues; when people have lost the ability to set their own agendas or knowledgeably question[ing] those in authority" (25). In *The Best of Humanism*, Norman Cousins discusses ideas of free will and determinism. Cousins says, "[t]he philosophers have been debating for years about whether man is primarily good or primarily evil, whether he is primarily altruistic or selfish, cooperative or competitive, gregarious or self-centered, whether he enjoys free will or whether everything is determined" (184). Ultimately, Cousins decides that humans are dualistic in nature. He compares determinism and free will to a card game: "the hand that is dealt you represents determinism. The way you play your hand represents free will" (184).

Preempting the upcoming apocalypse, Dean and Sam are chosen as the vessels for Heaven and Hell, respectively. Dean is chosen as Archangel Michael's surrogate; Sam as Lucifer's. If Dean and Sam were acting on religious belief, they would accept their destinies and "say yes" to Michael and Lucifer. However, this is not their reaction. They form, along with their fallen-angel friend, Castiel, Team Free Will; they fight against the demand from Heaven that they assume their roles in the apocalyptic battle. They know there must be a way to avoid the destruction of Earth and all humankind on it. As if addressing Sagan's concerns, the Winchesters do not submit to the religious demands of Heaven or Hell; they fight to maintain their individuality and fight for the benefit of human-kind. In true Winchester fashion, they follow their own path.

In their study of Team Free Will, Devon Fitzgerald Ralston and Carey F. Applegate conclude that the humanistic response was the correct one. This becomes even more apparent after Sam and Dean discover that the angels are just as manipulative and corrupt as the demons. Ralston and Applegate identify responsibility as the important element in Team Free Will: "Sam and Dean are responsible for their actions, which is better than you'd expect from an ex-blood junkie and a high school dropout with six dollars in his pocket" (46).

Mark A. Lutz and Kenneth Lux note: "The concept of humanism has gone through many changes and uses since its beginnings in the Renaissance, and today it can mean a great variety of things" (4). One of the many things it can mean includes secular humanism. Secular humanism "denies that religious voices should be given a privileged status" (Law 95). Thus, in the public sphere, religious discourse has no superiority over the secular.

Secular humanism comes into play in *Supernatural* when the Winchesters discover that the angels are just as harmful as the demons. The angel Uriel intends to smite an entire town to prevent a seal from breaking, as each broken seal brings Lucifer one step closer to rising. Uriel asserts that as an angel of Heaven, he manifests righteousness, power, and holiness. To Uriel, the decision to smite the town supersedes Sam and Dean's wish to save it and its inhabitants. Thus, the Winchesters' rebellion against Uriel becomes a battle for a secular public sphere. Neither the angels from Heaven nor the demons from Hell have special supreme power to hold dominion over humankind. Sam and Dean will fight to ensure that stays the case.

Gothic Parody

In "Gothic Parody," Natalie Neill establishes the relationship between the Gothic and parody by saying, "[f]ollowing the publication of *The Castle of Otranto*, parody—no less than haunted castles, prophetic dreams, and family curses—became a fixture of Gothic" (189). The three elements Neill describes are frequent fixtures of *Supernatural*. The Impala is the Winchesters' castle that frequently takes them to places haunted by the marvelous (Knowles 25). Sam develops prophetic dreams when his psychic powers begin to fully develop; which of course causes Dean to worry incessantly about what his brother is becoming. The family motto, "saving people, hunting things, the family business," can certainly be considered a curse. It seems quite unfair that the weight of the world rests on the shoulders of two brothers from rural Kansas. This provides evidence for the argument that *Supernatural* has always been functioning as Gothic. "Monster Movie," however, offers an example of Gothic parody within the series.

Northanger Abbey (1818) by Jane Austen is one of the most well-known examples of Gothic parody in literature. Neill remarks, "[i]n these parodies, depictions of deluded readers are used to expose Gothic's lack of realism and simultaneously to dramatize a range of social concerns" (197). The plot of *Northanger Abbey* follows a teenage girl, Catherine Morland, who after falling in love with a young man goes to stay at his family's home, called Northanger Abbey. Being an avid reader of Gothic novels, Catherine anticipates that the house will be frightening and rampant with the marvelous. She imagines all sorts of Gothic realities while staying at Northanger Abbey, one of which is that she develops a belief that a murder occurred in its vacant apartments. Catherine's realization that by reading Gothic novels she has developed an overactive imagination which creates a fantastic lens through which she sees the world is one of the ways the novel satirizes the Gothic perspective. Commenting on this satire, Neill notes, "*Northanger Abbey* adopts Gothic tropes yet ultimately asserts its own realism. Instead of amplifying Gothic's supposed faults, Austen sets out to correct them" (200).

The series of Abbott and Costello films parodying classic monster movies exemplifies an example of Gothic parody directly relating to the Universal horror movies that predates *Supernatural*'s parody of the same territory. These movies function as a cross between slapstick humor and horror suspense. In *Laughing Screaming*, William Paul critically explores this link between comedy and horror. He says, "[t]he conflation of screaming and laughing at the conclusion [of *Carrie*] is the satisfying culmination of a film that had occasionally seemed stranded between horror and comedy" (416). *Abbott and Costello Meet Frankenstein* (1948) builds upon feelings of suspension between horror and comedy.

Near the beginning of the film, Wilbur (Lou Costello) and Chick (Bud Abbott) arrive at a House of Horrors to assess two new deliveries: the supposed bodies of Dracula and Frankenstein. Wilbur, the obviously more superstitious and paranoid of the two, becomes the character who senses that something strange is afoot; while Chick, the rationalist, remains completely unaware of the potential dangers lurking in the two crates. In the scene, Dracula humorously taunts Wilbur. This taunting acts as horror for Wilbur but immense comedy for us, the audience. The humor of the scene recreates pure slapstick comedy as in the movies of Harold Lloyd, Buster Keaton, and Charlie Chaplin from the silent era. Wilbur places his candlestick on the top of Dracula's coffin to read a label on the side of the crate, whereupon the candle slides across the coffin when Dracula opens the lid. Dracula taunts him via playful gags such as this throughout the scene. Finally, Chick opens the lid of the coffin to show Wilbur that Dracula does not exist; and indeed, Dracula had snuck out of his coffin mere moments before and is hiding in the background. The physical humor of Lou Costello and the hilariously overacted gestures of Bela Lugosi's Dracula make this a comedy, for us. However, the Gothic nature of the narrative as well as the terror Wilbur feels makes it horror, to Wilbur.

A more direct precursor to *Supernatural*'s "Monster Movie" is *The X-Files*' episode, "The Post-Modern Prometheus" (5.05). This *X-Files* episode works much like the episode of *Supernatural* in that they both employ the visual aesthetics of the classic monster movies. Both episodes are shot in black and white and rework the narratives of Universal's horror films; "The Post-Modern Prometheus" reworks *Frankenstein*, as the episode title's allusion to the subtitle of Shelley's novel suggests, while "Monster Movie" acts as a loose adaptation of *Dracula*.

"The Post-Modern Prometheus" begins and ends with what Dru Jeffries calls "comic book film style" (2). The episode begins and ends with a still image from a fictitious comic book called *The Great Mutato*, the name of the episode's Frankenstein's creature-like monster. The opening comic book image looks like a reconstruction of a classic horror comic book à la *Tales from the Crypt*. The faux comic book cover shows the creature standing in front of a house that very much looks like the Gothic house from Alfred Hitchcock's *Psycho* (1960). This allusion perhaps serves to prime the audience for the remainder of the episode, as *Psycho* serves as the movie that took Gothic horror out of European Romanticism and into rural America, while the episode places a Gothic monster directly into an American town.

When the comic book flips open, the episode begins. The comic book reappears later in the episode when Scully finds it in the room of Izzy Berkowitz, the son of the victim of the episode, Shaineh, who claims to have been attacked by a creature suspiciously identical to the character on the cover of Izzy's comic book. The final comic book image at the end of the episode depicts Mulder and Scully dancing at the Cher concert to which they took the Cher-obsessed Mutato. The image morphs into a page from the comic book from the opening of the episode. Much as Mulder and Scully enter this comic book-like world of *The Great Mutato* during the episode, Sam and Dean move in and out of their adaptation of classic monster movies.

The plot of the episode follows the creature known as the Great Mutato, a monster with lumpy tumors on his head and who possesses two mouths. He was accidentally created by a Dr. Frankenstein-like mad scientist, Dr. Pollidori, named after John William Polidori, author of the Gothic short story "The Vampyre." In the *X-Files* episode, Dr. Pollidori disposes of his mistake but his father, Pollidori Sr., adopts Mutato and raises him as a son. Mutato and Pollidori Sr., attempt to create a mate for Mutato so he would not be lonely, by using an agricultural anesthetic and then raping and impregnating unconscious women. One of these attempts resulted in the conception of Izzy Berkowitz. Mulder and Scully visit Dr. Pollidori at his laboratory and become horrified at his experiments involving genetic mutations. When Mulder asks him, "why would you do that?" Dr. Pollidori responds, "because I can!" This parallels a similar secular arrogance seen in Dr. Frankenstein when he creates his creature by bypassing the laws of nature. At the climax of the episode, the town's people hunt Mutato down, in the same vein as Frankenstein's monster is hunted in the movies.

Gothic Parody in Supernatural

In season four, *Supernatural* concerns itself with questions of a religious nature after the angel Castiel resurrects Dean from Hell. Season three ends with Dean banished to Hell. Earlier, he made a deal with a demon, and the agreement left him with one year to live. When his year elapses, the demon holding his contract, Lilith, sends hellhounds after him. His exile in Hell is the result of making a deal with a demon, not a religious punishment for how he carried out his life on Earth.

After the angels enter the narrative, so does talk of God and Heaven. *Supernatural* takes on religious tones during season four. Season four begins with an angel rescuing Dean, and it ends with Sam breaking the final seal that allows Lucifer to escape his cage in Hell and ascend to Earth. Dean and Sam's looming fight against their supposed fate of becoming the vessels for Heaven and Hell for an upcoming grudge match featuring angelic brothers Michael and Lucifer acts as the ongoing tension of season four.

Supernatural's "Monster Movie" episode invokes the Gothic, via parody, to criticize blind religious fundamentalism in favor of a rational secular humanism. Up until this point, the marvelous elements of the show came without any implication of a religious framework. The series parodies the Gothic in exactly the moment that the tension between Heaven and Hell crystalizes. Angels and God were introduced to the *Supernatural* canon just a few episodes before "Monster Movie" first aired. In our real world, in some denominations of Christianity, we are taught through our Biblical mythologies that God and angels protect us, they care about us, and offer feelings of hope and justice. Very quickly in *Supernatural*, the benevolence of Heaven's entities comes into question.

Angels turn out to be horrible beings that are as corrupt and malicious as the demons. They think themselves above humans and believe they have the right to determine the destinies of every human on Earth. The angel Uriel refers to humans as "mud monkeys" in the episode "It's the Great Pumpkin, Sam Winchester" (4.07). Sam and Dean fight against the hegemony of Heaven to enact their own free will and to be the agents of their own destinies.

The religious fundamentalist would submit to his or her fate as it being God's will and not question the underlying motivations or consequences. The Winchesters, however, know that this Biblical grudge match accompanies an apocalypse that will destroy the Earth and all life on it; they approach it from a humanist perspective. The episode, then, breaks the expected boundaries of the series to provide a critique that calls for a life of critical thought and to approach decisions rationally, instead of acting upon blind faith or according to rules of a book.

This tension is alluded to in "Monster Movie" via Gothic parody. The entire episode acts as a statement about things not being as they seem. In the beginning of the episode, Sam and Dean travel to Pennsylvania in anticipation of hunting a vampire. However, when they arrive, they are greeted by strangeness. When they go to the morgue to see the first victim, she has two puncture wounds on her neck; vampires in *Supernatural* do not exsanguinate via two canine fangs as in the typical vampire mythology.

The monster of the episode, a shapeshifter, romanticizes the classic monsters. Here, the term shapeshifter is used in a specific context. Shapeshifters in *Supernatural* are creatures that can take on the visage of a human being—any human being—even fictional characters from classic monster movies, as in the case in this episode. This shapeshifter sees the classic monsters as being majestic in their films, dominant characters living elegant lives. This appeals to him much more than being the outcast monster having no place in society, one who was rejected by even his own father for being a freak. In the episode, he takes on the personae of the classic film versions of Dracula, the Wolf Man, and the Mummy, and he enacts classic scenes from the movies to reject his reality as being an abject Other. Instead, he creates a fantasy, alternate reality where classic monsters are real, and he is one of them.

The episode acts as an adaptation of *Dracula*: The shapeshifter falls in love with Jamie and begins calling her Mina. He starts referring to Dean as Mr. Harker and Sam as Van Helsing. While reenacting a scene from *Dracula*, the shapeshifter, in his vampire form, tells Jamie that she "[is] the reincarnation of his beloved and [he] must have [her]." However, the episode also shares connections with *Frankenstein*. Much like *Frankenstein*'s monster is kludged together via the assembled parts of cadavers, the shapeshifter's identity is a collection of the monsters he imitates.

My argument as to what "Monster Movie" attempts lies in the character of Ed Brewer. He witnesses the first murder and describes the killer as being a vampire; then, he describes traits associated with Dracula instead of the known traits for vampires on the show. Later in the episode, Sam and Dean suspect that Ed is the shapeshifter, as he has taken an excessive interest in Jamie. Sam goes to the Goethe Theater where Ed works to confront him. The invocation of Johann Wolfgang Goethe—author of the play *Faust* and the poem "Prometheus"—is a particularly amusing revelation within the context of the Gothic genre; however, it also acts as foreshadowing of the major story arc of the season. Much like season four of *Supernatural*, *Faust, Part One* (1808) concerns the tensions between Heaven and Hell. "Prometheus" depicts Prometheus's defiance of Zeus, much like Dean's rebellion against Heaven as he fights being forced to accept his fate as Michael's vessel. Ralston and Applegate advocate,

> Because of the heavy burden of responsibility, we don't always appreciate our ability to make free choices. Instead we are tempted to act in what Sartre calls "bad faith," lying to ourselves by denying our freedom and believing that luck, fate, or God's plan determine our choices and absolve us from responsibility. Dean is admirable in his ability to resist bad faith and act as captain for Team Free Will. Despite the pressure, he asserts that he has the choice to refuse as Michael's vessel [40].

If Dean subscribed to Sartre's bad faith, he would not fight against the forces of Heaven and Hell. He would pity himself for his bad luck, dwelling upon questions of why the fate of the world is constantly in his hands. Dean would curse his fate and all of the hardship and heartbreak that has fallen upon his family. He might even withdraw from his crusade against evil, thinking that if people were attacked by evil supernatural creatures, it must just be their time. In other words, if he acted in bad faith, he would not assume any responsibility for his actions nor feel any compelling reason to help others. He does not give God agency; instead, he takes responsibility for his actions and responds to the world around him with humanistic rationalism and skepticism.

Conclusion

Although appearing on screen in black and white, "Monster Movie" is anything but a straight-forward episode. It invokes elements of Gothic parody in order to break the expected aesthetic and narrative conventions of the show to alert the audience to more extreme broken boundaries in ideology on the horizon. On one hand, there are formalistic elements that parallel the classic monster movies. These include the episode appearing in black and white, the font of the credits, the music, and the editing (for example, the use of iris outs, optical wipes, and the old-fashioned kaleidoscope shot). These elements while similar to those used in the movies are atypical conventions in the *Supernatural* series. The sound design is immediately recognizable as straying from the norm of the series by trading its rock anthem soundtrack for instrumental music reminiscent of the Universal movies of the 1930s and 1940s. The editing of the episode makes generous use of the optical wipe, a technique common in classic monster movies, which was revived with the releases of *Young Frankenstein* (1974) and *Star Wars* (1977). This resurgence was due to directors having studied the techniques from Classic Hollywood in film school and then beginning to apply classic techniques to their films. "Monster Movie" also makes use of special effects and editing techniques more aligned with the Universal monster movies than the effects typically featured on the show. One such effect occurs at the second turning point of the episode, when Dean's and Jamie's drinks are drugged by the shapeshifter (in the form of Lucy). We, the audience, know that Dean is drugged via a subjective point of view shot, whereby we see the glass sitting on the table as the character Dean sees it. We first see the glass, then the glass multiplies, and the multiples of the glasses spin around the actual glass like a kaleidoscope within the frame.

Furthermore, the episode offers narrative parallels to the classic monster movies by recreating plots and tropes from Universal's movies. The episode features elements from *Dracula*, *The Wolf Man*, *The Mummy*, and *Frankenstein*. In addition to vastly reworking the plot of *Dracula*, the episode features scenes where a wolf-like creature murders teenagers under a full moon, a mummy rises from a seemingly ancient sarcophagus while ambient smoke stimulates a feeling of mysticism, and at the climax, Dean is strapped to a table in a room very reminiscent of Dr. Frankenstein's laboratory. Of course, these are faux recreations of the classic monster movies whereby the villain makes use of props from a local costume shop that aid him in playing out this cinematic fantasy, as the episode does not feature Dracula, Wolf Man, and a mummy in a classic monster mash up; instead, all the attacks were enacted by a singular creature—or "critter," as Dean calls him—a shapeshifter.

Additionally, Gothic parody is used in the episode in order to play with the established lore of the show and, instead, follows characteristics more in line with classic monster movies. In *Supernatural,* vampires do not suck the blood of their victims through two canine fangs, nor do they speak in eastern European accents or wear capes like Bela Lugosi's Dracula. Werewolves on the show also do not appear with black button noses, have canine hair, nor do they don torn clothing after transforming into their werewolf form. These are characteristics from the Universal movies, not of the well-established mythology of the series. Another way the episode playfully engages established lore is when the creature answers the door and greets the pizza delivery boy. He makes a big deal about whether the pizza contains garlic, garlic, of course, being a typical guard against vampires; however, it would have offered no protection from the vampires in the *Supernatural* universe.

"Monster Movie" makes use of Gothic parody to warn of the religious battle to come and urges Sam and Dean to lean towards humanism and rational thought over blind religious faith. This warning emerges most strongly via the episode's nod to Goethe. His writing establishes a tension between Heaven and Hell and deals in themes of defying wishes of the gods. This stress between Heaven and Hell in the series becomes apparent in season four of the show, fully materializing not long after "Monster Movie." Indeed, Sam and Dean can only save the world by defying the demands of Heaven. The nod to Goethe warns against trusting Biblical entities on blind faith and instead calls for a more rational approach. The oddities of the episode challenge Sam and Dean to make choices based on rational thought that benefits society over religious submission that would lead to the demise of humankind. If traditional Gothic narratives assure audiences that religion offers salvation by providing protection from the monsters via religious symbols and artifacts, the Gothic parody of *Supernatural* warns that religion is not a savior but in fact another persecutor.

WORKS CITED

Abbott and Costello Meet Frankenstein. Directed by Charles Barton, Universal, 1948.
Austen, Jane. *Northanger Abbey*. 1818. Norton, 2004.
Cooper, L. Andrew. *Gothic Realities*. McFarland, 2010.
Cousins, Norman. "Free Will and Determinism." *The Best of Humanism*, edited by Roger E. Greeley, Prometheus Books, 1988, pp. 184–185.
Dracula. Directed by Tod Browning, Universal, 1931.
Frankenstein. Directed by James Whale, Universal, 1931.
Herrick, Jim. *Humanism: An Introduction*. Prometheus Books, 2005.
Jeffries, Dru. *Comic Book Film Style*. U of Texas P, 2017.
Knowles, Thomas. "The Automobile as Moving Castle." *The Gothic Tradition in* Supernatural, edited by Melissa Edmundson, McFarland, 2016, pp. 25–36.
Kurtz, Paul. *What Is Secular Humanism?* Prometheus Books, 2007.
Law, Stephen. *Humanism: A Very Short Introduction*. Oxford UP, 2011.
Lutz, Mark A., and Kenneth Lux. *The Challenge of Humanistic Economics*. The Benjamins/Cummings Publishing Company, 1979.
The Mummy. Directed by Karl Freund, Universal, 1932.
Neill, Natalie. "Gothic Parody." *Romantic Gothic: An Edinburgh Companion*, edited by Angela Wright and Dale Townshend, Edinburgh UP, 2016, pp. 185–204.
Paul, William. *Laughing Screaming*. Columbia UP, 1994.
Polidori, John. "The Vampyre." 1819. *Three Vampire Tales*, edited by Anne Williams, Wadsworth, 2003, pp. 68–85.
"Post-Modern Prometheus." *The X-Files*, written and directed by by Chris Carter, season 5, episode 5, Fox, 1997.

192   Part Four: Breaking Out of the Box

Psycho. Directed by Alfred Hitchcock, Paramount, 1960.
Ralston, Devon Fitzgerald, and Carey F. Applegate. "Team Free Will: Something Worth Fighting For." Supernatural *and Philosophy: Metaphysics and Monsters ... for Idjits*, edited by Galen A. Foresman, Wiley Blackwell, 2013, pp. 37–46.
Sagan, Carl. *The Demon-Haunted World*. New York: Random House, 1995.
Shelley, Mary. *Frankenstein*. 1818. Oxford UP, 2008.
Smith, Andrew. "Gothic Science." *Romantic Gothic: An Edinburgh Companion*, edited by Angela Wright and Dale Townshend, Edinburgh UP, 2016, pp. 306–321.
Star Wars: Episode IV—A New Hope. Directed by George Lucas, Lucasfilm, 1977.
Stoker, Bram. *Dracula*. 1897. Oxford UP, 1990.
Todorov, Tzvetan. *The Fantastic: A Structural Approach to a Literary Genre*. Cornell UP, 1975.
Wells, Paul. *The Horror Genre: From Beelzebub to Blair Witch*. Wallflower, 2000.
The Wolf Man. Directed by George Waggner, Universal, 1941.
Yang, Sharon Rose, and Kathleen Healey. "Introduction: Haunted Landscapes and Fearful Spaces—Expanding Views on the Geography of the Gothic." *Gothic Landscapes: Changing Eras, Changing Cultures, Changing Anxieties*, edited by Sharon Rose Yang and Kathleen Healey, Palgrave Macmillan, 2016, pp. 1–18.
Young Frankenstein. Directed by Mel Brooks, 20th Century Fox, 1974.

Pamela Barnes as Pastiche
Supernatural's *Rock Muse and Blind Seer*

Kathleen Potts

Supernatural seems to have it all: great storylines, charismatic characters, and intriguing locales. Whether one is a lover of the horror genre, a die-hard fan of a specific actor, or a music fan who wants to rock out to the music that goes beyond enhancement of the episode to become an entity on its own, this show has something for everyone. One of *Supernatural*'s enduring features is the show's use of postmodern elements, such as pastiche, meta, and intertextuality. In his essay "Postmodernism and Consumer Society" theorist Fredric Jameson writes that "the second feature of this list of postmodernisms is the effacement of some key boundaries or separations, most notably the erosion of the older distinction between high culture and so-called mass or popular culture" (2). (On that list are the art of Andy Warhol, the music of John Cage, films by Godard, the writings of William Burroughs, etc.) He discusses how this was distressing from an academic standpoint, because academia had a vested interest in preserving the realm of high or elite culture and transmitting the skills necessary for interpreting it to its initiates. "But many of the newer postmodernisms have been fascinated precisely by that whole landscape" of low-cultural forms, he observes (2). This remains true today, and one way of incorporating both high- and low-culture forms is through the use of pastiche. The television series *Supernatural* goes beyond questioning the distinctions between high and low to actually celebrating the act of blending them through their use of pastiche. Jameson defines the term:

> Pastiche is, like parody, the imitation of a peculiar or unique style, the wearing of a stylistic mask, speech in a dead language: but it is a neutral practice of such mimicry, without laughter, without that still latent feeling that there exists something *normal* compared with which what is being imitated is rather comic. Pastiche is blank parody, parody that has lost its sense of humor [...] [5].

Pastiche in the context of *Supernatural* is not "blank parody" as Jameson describes. It could be seen as being more in line with Linda Hutcheon's ideas of parody in *A Theory of Parody: The Teachings of Twentieth-Century Art Forms*, in which she discusses pastiche as an imitation of an original and parody as an adaptation; nevertheless, utilizing the term pastiche (instead of parody) allows for the continued discussion of a multitude of texts that are essentially in conversation with one another within and throughout the individual episodes of *Supernatural*. Perhaps the ideas of Charles Jencks in *The Language of Post-modern Architecture* parallel the intent of the creator and writers of the television show when he discusses the use of pastiche in postmodern architecture and art as being a method for double-coding in a positive and often playful way. This certainly seems true for *Supernatural*.

This essay will explore the creation of a modern myth centered on the character of Pamela Barnes, whose story arc spans seasons four and five. The writers of *Supernatural* applied the concept of postmodern pastiche to two key elements: the creation of the character of Pamela Barnes and the structure of her storyline. Barnes, an under-examined example of the use of postmodernist pastiche, is a blend of the iconic "blind seer" from ancient Greek tragedies and the famed rock groupie Pamela Des Barres. Combining these high- and low-brow elements enables *Supernatural* to achieve a celebratory blurring of the distinctions between high culture as exemplified by the tragic dramas of ancient Greece and the low culture world of rock 'n' roll in the United States.

In addition, there is a purposeful use of pastiche in the creation of story structure within *Supernatural* and particularly concerning those episodes that include the character of Pamela Barnes. The structure for the series *Supernatural* is episodic. Aristotle says in his *Poetics* that "among simple plots and actions the episodic are the worst" (1976, 34). Since television began, episodic structure has been the norm, as it allows the majority of episodes to be of the "stand alone" variety. This facilitates the ability for viewers to enter into the series at any point and still enjoy the current episode. In the case of *Supernatural*, the protagonists of the series, Sam and Dean, hunt down the demon, ghost, ghoul, or monster of the week, and the episode ends with a type of "case closed" finality. Every television series begins with a story bible, and series creator Eric Kripke came armed with ideas and storylines for the first three years. In seasons four and five, the episodes featuring Barnes appear to be episodic, but ultimately unify into a traditional climactic structure. Consequently, this is one of the ways that a minor character like Pamela Barnes can seem fairly insignificant, yet has actually been purposefully threaded throughout a large swatch of the fabric of this show. Examined as a unit, the Pamela Barnes four-episode story arc is what Aristotle would classify as a well-constructed plot that is whole and has magnitude. In television, we have found a medium in which the commercial nature of the episodic plot and the artistic merits of Aristotelian structure can work together to create a long-form story that keeps audiences watching season after season. (And according to renowned workshop leader and author of *Story* Robert McKee, long-form television is the most exciting medium of today.) This essay will explore how the writers of *Supernatural* applied the concepts of postmodern pastiche to create a modern myth centered on Pamela Barnes as a reluctant hero.

"Lazarus Rising" (4.01) is season four's first episode and the first time we meet Pamela Barnes. This, as the title implies, is an episode focusing on the idea of rebirth. There are three instances of rebirth in this episode, including Dean's, the story structure for the series of *Supernatural*, and the beginning of Pamela Barnes's transition from a rock muse and psychic to a "blind seer." Lilith has sent Dean to Hell and, as the title indicates, in this episode he comes back from the dead. The title provides the first instance of intertextuality in this episode, linking Dean to Lazarus in the *Bible* (John. 11. 1–44). Dean is brought back from the dead completely healed of his wounds, both those he suffered on earth as Lilith's hounds mauled him while dragging him to Hell and any he suffered after death. The storyline of *Supernatural* has also experienced a rebirth at this point, with everything in the first three seasons becoming backstory to this new overarching series arc based around the entity that freed Dean. At this point, the essence of the new story arc is unknown, as is the entity that raised Dean from perdition. As Bobby Singer says, "No demon's letting you loose out of the goodness of their hearts. They got to have something nasty planned." Dean and Bobby set out to find the catalyst behind this new story arc's inciting incident, with Dean convinced that his brother has made a deal with a demon to free him from Hell. An inciting incident is that incident that sets the story in motion and the hero on his quest. In this case, the inciting incident is Dean being brought back from Hell, which raises the question, who brought Dean back? The quest in this episode is the search for the entity that brought Dean back.

Bobby and Dean find Sam, who explains that he tried, but was unsuccessful in saving his brother. Bobby replies, "Don't get me wrong. I'm gladdened that Sam's soul remains intact, but that does raise a sticky question." Dean continues the thought, "If he didn't pull me out, then what did?" As the conversation progresses, Sam states the obvious, "We got a pile of questions and no shovel. We need help." Bobby responds, "I know a psychic a few hours from here. Something this big maybe she's heard the other side talking." This statement seems almost innocuous in the *Supernatural* world, but as is the case in numerous Greek tragedies, it does not bode well for the one who uncovers the identity of the one who is sought.

This quest kicks off the inciting incident for Pamela Barnes's four-episode journey with the Winchester boys. In this episode, the plot will also include the Aristotelian elements of recognition and reversal. At the outset, psychic Pamela Barnes appears to be a rock muse. Immediately, we are confronted with multiple aspects of "low culture" when meeting Pamela Barnes. The door opens and reveals a character who could be categorized as a postmodern rock 'n' roll groupie and muse, with a beautiful face, shoulder-length, wavy black hair and a big smile. What the audience can see of her costume includes a sleeveless rock 'n' roll t-shirt featuring the innovative rock band, the Ramones, a black belt with studs, and jeans. Her jewelry includes a pendant necklace and a leather cuff bracelet. Like an Amazonian warrior, she appears strong; her sleeveless t-shirt shows off well-developed arms that not only embrace Bobby but also lift him up off the floor. Within her home, the camera shots reveal a number of other music-related items, evidence that points towards her being a groupie: a signed guitar on a stand and a portrait over the mantle of a rock legend, potentially Led Zeppelin guitarist Jimmy Page. Of course, the character might possibly be a musician herself, but there is no evidence of that in the dialogue. These conclusions are first fueled by the intertextuality drawn between the similar names of this character, Pamela Barnes, and the notorious, self-professed groupie Pamela Des Barres, author of two memoirs, *I'm with the Band: Confessions of a Groupie* (1987), and *Take Another Little Piece of My Heart: A Groupie Grows Up* (1992). In her first memoir, she describes ten years' worth of affairs with rock legends, including Jimmy Page. In her collection of interviews, *Let's Spend the Night Together: Backstage Secrets of Rock Muses and Supergroupies* (2008), Des Barres describes the first time she heard the term groupie:

> I was standing by Led Zeppelin's shiny black limo, smoothing my pink feather boa, reapplying my gooey Yardley Slicker lip gloss, preparing to slide in next to Jimmy Page for a hot night on the town. As the car door slammed, I heard a shrill voice from the gathered throng behind the roped-off area: "Look at *that* girl, she must be a *groupie*" [xii].

As Des Barres notes, it was not long before the word groupie became a scurrilous accusation. Interestingly, she pinpoints women as the ones who give the word groupie its negative connotation. She writes, "Some women, claiming to be forward-thinking, began branding groupies as backward-thinking concubines, when all we were doing was exactly what we wanted to do!" (xiii) In this declaration she highlights the sex-positive perspective of many groupies, including *Supernatural*'s character Pamela Barnes, who appears to be driving the underlying sexualized nature of this episode. Within moments of opening the door, Barnes looks Dean up and down and assesses him in what appears to be a totally lascivious way, ending with an "mm mm mm" and a knowing look at Bobby. Further, Pamela Des Barres equates the role of the rock groupie with that of a Greek Muse. In *Mythology* (2017), Edith Hamilton quotes the Greek poet Hesiod:

> He is happy whom the Muses love. For though a man has sorrow and grief in his soul, yet when the servant of the Muses sings, at once he forgets his dark thoughts and remembers not his troubles. Such is the holy gift of the Muses to men [33].

Whereas others shamed women who chose to be groupies, Des Barres celebrates the role of rock groupie and directly connects it to that of a Greek Muse, functioning as a source of inspiration and a guiding spirit for the men in their lives. Pamela Barnes arouses, inspires, and guides Dean and Sam in her four-episode arc.

In preparation for a séance in this episode, the mood is light; the banter between characters—especially between Pamela and Dean—remains sexy and playful. She is crouched down retrieving candles from a cupboard and her lower back tattoo (a.k.a. tramp stamp) "Jesse Forever" is showing. Although the spelling is different, this could be yet another musical intertextual reference to the song "Jessie's Girl" (1981) by pop and rock singer Rick Springfield (who in fact had an arc on the show himself, in season twelve). "Who's Jesse?" Dean asks. "Hahaha. Well, it wasn't forever," Pamela replies. "His loss," quips Dean. She moves very close to him and says quietly, "Might be your gain." Pamela says to Sam, "You're invited too, Grumpy" and winks. The incestuous implications are not to Dean's taste and he quickly retorts with finger pointed at Sam, "You are *not* invited!" The highly sexualized banter of Barnes continues, even when she begins the séance. Barnes says that she needs to touch something their "mystery monster" touched and she reaches under the table and touches Dean's lap. "Whoa! Well he didn't touch me *there*," he retorts. Pamela says teasingly, "My mistake." Next, she places her hand on the handprint branded on Dean's shoulder and begins the incantation of "I invoke, conjure, and command you, appear unto me before this circle."

At this point the focus shifts away from the sexualized qualities of Barnes to her more heroic qualities. Amid table shaking, static on the electronics, and high-pitched ringing, she receives a name, "Castiel." A dauntless hero, she boldly tells Castiel that she doesn't scare easily. Dean asks, "Castiel?" She answers, "Its name. It's whispering to me, warning me to turn back." Instead, she commands, "Show me your face now!" This is followed by each of the candles shooting up a high flame, and screaming by Pamela as her eyes also shoot flames. The fires die down, and cradled in Bobby's arms she opens her eyelids to reveal blackness where her eyes have been burned out of their sockets. This marks a reversal (*peripeteia*) in the Aristotelian structure of the story. In the *Poetics*, Aristotle says, "Reversal, as we have said, is a change from one state of affairs to its exact opposite, and this, too, as I say, should be according to probability or necessity" (2018, 15). Pamela has been permanently blinded by the act of spying on Castiel's true form; there is no turning back to her former life. This also sets up the element of "recognition" for Dean and Bobby (and eventually, Sam) who, having learned Castiel's name will end up having their first face-to-face encounter on this earthly plane with the angel Castiel. Aristotle describes the part of the plot called recognition (*anagnōrisis*) as "a change from ignorance to knowledge, leading either to friendship or to hostility on the part of those persons who are marked for good fortune or bad" (15). At the end of the episode we know the identity of the key player/catalyst in the inciting incident, Pamela Barnes has suffered a reversal (going from sighted to blind), and all involved achieve recognition in this new Aristotelian arc. While it may not appear evident within the confines of this episode's plot, the writers of *Supernatural* have initiated the creation of a modern myth centered on the character of Pamela Barnes.

Next, there is a gap of eight episodes between Pamela Barnes's introduction to the series and her following appearance. In "Heaven and Hell" (4.10), she helps unearth the pre-human identity of the character Anna Milton. This episode provides the elements of complication (*desis*) and rising action in Barnes's story arc structure. Aristotle explains that "the complication comprises everything from the beginning of the play up to the point of the change of fortune" (2018, 46). The angels Castiel and Uriel attempt to abduct Anna, presumably because she is eavesdropping on the plans of the angels. In mid-conflict, Anna makes the angels magically disappear. She has not killed them, but she has sent them far away. Anna claims, "That just popped in my head. I don't know how I did it. I just did it." Once they all reach a safe space, Anna swears that she doesn't know why her life has been leveled, with her parents dead and angels hunting her. She says, "I would give anything to know." Sam replies, "Okay. Let's find out." This is the cue for the return of the now blind psychic character of Pamela Barnes.

This episode retains much of Pamela Barnes's rock muse persona, but also continues her development as a blind seer. Pamela wears sunglasses (like rock stars Bono and Lenny Kravitz), a leather jacket, black nail polish, and with a hand on Dean's shoulder to lead her, she encounters Sam. She cannot see him, but she knows he's there. Pamela decides to play with him a little, stroking his face and asking, "Sam, is that you?" He responds, "I'm right here." She audaciously flirts with him by slapping him on the butt and exclaiming:

> Know how I can tell? That perky little ass of yours. You could bounce a nickel off that thing. Of course I know it's you, Grumpy. Same way I know that's a demon [Ruby], and that poor girl's Anna and that you've been eyeing my rack. [...] Don't sweat it, kiddo. I still got more senses than most.

Through her witty, sexually charged banter, we learn that Barnes's sense of humor is intact, as are all of her senses except sight. With her blindness,

Pamela Barnes joins the ranks of those characters in Greek mythology that are gathered under the umbrella of "blind seer." In Greek Golden Age drama, the character who stands out as emblematic of the blind seer is Teiresias, who is an active agent in a number of the tragedies that take place in Thebes, including Sophocles's *Oedipus Rex* and *Antigone*, as well as Euripides's *Bacchae*.

Barnes has been called in and says that she is excited to help, but she gives the audience a taste of her anger and edge when she replies, "Any chance I can dick over an angel, I'm taking it." Anna is shocked and asks why. Barnes gives visual evidence of how she has been wronged when she lifts her sunglasses and reveals white, plastic inserts in her eye sockets. Aristotle explains that "recognition may be by marks or tokens, such as a scar or necklace" (2018, 49). In this case, the moment of recognition has literally scarred this character, bringing to memory the fact that she saw the true face of the angel, Castiel.

Pamela Barnes puts Anna under hypnosis, showing yet another gift that belongs to this blind seer. Anna is resistant to going back far enough to remember, but Barnes fearlessly pushes forward, as she did in the first episode. She tells Anna it will be okay and says, "Just one look, that's all we need." Electricity crackles and Anna screams out, "He's gonna kill me." Barnes tells Anna to calm down and that she's safe. The door slams shut and Anna twists, turns, bolts upright, and causes sparks to fly. All through this melee Barnes remains incredibly calm and entreats Anna to calm down. She also warns Dean to stay back, as Dean jumps in to stop Anna's flailing and gets sent flying across the room. Barnes calmly counts up to bring Anna out of the trance. She strokes Anna's head, calls out her name, and asks, "You all right?" Anna sits up, looks directly at her and replies, "Thank you, Pamela." Anna reveals that now she remembers who she is—an angel—and is now sure that she has a death sentence on her head because she disobeyed and fell. Barnes clarifies for Dean, "She fell to earth, became human." The longer Anna was in human form the less she remembered about being an angel, which is why they needed someone with the extraordinary talents of Pamela Barnes to help uncover her past. Ruby interjects with a foreshadowing of the upcoming rising action when she says, "I don't think you all appreciate how completely screwed we are." Anna agrees, saying that Ruby's right and Heaven wants her dead. Ruby continues, "And Hell just wants her. A flesh-and-blood angel that you can question, torture, that bleeds. Sister, you're the Stanley Cup. And sooner or later, Heaven or Hell, they're gonna find you." In that last sentence Ruby provides an intertextual reference to the title of this episode. Anna replies to Ruby, "I know," and sets up the next level of rising action when she says, "And that's why I'm gonna get it back." After this point, Barnes disappears quietly from the episode, with a brief mention by Dean two scenes later about getting her back home safely and explaining to Anna that "she said she was sorry. It's just after last time, she, uh ... this is just a little too rich for her blood." This foreshadows the reluctant hero status that Barnes will attain in the next episode.

The third episode in the story arc is "Death Takes a Holiday" (4.15). Once again, the title provides the first example of intertextuality in the episode, this time referencing the 1934 film of the same name. Sam has been speaking to Bobby on his cellphone about a town where no one has died in the last week and a half. After beginning their interviews in a town in Wyoming, Sam and Dean come up empty for demon deals and skeevy faith healers. Together they construct a theory:

> DEAN: I mean, these souls just ain't getting dragged into the light.
> SAM: Maybe 'cause there's no one around to carry them. [...] Well, grim reapers—that's what they do, right? Schlep souls? So, if death ain't in town—
> DEAN: Then nobody's dying.

They decide to visit the graveside of the last victim to die in town, Cole Griffith. Here, Dean expresses how conflicted he is about this particular job: "This job is jacked, that's what. [...] You want me to gank a monster or torch a corpse, hey, let's light it up, right? But this? If we fix whatever this is, people are gonna start dropping dead. *Good people.*" In this statement, Dean foreshadows the deaths of "good people" in this episode, in particular Pamela Barnes. Dean and Sam's attempt to contact Cole is aborted when the demon Alastair arrives and attacks them. Sam prevails in the fight, but no new information is gained. Dean hatches plan B. Pamela Barnes is called into action again and asks, "Which one of you brainiacs came up with astral projection?" Dean raises a hand. Pamela's response, "Of course. Chachi." This is an allusion to the long-running television series *Happy Days* (1974–84), which features Fonzie and his younger cousin Chachi. A parallel can be inferred with Chachi and Dean being the immature counterparts to Fonzie and Bobby Singer (who, in this instance, should be read as a "stand-in" for Dean's missing father, John Winchester). Both Chachi and Dean are attempting to make their own path in the shadow of Fonzie and Bobby/John.

In the rest of the dialogue between Barnes and Dean, the overarching conflict in the episode is revealed and the idea of Barnes being a reluctant hero—foreshadowed at the end of "Heaven and Hell"—is elucidated. She asks Dean, "You want to rip your souls out of your bodies and take a little stroll through the spirit world? [...] Do you have any idea how heavy-duty insane that is?"

> DEAN: Maybe, but that's where the reaper is, so...
> BARNES: So, it's nuts.
> DEAN: Not if you know what you're doing.

BARNES: You don't know what you're doing.
DEAN: No, but you do.
BARNES: Yeah, I do.

At this point the character is showing reluctance, similar to how the Greek blind seers are reluctant to share their visions with those who are asking. Barnes complains that she is "sick of being hauled back into your angel-demon, Soc-Greaser crap." The "Soc-Greaser" reference is intertextual and stems from S.E. Hinton's novel, *The Outsiders* (1967), as well as the Francis Coppola film adaptation (1983). It relates to the major conflict between social and economic classes. Here it can be seen as reflecting the overarching conflict of the episode, which is the clash between the spirit world and the physical realm.

In response to her reluctance, Dean—who knows that she is the only one with the skills to be able to help them accomplish their task—reminds Barnes of the stakes at hand: "We're talking the end of the world here, okay?" He puts it in terms that he hopes she won't be able to resist: "No more tasseled leather pants, no more Ramones CDs, no more nothing." He attempts to close the deal with, "We need your help."

Like a true reluctant hero, in the face of danger Pamela Barnes does what is needed. With candles and incantations, she turns Sam and Dean into spirits. She gives them their last instructions with, "All right, so, I'm assuming you're somewhere over the rainbow. Remember I have to bring you back." Dean watches her stand up and approach Sam's body lying on the bed. In order to get him to return after the work, she tells him that she'll "whisper the incantation in your ear." She leans over Sam to do exactly that and says, in her rebel-sexy teasing voice, "You have got a great ass." Sam's spirit-self grins. Dean wants to know what she said, but Sam only shrugs. She remains in the motel room watching over the bodies of Sam and Dean. A demon has been sent by Alastair, and Barnes immediately senses it. She bolts and chains the door, then closes the window against the unseen intruder. She says, "I know you're here. What's the matter you reeking son of a bitch? You afraid of a skirt?" Taunting the demon with the idea of being beaten by a "skirt" implies that its masculinity is at stake in this fight. It is unusual to have a woman taunting a man (albeit a demon dressed as a man) about his masculinity. Quite often throughout the series Dean has taunted his brother with "feminine" insults, such as calling him a "bitch." Barnes's use of this taunt points up the troubling dichotomy between the fact that *Supernatural* often features female characters in strong roles while simultaneously encouraging a machismo that some have read as misogynistic.

As the scene continues, Barnes dramatically pulls back the shower curtain; the demon is not in the shower, but there is still a level of intertextuality in the gesture, bringing to mind Hitchcock's *Psycho* (1960). In her article

"What's Wrong with Hitchcock's Women," Bidisha describes Norman Bates as never having "grown out of his childlike Oedipal rage and his bedroom is a creepy preserved little kid's room, but as he grows older his feelings are overlaid by a very adult and pretty common place misogyny." The demon is lurking behind the door frame as Barnes exits the bathroom, lunging for her as she dashes to wake up Sam. She puts up a strong fight, but like so many other female characters on *Supernatural*, she is eventually killed off. As noted by Lorrie Palmer, "While female antagonists abound, it is in keeping with this determinedly masculine space that there are few storylines that feature women as allies to the Winchesters" (83). (It is beyond the scope of this essay to go into the fates of *Supernatural*'s numerous female characters who have been killed off, including the quashed spin-off series *Wayward Sisters*, but Bronwen Calvert investigates the issue more extensively in her essay, "Angels, Demons, and Damsels in Distress: The Representation of Women in *Supernatural*.") Barnes is given a fatal stab wound before she utters the incantation to bring Sam back. He vanquishes the demon with his psychic powers. She can't die right away, because the reapers aren't reaping yet. And before Dean can return to his body, Castiel has declined his request for a few exceptions and Tessa has already begun reaping "good people" like the young boy Cole. Sam tells Barnes, "We just gotta talk to Tessa, that's all. Get her to hold off reaping 'til we get you better." She leans back and says, "I'm pretty sure she's started up again." The evidence for this is the camera's close up on Barnes's left hand over her stomach wound, which begins to profusely spill blood. Dean has been brought back and gasps for air as he looks over at her. In true rock 'n' roll rebel style she takes a swig from a flask.

> SAM: Pamela, I'm so sorry.
> BARNES: Stop.
> SAM: You don't deserve this.
> BARNES: Yeah. I don't. (to Dean) I told you I didn't want anything to do with this.

As the reluctant hero of this episode, half-kidding and half-seriously she asks them to do her a favor: "Tell that bastard Bobby Singer to go to Hell for ever introducing me to you two in the first place." A parallel can be drawn to Teiresias's speech to Oedipus in Sophocles's *Oedipus Rex*: "How dreadful knowledge of the truth can be/When there's no help in truth! I knew this well,/But made myself forget. I should not have come" (16). Barnes rejects Dean's attempt to console her by saying she's going to a better place; she says, "You're lying." But, then in rebel style, she says, "But what the Hell, right? Everybody's got to go sometime." At the very end of this death scene she reveals more of her powers. She whispers to Sam, "I can feel what's inside of you. If you think you have good intentions, think again." This recalls when Creon asks the blind prophet Teiresias in Sophocles's *Antigone*, "What have you to say?" And Teiresias answers, "This Creon: you stand once more on the edge of fate" (224). Sam stands on the edge of fate and, despite her blindness and the fact that she has literally been stabbed, Pamela Barnes can still feel what's inside of Sam. A parallel can be drawn between the Winchester brothers and Oedipus utilizing this commentary by Fitts and Fitzgerald:

> Without reference to Freud we may perceive that in this whole fable of Oedipus the great poet is giving us to understand that the nature of man is darker than men believe it to be. Yet Oedipus is not penitent, for he has also recognized that the powers controlling life have, in a sense, chosen him as their example and instrument [176].

Both Dean and Sam have been chosen by the powers controlling their lives and, in spite of this, they constantly attempt to do the right thing and focus on saving people.

This scene ends the Aristotelian complication (*desis*) when it completes Barnes's change of fortune, which is her literal death. In today's story terms we would describe this scene as the climax of the Aristotelian arc for Pamela Barnes as reluctant hero, and her last words to Sam can be interpreted as a traditional cliff-hanger, leaving the audience to wonder what will become of him and his good intentions.

Finally, in season five, we have reached the catharsis and denouement of the Pamela Barnes arc. In "Dark Side of the Moon" (5.16), the title provides the episode with an instance of intertextuality by directly referencing the title of the very famous Pink Floyd album (1973). Sam and Dean are murdered and end up in Heaven. While searching for the Garden (in an effort to discover the whereabouts of God), they are saved by their friend Ash from the vengeful angel, Zachariah. Even though most people cannot leave their own private Heavens, Ash has skills and has been all over; he can also summon people into his Heaven (the Roadhouse), which he does with Pamela Barnes. It is in this scene that her arc enters into its denouement (*lusis*) as described by Aristotle:

> Every tragedy has a complication and denouement. The complication comprises events outside the play itself and often also some events within; the remainder is the denouement. I mean that the complication extends from the beginning up to the last moment before the change to good or bad fortune occurs, and that the denouement begins with that change and extends to the end of the play [2018, 24].

At the opening of this scene, Barnes has experienced catharsis (*katharsis*). Although Aristotle speaks of catharsis in *Poetics*, he does not specifically define it; therefore, over the centuries, scholars have advanced three major theories of catharsis. For her, the second theory of catharsis is most applicable:

> The second translates it as "purification" on the basis of its use in religious ritual, where it can refer to the cleansing of a person or place in order to bring it into a proper relationship with the divine. The interest here is in rendering someone or something pure and holy. According to its view, the emotions of pity and fear are not harmful, but in need of cleansing, refinement, or sublimation [2018, 46].

Pamela Barnes is, as she was when we encountered her for the first time in "Lazarus Rising," restored to her happy, rebel-sexy, sighted self. She sits with Dean and playfully swats his head, saying, "That's for getting me killed." Dean asks Pamela if she's good. She says, "I'm good. Really." Then she makes a metatheatrical gesture by describing what she calls her "death scene": "Remember my death scene? Gut shot. Coughing blood." Pamela Barnes did have a very theatrical death scene as the reluctant hero, much like many of the cinematic death scenes that have gone before hers in countless westerns, war movies, and tragic dramas, but in explicitly imaging her death in such terms, she calls attention to the constructedness of her narrative arc.

Having been purified and brought into relation with the divine, Barnes's Heaven, as she describes it, is distinctly suited to her role as rock muse. She exclaims, "My Heaven? It is one long show at the Meadowlands. It's amazing!" We come full circle back to the incredibly happy, rock 'n' roll groupie and muse that she started out as during the first episode. Like the ultimate groupie, she has slipped beyond the "velvet ropes" of Earth to get the ultimate seat in Heaven at an endless rock show at the Meadowlands.

Now that she is no longer a "blind seer" (because her eyesight has been restored), she appears to be less focused as one who sees things clearly beyond her realm. Apparently, she is still imbued with some version of second sight, for she "hears" about what is happening on Earth, and although she appears to be unconvinced herself, she suggests to Dean that being Michael's vessel (in the fight between Heaven and Hell) might not be so bad. Dean retorts that many people will die if that happens. She counters with, "And then they come here. Is that really so bad? Look. Maybe ... you don't have to fight it so hard. That's all I'm trying to say." It is almost as if, in regaining her eyesight, she has actually figuratively lost sight of who Dean is and what he must do—save people—on Earth.

Although the scene could have ended with animosity between Barnes and Dean, for her suggestion that he become Michael's vessel, instead the writers chose to bring resolution to the rock groupie and muse aspect of the story in regards to the sexual flirtation and connection that was begun in "Lazarus Rising." The end of this scene is the end of the denouement for the four-episode arc of the character of Pamela Barnes. Ash interrupts the conversation with news that he has found a shortcut to the Garden. He draws a sigil and gives the boys an "all access pass" (referencing credentials utilized by crew and visitors who are allowed to go anywhere and everywhere at a concert venue, neatly reflecting Pamela's groupie associations), but warns them that Zachariah will be watching every road to the Garden. They are ready to take their leave, and Sam engulfs Barnes in a hug. She tells him to watch his ass, a double-entendre relating to both the upcoming trip and her on-going comments through the episodes about his very nice derriere. In true rebel-sexy fashion, as Dean leans in to hug Barnes she takes control and pulls him in for a kiss. All of the flirting and built up sexual tension from their first meeting, and—in spite of her loss of sight—the continual flirtation in the next two episodes, has culminated in this last scene. If she has her classic cinematic "death scene" in "Death Takes a Holiday" then it could be said that she has her romantic comedy-style "first kiss scene" in "Dark Side of the Moon." Dean's hug transforms into her kiss, first short, but then they go for a second, much longer one. As their lips part, she pats his cheek and says, "Yup. Just how I imagined." This brings the characters full circle from their first meeting, where Dean had hoped to become intimate with this psychic/rock muse before fate took them down a different path. Instead of a love interest, Barnes became a reluctant hero in league with the Winchester brothers.

And, though the character experienced the second type of catharsis herself, the story arc culminates in the third type of catharsis as described by Aristotle:

> The third translates it as "clarification." Here the focus is on the tragic plot as an object of cognition, which we take in through a process that combines emotional arousal with intellectual understanding. Pity and fear are stirred up by the events we witness onstage, but they also undergo a process of clarification that releases us from their grip [2018, 46].

With her final good-byes to Sam and Dean, Barnes has been released from the grip of the Winchester brothers and their on-going battle to save the world from evil. As the reluctant hero, she has sacrificed herself for the sake of good and now is able to enjoy eternity in true rock muse fashion, watching a never-ending rock concert at the Meadowlands. Sam and Dean receive clarification in this episode, too. After leaving her, they reach the Garden and learn from Joshua that God is on Earth and He knows that the Apocalypse has begun, but He feels that it is not His problem. Joshua appears to pity the brothers, claiming that he is rooting for them and wishes he could do more to help. Joshua then resurrects the brothers on Earth, but this time, unlike before, God wants them to remember being in Heaven.

Pamela Barnes's arc has had its complication (including recognition and reversal) in the first two episodes, "Lazarus Rising" and "Heaven and Hell." It moved to the change to bad fortune (her death) in "Death Takes a Holiday." And, in "Dark Side of the Moon" the four-episode story arc transitioned into the denouement phase for Pamela Barnes. Although episodic television is the "norm" and utilized extensively throughout *Supernatural*, series creator Eric Kripke has achieved what Aristotle would classify as a well-constructed plot that is whole and has magnitude with the story arc encompassing the evolution of Pamela Barnes. The creators and writers of the show *Supernatural* utilized pastiche, meta, and intertextuality to achieve a celebratory blurring of the distinctions between high culture as exemplified by ancient Greek tragedies and the low culture world of rock 'n' roll in the United States. Via the trajectory of the overlain Aristotelian story arc, Barnes's on-going interactions with Dean and Sam were greatly enriched as she evolved from a rock groupie with psychic powers to a version of a Greek Muse, then to a "blind seer" and finally to a reluctant hero, leading to the creation of a new, modern myth centered on Pamela Barnes.

Works Cited

Aristotle. *Poetics*. Translated with an introduction by Gerald F. Else, U of Michigan P, 1976.
_____. *Poetics*. Edited and with a revised translation by Michelle Zerba and David Gorman, Norton, 2018.
Bidisha. "What's Wrong with Hitchcock's Women." *The Guardian*, 21 Oct. 2010, https://www.theguardian.com/film/2010/oct/21/alfred-hitchcock-women-psycho-the-birds-bidisha/.
Calvert, Bronwen. "Angels, Demons, and Damsels in Distress: Representations of Women in *Supernatural*." *TV Goes to Hell: An Unofficial Road Map of* Supernatural, edited by Stacey Abbott and David Lavery, ECW Press, 2011, pp. 90–104.
Death Takes a Holiday. Directed by Mitchell Leisen, performances by Fredric March, Evelyn Venable, and Guy Standing, Paramount Pictures, 1934.
Des Barres, Pamela. *I'm with the Band: Confessions of a Groupie*. William Morrow, 1987.
_____. *Let's Spend the Night Together: Backstage Secrets of Rock Muses and Supergroupies*. Chicago Review Press, 2008.
_____. *Take Another Little Piece of My Heart: A Groupie Grows Up*. William Morrow and Company, 1992.
Euripides. *Bacchae*. Translation, introduction, and notes by Stephen Esposito. Focus Publishing, 1998.
Hamilton, Edith. *Mythology: Timeless Tales of Gods and Heroes, 75th Anniversary Edition*. Black Dog & Leventhal, 2017.
Hinton, S.E. *The Outsiders*. Speak, 2006.
The Holy Bible: King James Version. Regency Publishing House, 1976.
Hutcheon, Linda. *A Theory of Parody: The Teachings of Twentieth-Century Art Forms*. Routledge, 1985.
Jameson, Fredric. *The Cultural Turn: Selected Writings on the Postmodern, 1983–1998*. Verso, 1998.
Jencks, Charles A. *The Language of Post-modern Architecture*. 6th ed. Rizzoli, 1997.
Marshall, Garry, creator. *Happy Days*. Miller-Milkis Productions, Henderson Productions, Miller-Milkis-Boyett Productions, Paramount Television, 1974.
McKee, Robert. *Story: Substance, Structure, Style and the Principles of Screenwriting*. HarperCollins, 1997.
The Outsiders. Directed by Francis Coppola, performances by C. Thomas Howell, Matt Dillon, Ralph Macchio, Patrick Swayze, Rob Lowe, Emilio Estevez, and Tom Cruise, Zoetrope Studios, 1983.
Palmer, Lorrie. "The Road to Lordsburg." *TV Goes to Hell: An Unofficial Road Map of* Supernatural, edited by Stacey Abbott and David Lavery, ECW Press, 2011, pp. 77–89.
Pink Floyd. *The Dark Side of the Moon*. Harvest Records, 1973.

Psycho. Directed by Alfred Hitchcock, performances by Anthony Perkins, Janet Leigh, and Vera Miles, Shamley Productions, 1960.
Sophocles. *The Oedipus Cycle*. Translated by Dudley Fitts & Robert Fitzgerald. Harcourt Brace Jovanovich, 1977.
Springfield, Rick. "Jessie's Girl." *Working Class Dog*. RCA Records, 1981.

Appendix One: Episodes Cited

Episodes are cited throughout the volume by episode name and year/season number only, to avoid unnecessary repetition. Full bibliographical information, season by season, is provided below. To find details about an episode, check by the year/season number cited in the essay. All seasons are available on Warner home video, in both DVD and Blu-Ray formats.

Season 1

1.01, "Pilot" (Sept. 13, 2005). Written by Eric Kripke, directed by David Nutter.

1.02, "Wendigo" (Sept. 20, 2005). Written by Eric Kripke, Ron Milbauer, and Terri Hughes Barton, directed by David Nutter.

1.04, "Phantom Traveler" (Oct. 4, 2005). Written by Richard Hatem, directed by Robert Singer.

1.05, "Bloody Mary" (October 11, 2005). Written by Ron Milbauer and Terri Hughes Burton, story by Eric Kripke, directed by Peter Ellis.

1.07, "Hook Man" (Oct. 25, 2005). Written by John Shiban, directed by David Jackson.

1.08, "Bugs" (Nov. 8, 2005). Written by Rachel Nave and Bill Coakley, directed by Kim Manners.

1.11, "Scarecrow" (Jan. 10, 2006). Written by John Shiban and Patrick Sean Smith, directed by Kim Manners.

1.13, "Route 666" (Jan. 31, 2006). Written by Eugenie Ross-Leming and Brad Buchner, directed by Paul Shapiro.

1.17, "Hell House" (March 30, 2006). Written by Trey Callaway, directed by Chris Long.

Season 2

2.01, "In My Time of Dying" (Sept. 28, 2006). Written by Eric Kripke, directed by Kim Manners.

2.03, "Bloodlust" (Oct. 12, 2006). Written by Sera Gamble, directed by Robert Singer.

2.07, "The Usual Suspects" (November 9, 2006). Written by Catherine Humphris, directed by Mike Rohl.

2.10, "Hunted" (Jan. 11, 2007). Written by Raelle Tucker, directed by Rachel Talalay.

2.15, "Tall Tales" (February 15, 2007). Written by John Shiban, directed by Bradford May.

2.16, "Roadkill" (March 15, 2007). Written by Raelle Tucker, directed by Charles Beeson.

2.17, "Heart" (March 22, 2007). Written by Sera Gamble, directed by Kim Manners.

2.18, "Hollywood Babylon" (April 19, 2007). Written by Ben Edlund, directed by Phil Sgriccia.

2.19, "Folsom Prison Blues" (April 26, 2007). Written by John Shiban, directed by Mike Rohl.

2.20, "What Is and What Should Never Be" (May 3, 2007). Written by Raelle Tucker, directed by Eric Kripke.

2.22, "All Hell Breaks Loose, Part 2" (May 17, 2007). Written by Sera Gamble, directed by Robert Singer.

Season 3

3.01, "The Magnificent Seven" (Oct. 4, 2007). Written by Eric Kripke, directed by Kim Manners.

3.03, "Bad Day at Black Rock" (Oct. 18, 2007). Written by Ben Edlund, directed by Robert Singer.

3.04, "Sin City" (Oct. 25, 2007). Written by Robert Singer and Jeremy Carver, directed by Charles Beeson.

3.05, "Bedtime Stories" (Nov. 1, 2007). Written by Cathryn Humphris, directed by Mike Rohl.

3.06, "Red Sky at Morning" (Nov. 8, 2007). Written by Laurence Andries, directed by Cliff Bole.

3.08, "A Very Supernatural Christmas" (Dec. 13, 2007). Written by Jeremy Carver, directed by J. Miller Tobin.

3.09, "Malleus Maleficarum" (Jan. 31, 2008). Written by Ben Edlund, directed by Robert Singer.

3.10, "Dream a Little Dream of Me" (Feb. 7, 2008). Written by Sera Gamble and Cathryn Humphris, directed by Steve Boyum.

Appendix One: Episodes Cited

3.11, "Mystery Spot" (Feb. 14, 2008). Written by Eric Kripke, directed by Kim Manners.

3.12, "Jus in Bello" (Feb. 21, 2008). Written by Sera Gamble, directed by Phil Sgriccia.

3.13, "Ghostfacers" (April 24, 2008). Written by Ben Edlund, directed by Phil Sgriccia.

3.15, "Time Is on My Side" (May 8, 2008). Written by Sera Gamble, directed by Charles Beeson.

3.16, "No Rest for the Wicked" (May 15, 2008). Written by Eric Kripke, directed by Kim Manners.

Season 4

4.01, "Lazarus Rising" (Sept. 18, 2008). Written by Eric Kripke, directed by Kim Manners.

4.03, "In the Beginning" (Oct. 2, 2008). Written by Jeremy Carver, directed by Steve Boyum.

4.04, "Metamorphosis" (Oct. 9, 2008). Written by Cathryn Humphris, directed by Kim Manners.

4.05, "Monster Movie" (Oct. 16, 2008). Written by Ben Edlund, directed by Robert Singer.

4.07, "It's the Great Pumpkin, Sam Winchester" (Oct. 30, 2008). Written by Julie Siege, directed by Charles Beeson.

4.08, "Wishful Thinking" (Nov. 6, 2008). Written by Ben Edlund and Lou Bollo, directed by Robert Singer.

4.10, "Heaven and Hell" (Nov. 20, 2008). Written by Eric Kripke and Trevor Sands, directed by J. Miller Tobin.

4.13, "After School Special" (Jan. 29, 2009). Written by Daniel Loflin and Andrew Dabb, directed by Adam Kane.

4.15, "Death Takes a Holiday" (March 12, 2009). Written by Jeremy Carver, directed by Steve Boyum.

4.17, "It's a Terrible Life" (March 26, 2009). Written by Sera Gamble, directed by James L. Conway.

4.18, "The Monster at the End of This Book" (April 2, 2009). Written by Julie Siege, directed by Mike Rohl.

4.21, "When the Levee Breaks" (May 7, 2009). Written by Sera Gamble, directed by Robert Singer.

Season 5

5.01, "Sympathy for the Devil" (Sept 10, 2009). Written by Eric Kripke, directed by Robert Singer.

5.05, "Fallen Idols" (Oct. 8, 2009). Written by Julie Siege, directed by James L. Conway.

5.06, "I Believe the Children Are Our Future" (Oct. 15, 2009). Written by Daniel Loflin and Andrew Dabb, directed by Charles Beeson.

5.07, "The Curious Case of Dean Winchester" (Oct. 29, 2009). Written by Sera Gamble, story by Sera Gamble and Jenny Klein, directed by Robert Singer.

5.08, "Changing Channels" (Nov. 5, 2009). Written by Eric Kripke, directed by Charles Beeson.

5.09, "The Real Ghostbusters" (Nov. 12, 2009). Written by Eric Kripke, directed by James L. Conway.

5.10, "Abandon All Hope..." (Nov. 19, 2009). Written by Ben Edlund, directed by Phil Sgriccia.

5.11, "Sam, Interrupted" (Jan. 21, 2010). Written by Andrew Dabb and Daniel Loflin, directed by James L. Conway.

5.14, "My Bloody Valentine" (Feb. 11, 2010). Written by Ben Edlund, directed by Mike Rohl.

5.15, "Dead Men Don't Wear Plaid" (March 25, 2010). Written by Jeremy Carver, directed by John F. Showalter.

5.16, "Dark Side of the Moon" (April 1, 2010). Written by Andrew Dabb and Daniel Loflin, directed by Jeff Woolnough.

5.17, "99 Problems" (April 8, 2010). Written by Julie Siege, directed by Charles Beeson.

5.21, "Two Minutes to Midnight" (May 6, 2010). Written by Sera Gamble, directed by Phil Sgriccia.

5.22, "Swan Song" (May 13, 2010). Written by Eric Kripke, directed by Steve Boyum.

Season 6

6.01, "Exile on Main St." (Sept. 24, 1010). Written by Sera Gamble, directed by Phil Sgriccia.

6.02, "Two and a Half Men" (Oct. 1, 2010). Written by Adam Glass, directed by John Showalter.

6.03, "The Third Man" (Oct. 8, 2010). Written by Ben Edlund, directed by Robert Singer.

6.05, "Live Free or Twihard" (Oct. 22, 2010). Written by Brett Matthews, directed by Rod Hardy.

6.06, "You Can't Handle the Truth" (Oct. 29, 2010). Written by Eric Charmelo and Nicole Snyder, directed by Jan Eliasberg.

6.07, "Family Matters" (Nov. 5, 2010). Written by Andrew Dabb and Daniel Loflin, directed by Guy Bee.

Appendix One: Episodes Cited

6.09, "Clap Your Hands If You Believe" (6.09). Written by Ben Edlund, directed by John F. Showalter.

6.11, "Appointment in Samarra" (December 10, 2010). Written by Sera Gamble and Robert Singer, directed by Mike Rohl.

6.13, "Unforgiven" (Feb. 7, 2011). Written by Andrew Dabb and Daniel Loflin, directed by David Barrett.

6.14, "Mannequin 3: The Reckoning" (Feb. 18, 2011). Written by Eric Charmelo and Nicole Snyder, directed by Jeannot Szwarc.

6.15, "The French Mistake" (Feb. 25, 2011). Written by Ben Edlund, directed by Charles Beeson.

6.17, "My Heart Will Go On" (April 15, 2011). Written by Eric Charmelo and Nicole Snyder, directed by Phil Sgriccia.

6.18, "Frontierland" (April 22, 2001). Written by Andrew Dabb and Daniel Loflin, directed by Guy Norman Bee.

6.19, "Mommy Dearest" (April 29, 2011). Written by Adam Glass, directed by John F. Showalter.

6.20, "The Man Who Would Be King" (May 6, 2011). Written and directed by Ben Edlund.

6.22, "The Man Who Knew Too Much" (May 20, 2011). Written by Eric Kripke, directed by Robert Singer.

Season 7

7.01, "Meet the New Boss" (Sept. 23, 2011). Written by Sera Gamble, directed by Phil Sgriccia.

7.02, "Hello Cruel World" (Sept. 30, 2011). Written by Ben Edlund, directed by Guy Bee.

7.03, "The Girl Next Door" (Oct. 7, 2011). Written by Andrew Debb and Daniel Loflin, directed by Jensen Ackles.

7.06, "Slash Fiction" (Oct. 28, 2011). Written by Robbie Thompson, directed by John Showalter.

7.08, "Season Seven, Time for a Wedding!" (Nov. 11, 2011). Written by Andrew Dabb and Daniel Loflin, directed by Tim Andrew.

7.09, "How to Win Friends and Influence Monsters" (Nov. 18, 2011). Written by Ben Edlund, directed by Guy Bee.

7.12, "Time After Time" (Jan. 13, 2012). Written by Robbie Thompson, directed by Phil Sgriccia.

7.16, "Out with the Old" (March 16, 2012). Written by Robert Singer and Jenny Klein, directed by John Showalter.

7.20, "The Girl with the Dungeons and Dragons Tattoo" (April 27, 2012). Written by Robbie Thompson, directed by John MacCarthy.

7.22, "There Will Be Blood" (May 11, 2012). Written by Andrew Dabb and Daniel Loflin, directed by Guy Norman Bee.

7.23, "Survival of the Fittest" (May 18, 2012). Written by Sera Gamble, directed by Robert Singer.

Season 8

8.01, "We Need to Talk About Kevin" (Oct. 3, 2012). Written by Jeremy Carver, directed by Robert Singer.

8.04, "Bitten" (Oct. 24, 2012). Written by Robbie Thompson, directed by Thomas J. Wright.

8.06, "Southern Comfort" (Nov. 7, 2012). Written by Adam Glass, directed by Tim Andrew.

8.08 "Hunteri Heroici" (Nov. 28, 2012). Written by Andrew Dabb, directed by Paul Edwards.

8.11, "LARP and the Real Girl" (Jan. 23, 2013). Written by Robbie Thompson, directed by Jeannot Szwarc.

8.12, "As Time Goes By" (Jan. 30, 2013). Written by Adam Glass, directed by Serge Ladouceur.

8.14, "Trial and Error" (Feb. 13, 2013). Written by Andrew Dabb, directed by Kevin Parks.

8.19, "Taxi Driver" (April 3, 2013). Written by Eugenie Ross-Leming and Brad Buckner, directed by Guy Norman Bee.

8.20, "Pac Man Fever" (April 24, 2013). Written by Robbie Thompson, directed by Robert Singer.

8.21, "The Great Escapist" (May 1, 2013). Written by Ben Edlund, directed by Robert Duncan McNeill.

Season 9

9.04, "Slumber Party" (Oct. 29, 2013). Written by Robbie Thompson, directed by Robert Singer.

9.11, "First Born" (Jan. 21, 2014). Written by Robbie Thompson, directed by Jon Badham.

9.12, "Sharp Teeth" (Jan. 28, 2014). Written by Adam Glass, directed by John Showalter.

9.15, "#thinman" (March 4, 2014). Written by Jenny Klein, directed by Jeannot Szwarc.

9.16, "Blade Runners" (March 18, 2014). Written by Brad Buckner and Eugenie Ross-Leming, directed by Serge Ladouceur.

9.18, "Meta Fiction" (April 15, 2014). Written by Robbie Thompson, directed by Thomas J. Wright.

9.23, "Do You Believe in Miracles?" (May 20, 2014). Written by Jeremy Carver, directed by Thomas J. Wright.

Appendix One: Episodes Cited

Season 10

10.01, "Black" (Oct. 7, 2014). Written by Jeremy Carver, directed by Robert Singer.

10.02, "Reichenbach" (Oct. 14, 2014). Written by Andrew Dabb, directed by Thomas J. Wright.

10.03, "Soul Survivor" (Oct. 21, 2014). Written by Brad Buckner and Eugenie Ross-Leming, directed by Jensen Ackles.

10.04, "Paper Moon" (Oct. 28, 2014). Written by Adam Glass, directed by Jeannot Szwarc.

10.05, "Fan Fiction" (Nov. 11, 2014). Written by Robbie Thompson, directed by Phil Sgriccia.

10.06, "Ask Jeeves" (Nov. 18, 2014). Written by Eric Charmelo and Nicole Snyder, directed by John MacCarthy.

10.11, "There's No Place Like Home" (Jan. 27, 2015). Written by Robbie Thompson, directed by Phil Sgriccia.

10.13, "Halt & Catch Fire" (Feb. 10, 2015). Written by Eric Charmelo and Nicole Snyder, directed by John F. Showalter.

10.21, "Dark Dynasty" (May 6, 2015). Written by Eugenie Ross-Leming and Benjamin Buckner, directed by Robert Singer.

10.23, "Brother's Keeper" (May 20, 2015). Written by Jeremy Carver, directed by Phil Sgriccia.

Season 11

11.01, "Out of the Darkness, Into the Fire" (Oct. 7, 2015). Written by Jeremy Carver, directed by Robert Singer.

11.02, "Form and Void" (Oct. 14, 2015). Written by Andrew Dabb, directed by Phil Sgriccia.

11.04, "Baby" (Oct. 28, 2015). Written by Robbie Thompson, directed by Thomas J. Wright.

11.05, "Thin Lizzie" (Nov. 4, 2015). Written by Nancy Won, directed by Rashaad Ernesto Green.

11.06, "Our Little World" (Nov. 11, 2015). Written by Robert Berens, directed by John Showalter.

11.08, "Just My Imagination" (Dec. 2, 2015). Written by Jenny Klein, directed by Richard Speight, Jr.

11.12, "Don't You Forget About Me" (Feb. 3, 2016). Written by Nancy Won, directed by Stefan Pieszczynksi.

11.20, "Don't Call Me Shurley" (May 4, 2016). Written by Robbie Thompson, directed by Robert Singer.

11.23, "Alpha and Omega" (May 25, 2016). Written by Andrew Dabb, directed by Phil Sgriccia.

Season 12

12.02, "Mamma Mia" (Oct. 20, 2016). Written by Brad Buckner and Eugenie Ross-Leming, directed by Thomas J. Wright.

12.04, "American Nightmare" (Nov. 3, 2016). Written by Davy Perez, directed by John F. Showalter.

12.06, "Celebrating the Life of Asa Fox" (Nov. 17, 2016). Written by Steve Yockey, directed by John Badham.

12.09, "First Blood" ((Jan. 26, 2017). Written by Andrew Dabb, directed by Robert Singer.

12.15, "Somewhere Between Heaven and Hell" (March 9, 2017). Written by Davy Perez, directed by Lopez Corrado.

12.17, "The British Invasion" (April 6, 2017). Written by Eugenie Ross-Leming and Brad Buckner, directed by John F. Showalter.

12.18, "The Memory Remains" (April 13, 2017). Written by John Bring, directed by Phil Sgriccia.

Season 13

13.16, "Scoobynatural" (March 29, 2018). Written by Jeremy Krieg and James Adams, directed by Robert Singer and Spike Brandt.

13.23, "Let the Good Times Roll" (May 17, 2018). Written by Andrew Dabb, directed by Robert Singer.

Season 14

14.04, "Mint Condition" (November 1, 2018). Written by Davy Perez, directed by Amyn Kaderali.

Appendix Two: Main and Major Characters

Brief information about all major characters and about secondary ones who are relevant to the essays in this volume appears below.

Main Cast (Regulars)

Dean Winchester*	Jensen Ackles
Sam Winchester**	Jared Padalecki
Ruby (Season 3)†	Katie Cassidy
Bela Talbot (Season 3)	Lauren Cohan
Castiel	Misha Collins
Crowley	Mark Sheppard
Lucifer/Nick***	Mark Pellegrino
Jack Kline	Alexander Calvert

*Young Dean was played by Dylan Everett (9.07, 10.12, 11.08), Ridge Canipe (1.18, 3.08), Brock Kelly (4.13), Nicolai Guistra (5.22, 7.10), and Anthony Bolognese (12.22), and Elderly Dean was played by Chad Everett (5.07).

**Young Sam was played by Colin Ford (3.08, 4.13, 4.21, 5.16, 7.03, 11.10), Alex Ferris (1.18), Nathan Smith (5.22), Hunter Dillon (9.07), and Dylan Kingwell (11.08).

***Lucifer has also been played briefly by Bellamy Young (5.01) Jared Padalecki (5.04, 5.22), Misha Collins (11.10, 11.11, 11.14, 11.15, 11.18, 11.21, 11.22), Rick Springfield (13.02, 12.03, 12.07), David Chisum (12.08), Michael Querin (12.08), Emma Johnson (12.02), and Adrianne Palicki (5.03).

†Ruby was recurring and played by Genevieve Padalecki (née Cortese) in season four and by Anna Williams (4.09) and Michelle Hewitt-Williams (4.09). Padalecki also played herself in "The French Mistake" (6.15).

Major Recurring Characters/Characters Referenced

Abaddon/Josie Sands	Alaina Huffman
Adina	Jud Tylor
Ajay	Assaf Cohen

Appendix Two: Main and Major Characters

Alastair°°	Christopher Heyerdahl
Alice	Kelli Ogmundson
Alpha Vamp	Rick Worthy
Amara°†	Emily Swallow
Antichrist	see Jesse Turner below
Ash	Chad Lindberg
Azazel	Frederic Lehne
Balthazar	Sebastian Roche
Alicia Banes	Kara Royster
Max Banes	Kendrick Sampson
Barnes	Ernie Grunwald
Pamela Barnes	Traci Dinwiddie
Tara Benchley	Elizabeth Whitmere
Doc Benton	Billy Drago
Lady Toni Bevell	Elizabeth Blackmore
Billie	Lisa Berry
Stuart Blake	Kurt Ostlund
Lou Bollo	Himself
Boltar	Hank Harris
Boris	Joseph D. Reitman
Charlie Bradbury	Felicia Day
Ben Braeden	Nicholas Elia
Lisa Braeden	Cindy Sampson
Brandon	Jason McKinnon
Ed Brewer	Michael Eklund
Bucky	Mac Brandt
Cain	Timothy Omundson
Jimmy Caldwell	Connor Levins
Callie	Tracy Froese
Young Callie	Ava Rebecca Hughes
Calliope	Hannah Levien
Christian Campbell	Corin Nemec
Deanna Campbell	Allison Hossack
Gwen Campbell	Jessica Heafey
Samuel Campbell	Mitch Pileggi
Edward Carrigan	Spencer Garrett
Madge Carrigan	Merrilyn Gann
Casey	Sasha Barrese
Mrs. Chandler	Alberta Mayne
Chet	Sean Owen Roberts
Ben Collins	Alden Ehrenreich
Haley Collins	Gina Holden

Appendix Two: Main and Major Characters

Tommy Collins	Graham Wardle
Samuel Colt	Sam Hennings
Alan J. Corbett	Dustin Mulligan
Cronos	Jason Dohring
Freeman Daggett	John DeSantis
Dagon	Ali Ahn
Daphne	Grey Griffin (voice)
Mick Davies	Adam Fergus
Death	Julian Richings
Demian	Devin Ratray
Frank Devereaux	Kevin McNally
Dirk	Aaron Paul Stewart
Walter Dixon	Benjamin Ratner
Dorothy	Kaniehtiio Horn
Dracula	Todd Stashwick
Edgar	Benito Martinez
Eve°°°	Julie Maxwell
Fate/Atropos	Katie Walder
Garth Fitzgerald IV	DJ Qualls
Marty Flagg	Michael B. Silver
Len Fletcher	Jared Gertner
Fritz	Ken Lawson
Gabriel/Trickster	Richard Speight, Jr.
Gadreel	Tahmoh Penikett
Dr. Gaines	Cameron Bancroft
Sera Gamble	Hilary Jardine (voice)
Game Show Host	Hiro Kanagawa
Gandhi	Paul Statman
Dr. Garrison	Christopher Cousins
Father Gil	Robert Curtis Brown
Gilda	Tiffany Dupont
God/Chuck Shurley	Rob Benedict
Leticia Gore	Teagan Rae Avoledo
Grandpa	Don Mackay
Guy/Demon	Leslie Odom, Jr.
Hannah	Erica Carroll
Donna Hanscum	Briana Buckmaster
Ellen Harvelle	Samantha Ferris
Jo Harvelle	Alona Tal
Hatchet Man	Barry Nerling
Victor Henriksen	Charles Malik Whitfield
Dr. Hess	Gillian Barber

Isaac	Peter Macon
Jamie	Melinda Sward
Alex Jones	Katherine Ramdeen
Fred Jones	Mike Farrell
Joshua	Roger Aaron Brown
Kate	Brit Sheridan
Katie	Vivien Elizabeth Armour
Arthur Ketch	David Haydn-Jones
Kelly Kline	Courtney Ford
Clif Kosterman	Philip Maurice Hayes
Eric Kripke	Micah Hauptman
Kristen	Nina Winkler
Kubrick	Michael Massee
Serge Ladouceur	Art Kitching
Benny Lafitte	Ty Olsson
Lenore	Amber Benson
Leshii	Paris Hilton
Leticia (Actress)	Crystal Lowe
Lilith°	Katherine Boecher
Abraham Lincoln	David Livingstone
Lucy	Holly Elissa
Madison	Emmanuelle Vaugier
Maeve	Joy Regullano
Marie	Katie Sarife
Meg Masters	Nicki Aycox (Seasons 1 and 3)
Meg Masters	Rachel Miner (Seasons 5–8)
McG	Regan Burns
David McNamara	Dan Gauthier
Molly McNamara	Tricia Helfer
Nicky Mermaid	Ida Segerhagen
Metatron	Curtis Armstrong
Michael††	Christian Keyes
Jim Michaels	Garwin Sanford
Jody Mills	Kim Rhodes
Anna Milton	Julie McNiven
Jack Montgomery	Dameon Clarke
Jessica Moore	Adrianne Palicki
Missouri Moseley	Loretta Devine
Nate Mulligan	David Quinlan
Naomi	Amanda Tapping
Eliot Ness	Nicholas Lea
Nicole/Demon	Nicole "Snooki" Polizzi

Appendix Two: Main and Major Characters 221

Claire Novak	Kathryn Newton
Olivia	Izabella Miko/Wendy Abbott/Robert Underwood/Kevin McNulty
Kevin Parks	Jason Bryden
Jerry Penowski	Brian Markinson
Pestilence	Matt Frewer
Phoenix/Elias Finch	Matthew Armstrong
Amy Pond	Jewel Staite
Young Amy Pond	Emma Grabinsky
Jacob Pond	Lyova Beckwitt
Carmen Porter	Michelle Borth
Raphael†††	Demore Barnes
Brad Redding	Gary Cole
Amelia Richardson	Liane Balaban
Dr. Robert	Robert Englund
Cassie Robinson	Megalyn Echikunwoke
Dick Roman	James Patrick Stuart
Becky Rosen	Emily Perkins
Rowena	Ruth Connell
Roy	Kerry Van Der Griend
Samandriel	Tyler Johnston
Samantha	Genevieve Buechner
Samhain	Don McManus
Santa (Drunk)	Alex Bruhanski
Scooby-Doo	Frank Welker (also the voice of Fred Jones)
Dr Sexy	Steve Bacic
Shaggy	Matthew Lillard (voice)
Sera Siege	Keegan Connor Tracy
Cuthbert Sinclair	Kavan Smith
Bobby Singer	Jim Beaver
Karen Singer	Carrie Ann Fleming
Robert Singer	Brian Doyle-Murray
Siobhan	Alyssa Lynch
Sparkle	Everett Shea
Harry Spengler	Travis Wester
Kenny Spruce	Austin Basis
Stevie	Zak Ludwig
Cyrus Styne	Connor Price
Eldon Styne	David Hoflin
Eli Styne	Matt Bellefleur
Monroe Styne	Markus Flanagan
Sully	Nate Torrence

Jake Talley	Aldis Hodge
Tamara	Caroline Chikezie
Tammy	Rachel Warkentin
Tara	Rachel Hayward
Tasha	Emily Tennant
Tessa/Reaper	Lindsey McKeon
Corbin Tilghman	Blair Penner
Tiny	Clif Kosterman
Tooth Fairy	Mark Acheson
Kevin Tran	Osric Chau
Travis	Ron Lea
Cole Trenton	Travis Aaron Wade
Jesse Turner	Gattlin Griffith
Rufus Turner	Steven Williams
Uriel	Robert Wisdom
Velma	Kate Micucci (voice)
Veritas	Serinda Swan
Vince Vincente	Rick Springfield
Eleanor Visyak	Kim Johnston Ulrich
Gordon Walker	Sterling K. Brown
Walt	Nels Lennarson
Michael Wheeler	Brandon W. Jones
Brian Wilcox	Leigh Parker
Ava Wilson	Katherine Isabelle
Henry Winchester	Gil McKinney
John Winchester	Jeffrey Dean Morgan
Young John Winchester	Matt Cohen
Mary Winchester	Samantha Smith
Young Mary Winchester	Amy Gumenick
Zachariah	Kurt Fuller
Ed Zeddmore	AJ Buckley
Maggie Zeddmore	Brittany Ishibashi

†† Michael also briefly played by Jake Abel (5.22), Matthew Cohen (5.13), Felisha Terrell (14.09), and Jensen Ackles (13.23 and in season fourteen).

††† Raphael was also played by Lanette Ware (6.15).

° Lilith was also played by Sierra McCormick and Katie Cassidy (3.16).

°° Alastair was also played by Mark Rolston (4.10) and briefly by Andrew Wheeler (4.15).

°°° Eve was also played by Samantha Smith (6.19).

°† Amara was also played by Gracyn Shinyei (11.02), Yameene Ball (11.05), and Samantha Isler (11.06).

About the Contributors

Stella **Castelli** has an MA in English literature and linguistics from the University of Zurich. Her thesis, "Aestheticized Representations of Death in American Literature and Film," explores representations of death and their symptomatic reappearance in contemporary American culture. She is working on her doctoral dissertation furthering her research within this field with a specific interest in the serial depiction of death.

Erin M. **Giannini**, Ph.D., is an independent scholar in television studies whose work has focused on industrial contexts surrounding corporate culture on television, and the portrayals thereof, including a monograph on corporate culture in the works of Joss Whedon. She has also published and presented work on religion, socioeconomics, and technology in series such as *Supernatural*, *Dollhouse*, *iZombie*, and *Mystery Science Theater 3000*, and is a contributor at PopMatters.

Annika **Gonnermann** is a lecturer of English literature at the University of Mannheim, Germany. She specializes in utopian and dystopian literature, focusing on contemporary novels from British and American authors. She is also interested in social and political theory connected to the construction of a better society, as well as Gothic literature, contemporary television series, superhero narratives, and popular culture in cinema and television.

Dominick **Grace** is a professor of English at Brescia University College. He is the author of *The Science Fiction of Phyllis Gotlieb* (2015) and coeditor, with Eric Hoffman, of *Approaching* Twin Peaks (2017). He has written numerous articles on popular culture and coedited several other books, including the forthcoming *A Supernatural Politics*, with Lisa Macklem.

Stephanie A. **Graves** is a Ph.D. candidate in English with a focus in rhetoric and composition studies at Georgia State University. She is particularly interested in rhetoric in film, television, and popular culture, which is informed by her background in theatrical design. Her research interests include the grotesque and the southern Gothic, horror, film and television, and queer and feminist studies.

Linda **Howell** holds a Ph.D. in English from the University of Florida. She has been with the university since 2005 and has been director of the Writing Program &

Center since 2012. Her administrative work focuses on student engagement with writing, writing across the curriculum, and first-year writing curriculum design. Her research centers on digital literacy practices with an emphasis in plagiarism and citation studies, which informs her fan studies research.

Eden Lee Lackner has a Ph.D. in English literature from Victoria University of Wellington, New Zealand. She teaches at the University of Calgary and is a member of the Horror Writers Association. Her publications include contributions to *Fan Fiction and Fan Studies in the Age of the Internet* (2006), *Women in Science Fiction and Fantasy* (2008), *The Works of Tim Burton* (2013), as well as several forthcoming works.

Khara Lukancic is a doctoral student in mass communication and media arts at Southern Illinois University. She has published two chapters on horror film and television: "'I Seek the White Mask': The Intertextuality of *Halloween* and *Moby-Dick*" (2018) and "Weeping Angels: *Doctor Who*'s (De)Monstrous Feminine" (2019). She is also the author of several film and book reviews published in *Film Criticism*, *Gateway Journal Review*, and *Gothic Nature*.

Lisa Macklem is a Ph.D. candidate in law at the University of Western Ontario. She has a JD with a specialization IP and IT, an LLM in entertainment and media law and an MA in media studies. Her MA thesis is "We're on This Road Together: The Changing Fan/Producer Relationship in Television as Demonstrated by *Supernatural*" (2013). She also serves on the editorial board of *The Journal of Fandom Studies*.

Kathleen Potts received a Ph.D. from the Graduate Center at the City University of New York. An award-winning playwright and professional dramaturge, she is a faculty member in the Department of Theatre and Speech at the City College of New York. She is co-author, with Julio Agustin, of *The Professional Actor's Handbook: From Casting Call to Curtain Call* (2017).

Kari Sawden is a Canadian folklorist whose research focuses on folk belief, alternative spiritual practices, and the power of narrative to articulate numinous experiences in both fiction and non-fiction. Her doctoral thesis, "Maps of Our Own Making: Practicing Divination in 21st Century Canada," was completed at the Memorial University of Newfoundland, where she has taught as a sessional instructor. She is a lecturer in folklore at Memorial's Grenfell Campus.

Kwasu David Tembo has a Ph.D. from the University of Edinburgh's Language, Literatures, and Cultures Department. His research interests include media studies, comics studies, literary theory and criticism, and philosophy, particularly the so-called "prophets of extremity"—Nietzsche, Heidegger, Foucault, and Derrida.

Kevin J. Wetmore, Jr., is the author and editor of more than a dozen and a half books, including *Uncovering Stranger Things* (2018) and *The Streaming of Hill House* (2020), as well as *Post–9/11 Horror in American Cinema* (2012). He has also written dozens of book chapters on horror cinema and culture. He teaches at Loyola Marymount University in Los Angeles.

About the Contributors

Kelli **Wilhelm** is a doctoral candidate in English at West Virginia University. Her interests include British Romanticism as well as the intersections of folklore and studies of contemporary popular culture. She is completing her dissertation, which explores relationships between silence and women in British novels of the 18th and 19th centuries.

Index

"Abandon All Hope…" 86
Abbott, Stacy 58, 59, 92, 94, 98
Abbott and Costello 185–186
Ackles, Jensen 5, 6, 33, 35, 36, 45, 48, 52, 53, 126
"After School Special" 99
Alastair 200, 201
Alexander, Jeffrey 121–124, 130, 133
"All Hell Breaks Loose, Part 2" 34, 82
"Alpha and Omega" 35, 37, 112, 122, 132
Amara 9, 30, 34–35, 36–39, 125, 132–133, 141–142
Amateur Research and Investigation Groups (ARIGs) 164, 167–168, 170
"American Nightmare" 142
The Amityville Horror 166
Anna *see* Milton, Anna
Antigone 199, 202
The Apocalypse 31–32, 37, 40*n*5, 57–63, 65, 67, 69, 71, 74, 82, 88, 107–109, 114–118, 132, 137, 139–140, 178, 182, 184, 188, 205
Applegate, Carey F. 184, 189
"Appointment in Samarra" 31
Aristotle 10, 194–199, 203–206
Aronofsky, Darren 32, 62
"As Time Goes By" 111
Ash 203. 204–205
"Ask Jeeves" 144
authorship 1–2, 9–10, 19–26, 28, 35–37, 39, 53, 57–73, 75–88, 120, 121–124, 130–132, 140–141, 145

"Baby" 34
Baby *see* The Impala
"Bad Day at Black Rock" 5
Balthazar 35–36, 45, 140
Barker, Cory 33
Barnes 21–22, 29, 39*n*2, 70, 86–88, 125
Barnes, Pamela 10, 193–206
Barnett, Richard-Laurent 46
Barthes, Roland 8, 15–26, 63, 64–69, 70–71, 73

Baudrillard, Jean 69, 174
Becky *see* Rosen, Becky
"Bedtime Stories" 44, 107, 138
Bela *see* Talbot, Bela
Benchley, Tara 7, 47
Benedict, Rob 62, 80
Benefiel, Candace 29, 39*n*4, 127
Benjamin, Walter 19–21, 22–23
Benny *see* Lafitte, Benny
Bezos, Jeff 4
The Bible 45, 58–59, 60–61, 63, 64, 69, 70, 82, 88, 108, 136, 138–139, 140, 145–146, 178, 183, 188, 191, 195
Bidisha 202
"Bitten" 144
"Black" 34
"Blade Runners" 5
Blake, Linnie 93, 94, 97
Blazing Saddles 36, 51–52, 131
"Bloodlust" 95, 143
"Bloody Mary" 44, 145
Bobby *see* Singer, Bobby
Bon Jovi 1
Boogeyman 7, 47
Botting, Fred 92, 101*n*3
Bradbury, Charlie 45–46, 122, 124, 126–130, 132
Branea, Silvia 58
"The British Invasion" 141
"Brother's Keeper" 35, 39*n*1
Brown, Charlie 45, 152, 154, 156, 159–160
Buffy the Vampire Slayer 30–32, 39*n*3, 43, 44, 57, 165–166
"Bugs" 93
Busse, Kristina 128

Callie 138
Calvert, Bronwen 95, 109, 202
Campbell family 32
Canfield, Dave 154, 159–160
canon 28, 125–126, 131–132, 136, 187, 97; canonical 49

227

"Carry On Wayward Son" 2, 54*n*2
Caruth, Cathy 121
Carver, Jeremy 7, 29, 36, 39, 48, 49, 123
Castiel 28, 32, 35, 36–38, 52, 65–66, 71–73, 99, 136, 140–141, 184, 187, 197–199, 202
Cavell, Stanley 25
"Celebrating the Life of Asa Fox" 142
"Changing Channels" 2, 6–7, 15, 49, 53, 137
Charlie *see* Bradbury, Charlie
Charlie Brown *see* Brown, Charlie
Cherry, Brigid 83–84, 145
Chuck *see* Shurley, Chuck
"Clap Your Hands If You Believe" 2, 6, 7, 15, 49, 53, 137
Cohen, Jeffrey Jerome 91–92
Coker, Cait 29, 39*n*4, 127
Collins, Misha 6
The Colt 24, 69–70, 87, 127
Cooper, L. Andrew 180
Corbett, Alan 162–165, 167–171, 173–176
Cortese, Genevieve 35, 52
cosplay 17, 86, 125, 145, 146; *see also* LARPing
Cousins, Norman 183
Crome, Andrew 82
Crowley 24, 35, 37, 91, 140–141
Crowther, Gillian 114
"The Curious Case of Dean Winchester" 45

D'Acci, Julie 3
Daggett, Freeman 164, 166–167, 173, 174, 175, 176
"Dark Dynasty" 122
"Dark Side of the Moon" 34, 82, 110–111, 139, 203, 205–206
The Darkness *see* Amara
Davis, Tracy C. 22
"Dead Men Don't Wear Plaid" 111
Death 35, 39*n*1, 60, 62
"Death Takes a Holiday" 98, 200, 205
DeCandido, Keith R.A. 57
Demian 20–23, 29, 39*n*2, 70, 86–88, 125
demon blood 97–98, 136, 143, 183,
demons 5, 24, 31–32, 34–35, 38, 50, 51–52, 57–59, 65, 82, 90–91, 93, 95–99, 128, 136–138, 141, 142–144, 166, 179–180, 182–184, 187–188, 194–195, 198, 200–202
DeRosa, Robin 58
Derrida, Jacques 59, 61
Des Barres, Pamela 194, 196–197
destiny 9, 57, 59, 61, 79, 91, 94, 99–100, 137–138
determinism 94–101, 183
The Devil *see* Lucifer
diegesis 8–9, 16–26, 42–53, 58, 60, 62–64, 67–72, 98, 123, 179
Dion, Celine 44, 45
djinns 90, 93, 110
"Do You Believe in Miracles?" 35
Dr. Sexy 7, 49, 54*n*8

"Don't Call Me Shurley" 35, 38, 141
"Don't You Forget about Me" 112
Dracula 44, 50, 92–93, 101*n*3, 180–181, 185–186, 188–189, 190
Dracula (1931 movie) 178, 180, 188–189, 190
Dracula (novel) *see* Stoker, Bram
"Dream a Little Dream of Me" 31
Dundes, Alan 135, 140, 145

The Easter Bunny Is Coming to Town 152, 160
Edlund, Ben 6, 7, 11*n*3, 33, 39, 47, 48, 49, 51, 123, 179
Edlund, Carver *see* Shurley, Chuck
Edmundson, Melissa 58, 91, 92
Emerson, Ralph Waldo 24–26
Engstrom, Erika 58–59, 60, 61
Euripides 199
Eve 32, 112, 143–144
"Exile on Main Street" 31

fairy tales 44, 107, 138
"Fallen Idols" 5, 46
"Family Matters" 31
fan fiction 18, 28–29, 33, 48, 51, 52–53, 83, 109, 123, 127, 145; *see also* slash
"Fan Fiction" 7, 9, 28–39, 51 52–53, 54*n*4, 54*n*5, 54*n*7, 86, 125, 126–127, 128, 131, 135, 146–147
fan practice 4, 7, 33, 39*n*4, 50–53, 125–129, 131
fandom 3–5, 6–9, 16–17, 28–29, 30–33, 34, 36, 39–40, 42–43, 45–46, 47, 50–51, 52, 57, 58, 62, 65, 67, 69–70, 76–77, 79, 82–84, 85–88, 100, 101*n*4, 109, 121–33, 135, 136, 145–47, 193
fanspace 121, 126, 128–129, 133
Felschow, Laura E. 83–84, 123
Finkelstein, Joanne 110
"First Blood" 142
"First Born" 35
Fiske, John 46
Fitts, Dudley 203
Fitzgerald, Garth IV 125, 144
Fitzgerald, Robert 203
folklore 10, 57, 59, 93, 118*n*3, 135–140, 143, 147
"Folsom Prison Blues" 98
food 8, 9, 31, 32, 93, 107–118, 158
"Form and Void" 34
Foster, Michael Dylan 136
Frankenstein 92, 95, 180–181, 186, 189, 190
Frankenstein, Victor 92–93, 181, 187, 190
Frankenstein's Monster 92–93, 181, 185–187, 189
free will 9, 51, 58–61, 62–64, 67, 72, 76, 81, 84–85, 90–101, 136–137, 141, 144, 183–184, 188, 189
"The French Mistake" 2, 6, 11*n*3, 15, 35–36, 38, 47, 48, 51–52, 54*n*9, 126, 130–31, 147
Freud, Sigmund 23, 121, 203

Index   229

"Frontierland" 2, 7
Fuchs, Michael 33

Gabriel 6, 44, 49, 53, 137
Gadreel 142
Gamble, Sera 6–7, 29–30, 31–34, 35–36, 37–38, 39, 47, 130–131
García, Alberto N. 93, 145
Garth *see* Fitzgerald, Garth, IV
gender *see* sexuality
Genette, Gérard 2–3, 5, 10
Ghost Hunters 162–167, 172, 174
Ghostbusters (1984) 5, 54n4, 162–163, 169
Ghostfacers 5, 7, 10, 48, 54n4, 162–177
"Ghostfacers" 162–177
ghosts 4, 5, 6, 8, 16, 21–24, 29, 44, 45, 48, 50–51, 54n8, 57, 69, 90, 92, 93, 94–95, 100, 130, 138, 143, 163–165, 166–168, 171, 173, 174–175, 176, 179–180, 194, 200–201
Gilmore Girls 46
"The Girl Next Door" 97
"The Girl with the Dungeons and Dragons Tattoo" 45
God 7, 57–61, 62–65, 157, 159, 181, 182, 183, 187–189, 203, 205; *see also* Shurley, Chuck
Goethe, Johann Wolfgang 189, 191
Gore, Leticia 69
the gothic 9, 10, 91–96, 100–101, 178–191
Gray, Jonathan 2
"The Great Escapist" 118n6, 131, 140–141
Greek muse 197, 206
Greeley, Andrew 80

Hale, Mike 164–165, 169–170
"Halt & Catch Fire" 93
Hamilton, Edith 197
Hartman, Geoffrey 121
Hatchet Man 8
Healey, Kathleen 179–180
"Heart" 32, 95, 144
Heaven 32, 36–37, 59, 62, 71, 110–111, 137, 139–140, 183–184, 187–189, 191, 199–200, 203–205
"Heaven and Hell" 198, 200, 204–205
Hell 30–31, 32, 36–37, 38, 45, 62, 73, 77, 95, 98, 99–100, 137, 140, 161, 183–184, 187–188, 189, 191, 195, 199, 202
"Hell House" 5, 7, 48, 93, 111, 165, 166
"Hello, Cruel World" 37
Herrick, Jim 181–182
Hill, Sharon A. 164, 166
Hilton, Paris 5, 46
Hinton, S.E. 201
Hitchcock, Alfred 186, 201–202
Hofer, Johaness 152
Hogle, Jerold E. 92
Hollywood 47, 50–51, 78, 163, 190
"Hollywood Babylon" 6, 7, 46, 47, 123, 130, 151
"Hook Man" 4, 44, 50, 93, 135

House of Wax (2005) 46
"How to Win Friends and Influence Monsters" 32, 94, 111
Howell, Charlotte 127
humanism 179, 181–184, 187, 191
"Hunted" 98, 143
"Hunteri Heroici" 5–6
Hutcheon, Linda 194

"I Believe the Children Are Our Future" 137
The Impala 1, 16, 32, 34, 43, 49, 52, 57, 71–72, 79, 100, 111, 135, 139, 147, 160–161, 178, 179–181, 185
"In My Time of Dying" 94
"In the Beginning" 99
Inness, Sherrie A. 108, 114, 117
intertextuality 2–3, 8,15–16, 43–45, 46, 53, 92, 101n4, 162–176, 193, 195–197, 199–203, 206
"It's a Terrible Life" 45, 47, 99, 101n4
It's a Wonderful Life 45, 154, 156
"It's the Great Pumpkin, Sam Winchester" 45, 188

Jameson, Fredric 92–93, 193–194
Jeffries, Dru 186
Jencks, Charles 194
Jenkins, Henry 4, 145
Jesse 137–138
Jesus 69, 138, 154, 158–159
Joshua 62, 205
Jowett, 92, 93
"Jus in Bello" 31–32
"Just My Imagination" 11

Kelleter, Frank 18, 21, 26, 27
Knowles, Thomas 181, 185
Koven, Mikel J. 92, 108, 136, 143
Krampus 155, 157
Kripke, Eric 6–7, 9, 28–30, 31, 33, 34, 35, 36–39, 47, 50, 52, 57, 59, 60–61, 66, 72, 75–81, 83–88, 91, 97, 123, 130, 151, 152–153, 157, 194, 206
Kurtz, Paul 182

Lafitte, Benny 96, 144
"LARP and the Real Girl" 7, 129
LARPing 7–8, 16, 18–23, 25, 29, 50–51, 67, 69, 84–86, 129; *see also* cosplay
Larsen, Katherine 33, 123, 145, 146
"Lazarus Rising" 35, 82, 111, 183, 195, 204–205
Led Zeppelin 54n2, 196
Lenore 143–144
Leviathans 9, 32, 37, 45, 93–4, 108, 114–118
Lilith 24, 31–32, 87, 100, 124, 139, 187, 195
The Little Drummer Boy 152, 159
Live Action Role Playing *see* LARPing
"Live Free or Twihard" 29, 31, 34, 48–49

Lucifer 31, 58, 59, 62, 65–66, 71–73, 97, 124, 137, 139–140, 142, 184, 187
Łuksza, Agata 101
Lutz, Mark A. 182, 184
Lux, Kenneth 182, 184

Madison 144
"The Magnificent Seven" 4–5
"Malleus Maleficarum" 95
"Mamma Mia" 101n4, 111, 141
"The Man Who Knew Too Much" 37
"The Man Who Would Be King" 140
"Mannequin 3: The Reckoning" 45
Marescu, Valentina 58
Marie 28, 29, 39n1, 39n4, 52–53, 126, 146–147
Mark of Cain 34–35, 39n1, 136, 142
masculinity 33–34, 83, 86, 109, 114, 125, 128, 165, 174–175, 201–202
Mathis, Cori 31
McG 47
McKee, Robert 195
McNeill, Lynne S 136
Mechling, Jay 145
"Meet the New Boss" 37
"The Memory Remains" 100, 147
Men of Letters 117, 135, 136, 138, 141; British Men of Letters 135, 142
"Meta Fiction" 49, 54n7, 131, 141
metafiction 1, 36, 42, 49–51, 53, 122–3, 125
"Metamorphosis" 91, 96–97
metanarrative 7, 10, 25, 30, 34, 39, 120–121, 123–126, 128, 130–133, 135
metatext 1–5, 9, 15–16, 18–19, 25–26, 35, 39n2, 42, 46, 48–49, 53, 67, 75–76, 78, 81, 83, 85, 128, 164;
Metatron 7, 34–35, 38, 49, 62, 122, 125, 127, 130, 131–132, 140–141
Michael 8, 31, 40n5, 58, 65–66, 71, 73, 137, 139–140, 184, 187, 189, 204
Mills, Jody 5, 112
Milton, Anna 198–200
"Mint Condition" 8
Mintz, Sidney 107–108
Mittell, Jason 42–43, 49
Mitu, Bianca 58
"Mommy Dearest" 112, 143–144
"The Monster at the End of This Book" 7–8, 29, 47, 48, 50, 52, 53, 54n8, 54n10, 62, 67–68, 77, 84–85, 86, 88, 99–100, 111, 120, 122, 124–125, 132, 139
"Monster Movie" 10, 28, 49–50, 92, 178–191
Morton House 163, 166–168, 170–173, 175–176
Most Haunted 162, 164
Mother of All Demons *see* Eve
The Mummy (1932 movie) 50, 93, 178, 188, 190
My Bloody Valentine (2009) 45
"My Bloody Valentine" 45

"My Heart Will Go On" 37, 45
"Mystery Spot" 15

Naomi 140
Neill, Natalie 184–185
Newbury, Michael 108–109, 115–117
Nicol, Rhonda 34
Nietzsche, Freidrich 63–64, 101
"No Rest for the Wicked" 32, 80
Northanger Abbey 185
nostalgia 108–114, 117–118, 151–154
Noxon, Marti 30–32, 39n3

Oedipus 199, 202–203
O'Hara, Jessica 167, 174
"Our Little World" 35, 36
"Out of the Darkness, into the Fire" 101n4
"Out with the Old" 33–34

"Pac Man Fever" 129
Padalecki, Jared 5, 6, 31, 33, 35, 36, 46, 48, 52, 53, 126, 160
Palmer, Lorrie 202
"Paper Moon" 144
Paradise Lost 181
Paranormal State 162–163, 165
paratext 2–3, 45, 48, 52, 122, 131
parody 1, 2, 10, 15, 42, 44, 47–49, 52, 53, 54n3, 82, 92–93, 123–125, 151–161, 162–176, 178–191, 193–194
pastiche 2, 8, 10, 93, 193–206
Paul, William 185
"Phantom Traveler" 93
"Pilot" 34, 37, 109–110, 169, 179, 182
Pitt, Brad 5, 45
Pond, Amy 97, 98
Postlewait, Thomas 22
postmodern 8, 10, 42, 46, 51, 92, 108, 122, 135, 193–196,
Prickett, Stephen 145
Primiano, Leonard Norman 138
prophet 16, 19, 28, 35, 45, 47, 50, 61–62, 65–67, 72, 78, 85, 99, 123–124, 139, 142, 202
Psycho (1960) 186, 201
Purgatory 32–33, 36–37, 82, 140, 144

Ralston, Devon Fitzgerald 184, 189
The Ramones 196, 201
Raphael 37
"The Real Ghostbusters" 8, 15–26, 28–29, 50–51, 54n4, 67, 69–70, 77–78, 83, 86–87, 101n4, 125, 126, 127–128, 146
Reality TV 5, 10, 46, 162–176
Reapers 90, 94–95, 200, 202
"Red Sky at Morning" 98
"Reichenbach" 34
Reiter, Ester 113, 115
reluctant hero 10, 195, 200–206
Renner, Karen J. 174–175
Revolution (TV series) 38

Rimmon Kenan, Shlomith 18, 21, 22
"Roadkill" 95
Roman, Dick 93–94, 116
Rosen, Becky 8, 24, 28–29, 39n4, 50–51, 65, 69–70, 83, 85–88, 122, 124–130, 132, 146
Rosenberg, Bruce A. 139
Roth, LuAnn 108
"Route 666" 77, 93
Rowena 35, 141; see also Witches
Ruby 35, 52, 95, 183, 198–199
Rudolph the Red-Nosed Reindeer 152, 154, 160
Rugarou 96–97

Sagan, Carl 183
"Sam, Interrupted" 45
Samulet 146, 160
Santa Claus Is Coming to Town 152, 156–157, 159–161
Sartre, Jean-Paul 189
Satan see Lucifer
"Scarecrow" 109, 110
Schlosser, Eric 108, 113
Schmidt, Lisa 94, 96, 101
Scooby-Doo 6
"Scoobynatural" 6
scripture see The Bible
"Season Seven, Time for a Wedding!" 8, 28–29, 51, 87, 125, 126, 128, 147
seriality 18, 24–26, 42, 51
sexuality 29, 37, 39n4, 50, 57, 86, 101n3, 107–108, 117–118, 124–125, 127–129, 132, 167, 174–175, 179, 180, 196–197, 198–199, 204–205
shapeshifters 28, 50, 90, 97, 144, 179, 188–190
"Sharp Teeth" 144
Shelley, Mary see Frankenstein
Shuman, Amy 139
Shurley, Chuck 7–10, 11, 16, 19, 28–30, 35, 36–39, 47, 48, 50–52, 53, 61–62 66–74, 75–88, 99–100, 120, 122–125, 127–128, 130–132, 138–142, 147
Siege, Julie 39, 46
Siege, Sera 39, 123–5
Simmons, David 138
"Sin City" 95
Singer, Bobby 4–5, 21, 32, 37, 44, 48, 63, 65, 80, 111, 114–115, 117, 154–155, 159–160, 195–198, 200, 202
Singer, Karen 111–112, 117
Singer, Robert 6, 48, 52
Singer, Robert (character in "The French Mistake") 35, 38, 48, 42, 52
slash 51, 52, 109, 125; see also fan fiction
"Slash Fiction" 32, 44, 54n7, 111
"Slumber Party" 129
Smith, Andrew F. 113
Snooki 5
"Somewhere Between Heaven and Hell" 48

Sophocles 199, 202–203
"Soul Survivor" 35
"Southern Comfort" 111
Spengler, Harry 5, 7, 48, 54n4, 162–163, 165–166, 168–169, 172–173, 174, 175–176
spirits see ghosts
Spooner, Catherine 92
Spruce, Kenny 162–163, 165–167, 169, 171–173
Spurlock, Morgan 113, 115, 116
Stevens, Morton 152
Stevenson, Robert Louis 92
Stoker, Bram 92, 101n3, 180
Storey, John 137
Stout, Nathan 93, 94, 95
"Survival of the Fittest" 32
"Swan Song" 7, 28, 31, 35, 37–38, 70–74, 78–81, 82–83, 127–128, 139–140
"Sympathy for the Devil" 8, 28–29, 51, 61, 65–67, 83, 85–87, 125, 127

Talbot, Bela 24, 87, 98
"Tall Tales" 44
Tara see Benchley, Tara
Team Free Will 136, 184, 189
Teiresias 199, 202–203
Tessa see Reapers
Thatcher, Adrian 138
"There Will Be Blood" 116
"Thin Lizzie" 37
"#thinman" 44
Thorgeirsdottir, Gunnel 92, 108, 136, 143
"Time After Time" 7
"Time Is on My Side" 92
Titanic (1997) 37, 47
Todorov, Tzvetan 180
Tolbert, Jeffrey A. 136
Torrey, KT 50
Tran, Kevin 142
trauma 9–10, 30, 66, 120–133, 146
"Trial and Error" 34, 118n6
Trickster see Gabriel
Tulpa 7, 93, 166
Turner, Rufus 21
Twilight 29, 44, 48–49, 54n6
"Two and a Half Men" 34
"Two Minutes to Midnight" 45, 60

the uncanny 23–24, 26, 80, 91
"Unforgiven" 31
Uriel 184, 188, 198
"The Usual Suspects" 46

Valenzano, Joseph M., III 58–59, 60, 61
vampires 29, 34, 48–49, 90, 92, 95, 96, 97, 113, 143–144, 165, 178–180, 188–189, 190–191
"A Very Brady Christmas" 153–154
"A Very Supernatural Christmas" 10, 151–161
violence 31, 32, 34–35, 48, 71, 82, 94, 115, 124–125, 128, 130, 131, 141, 151–152, 164, 167–168, 202; see also trauma

The Walking Dead 48, 123
Walton, Ashley 128
"We Need to Talk About Kevin" 82
Wells, Paul 180–181
"Wendigo" 4, 43, 90, 93, 96, 110, 113, 135
Werewolf 32, 50, 97, 144, 178, 188, 190–191
Wexelblat, Alan 33
"What Is and What Should Never Be" 34, 99, 110
Whedon, Joss 30, 39*n*3, 43
"When the Levee Breaks" 98–99, 101*n*4
Wincest 29, 127
Winchester, John 2, 4, 48, 68, 80, 111, 137, 143, 154, 155, 156–158, 159–160, 161, 183, 200
Winchester, Mary 34, 37, 68, 99, 109–112, 117, 133, 137, 142, 156
Winchester Gospels 53, 62, 67, 99, 123, 139
Winter Warlock 156, 160
"Wishful Thinking" 5
witches 45, 90, 92, 180; *see also* Rowena
Wolf Man *see* Werewolf
The Wolf Man (1941 movie) 50, 178, 188, 190
Wood, Tahir 75–76, 88
writerliness 8–9, 16–19, 21, 25–26, 47

The X-Files 2, 43, 123, 186–87

Yang, Sharon Rose 179–180
"You Can't Handle the Truth" 31

Zachariah 47, 58, 61, 65–66, 99, 203, 205
Zeddmore, Ed 5, 7, 48, 54*n*4, 162–163, 165–166, 168–169, 170–173, 174, 175–176
Zeddmore, Maggie 162, 165, 169, 173
zombies 108, 109, 112, 115–118
Zubernis, Lynn 33, 123, 145, 146

www.ingramcontent.com/pod-product-compliance
Ingram Content Group UK Ltd.
Pitfield, Milton Keynes, MK11 3LW, UK
UKHW041945140426
5217IPUK00014B/670